# WHY JACKIE SCOWLED

Stephen F. Zeigler

Why Jackie Scowled





Published by Spines

ISBN: 979-8-89691-052-7

# WHY JACKIE SCOWLED

LEFTIST OSWALD SHOT RIGHTIST JOHN
CONNALLY, POLARIZED AMERICA PAYS A
TERRIBLE PRICE

STEPHEN F. ZEIGLER

# ACKNOWLEDGMENTS

Any book involving John F. Kennedy's murder is built on the work of thousands of researchers. Some are published authors in the bibliography. Many, many others spend hours, days or even years culling through the evidence, talking with witnesses and fellow researchers, and reading books to critique or suggest new views of the disaster - a measure of both the continuing importance of the event and of the complexities surrounding it.

Much of the initial internet discussions happened on the newsgroup alt.assassination.jfk, or Compuserve, is now continued on Quora (e. g. jfkassassination) and most recently on Facebook (e. g. JFK Assassination Discussion Group). All kinds of views are represented, and all kinds are valuable - perhaps especially when they disagree. The topics are so nuanced that essentially, no one ever agrees completely. Some salient posters, most of whom I have never met in person and sometimes are known only by their posting names, include: John McAdams, Dale Myers, JLeyden900, Dave Dix, Dave Reitzes, DRoberdeau, Caeruleo, Jefferson Morley, Joe Durnavich, Chris Farrer, Gary Mack, Clark Wilkins, AjHidell99, Bill Kell, Mark Dixon, Fred Litwin, and Barb Junkkarinen.

This topic is so vast that no one can know its entirety. New facts may be found, for example, if the CIA ever reveals its last documents. It is rare to be able to suggest a completely new idea; for example, my analysis of the Single Bullet neuromuscular impact was already suggested back in 1994 by Dr. Kenneth Strully and Dr. Robert Artwohl - as I discovered as this book was going to print. Even so, this book does present a cohesive interpretation that is mostly dependent on physical evidence - evidence that is unlikely to change significantly.

Any book depends on early readers who take the time to provide feedback. First among those, I list my brother, Robert Zeigler, who not only read the book but immediately encouraged me to spend years refining it for its future readers. Other helpful readers include Gary Raetz, Gary Funck, Rich LeBlanc, Jeff Tash, Julian Banerji, Ellen Salvatore, Peter Schmidt, William Churchill, John Bellatti, Pierre Sundborg, and the P2P Nonfiction Group. I thank my publisher, Spines, especially Melina Honorato and Kira Gill.

A special thanks to my wife of many decades, Marti Oas-Zeigler.

Please enjoy,

Stephen F. Zeigler

# CONTENTS

# AUTHOR'S NOTE

I was twelve years old when the middle-school principal interrupted our class with his bulletin. I recall the class sat in silence for a long or short time – sometimes I remember it one way and sometimes the other. Then he announced we should all go home, which seemed weird since my house would be empty. But it wasn't. My mom was soon home, then my whole family. My father arrived with a black and white TV; we'd never had one, as my parents considered them a waste of time. We plugged in that rental and fumbled with its rabbit-ear antenna, and a fuzzy picture appeared. We sat in front of our first family TV experience for much of the next two days –Oswald was murdered in front of us, then we watched the solemn funeral with its never-forgotten drumbeat.

The rental TV went home, our homework and readings resumed, and life was sad for a long while. I was oblivious. Soon, the Beatles came and we kids were on to the excitements of growing up.

My parents had loved Kennedy. They were very politically aware.

My father had come from the old subsistence farms in the rocky hills of Southern Tennessee. He was the first to go to Junior College from his area. He was drafted, IQ-tested impressively, and sent to Iran to help build resistance to a possible

German invasion. After some secretive interviews, he was tapped to type notes at the Teheran Conference, where he met FDR, Churchill and Stalin as one of a handful of Americans allowed into the Soviet embassy. He got a new "shadow" man in his unit whose job was to arrest or kill him if he said anything to anyone. His good behavior got him into the OSS and later the CIA, where eventually he worked for a scary man named Bill Harvey as "Director of Plans." The CIA was changing from intelligence gathering to worldwide interference, but it was also repopulating itself with Harvard-type men. My father broke security by marrying another CIA officer – they joked they didn't need to hire a wedding photographer because the KGB took so many photos. But my "farm boy" father did not fit in the new elites' CIA and finally talked my mother into buying a black-soil farm back in Tennessee.

My mom had become the 12-year-old "mother" of her family when her father died and her mom collapsed with a stroke in grief. Mom raised her two sisters while taking care of her mother, thanks to family friends. She was superb in school but had no money for college and became a "paid teacher's assistant" – women were blocked from many other careers. Eventually, her siblings could help, and she won a scholarship to college. With a Masters in Political Science, she eventually became an aide to her Congressman. When WW2 began, her Congressman went to London but left when bombs started falling. My mom was asked to stay as a code-breaker because of her skill at crosswords and she eventually worked for British Intelligence. With her Political Science schooling, she was soon in counter-intelligence, eventually joined the OSS, and tracked hostile spies in Greece and Turkey after the war. The CIA hired her as a director of the Middle East department.

I never knew anything about my parents' careers. The first time I realized they might be a little different was when my brother and I went to complain about a water moccasin sunning on our favorite swimming hole rock; with my dad gone, we gave up and expected to find new fun, but to our surprise, my mom walked out holding a .22 rifle. We stood stunned as she calmly shot that snake from about a mile away.

It turned out my mom had been the captain of her rifle team and that in the war years, she kept up her skills with pistols enough to win contests at the FBI firing range when it was lent out to the initially homeless CIA. We got a lot more obedient after that.

Still, my parents were sworn to secrecy and never spoke about anything – unless it was reported in the press by at least two reputable sources. It was a bit hard for them to get jobs because they had no real references from the intelligence world. My father's farming experiment ended in bankruptcy, which forced him into the personnel manager trade, while my mom struggled through cancer and eventually became a college professor.

I have no such exciting resume. I learned only not to trust what people say until I could verify it; the more powerful the person, the more difficult the verification.

When LBJ pumped up his Gulf of Tonkin Resolution to start a war in Vietnam, everyone I knew was excited to "get those evil SOBs." We were shocked when my mom and dad quietly advised us that "people who start wars over 'incidents' are usually wanting the war and manufacturing the "incident."" Wow, they were cynical. I guess I inherited that. I began to reject any received "history" unless I could verify it.

My parents were not happy with me – I rejected their authority along with everyone else's. My father was from the South, where kids were supposed to obey their elders and not argue with them. So, there was a lot of combat and temporary "vacations" for me out from under the parental roof. I married very young and with astounding good luck, and left home. However, to support my new family, I had to work, and I was lucky to get a job in the local hospital as a lab technician in the same suite as our pathologist.

Our pathologist's extensive desk and tables were normally clean. One late 1970 night, I found them covered with bloody photos and x-rays of a gruesomely wounded man. Leaning closer, I saw John F. Kennedy.

Vaguely curious (I was a science major, not a historian!) I snooped enough to see a clear "bone cone" entry in a bone fragment from the back of Kennedy's skull. I didn't even discuss the discovery with my bosses or my friends. At the time, I had no idea they were to be viewed by only a select few experts. I knew nothing about the assassination or Kennedy. Of course, I knew a lot about our presidents, "Lying Lyndon" and "Tricky Dick," and about the Vietnam War that had killed one friend, scared us all, and encouraged our protests. But I filed those autopsy materials away, maybe for future investigation.

What I did notice as I got on with my life in software engineering: people were having a harder and harder time agreeing about what was true in the political world. The Watergate hearings exposed some sordid election cheating, the Church Committee exposed some sordid CIA operations, and the House Select Committee on Assassinations eventually declared that my parents' hero JFK had been killed by an unknown conspiracy. I watched as President Carter struggled to be righteous but was pilloried by what I thought was unfair propaganda. The Pew Polling periodically confirmed what I was thinking: people were losing faith and trust in their government. When Reagan got rid of regulations that curbed lying on TV and radio, I saw the growth of more and more fake news. And soon, the fake news was accompanied by what could only be called "hate speech," as each "side" vilified the other.

America was polarized. It was getting more polarized. The Federal Government was getting paralyzed and lost the point of compromising. If one side eventually made a change, the other side would immediately cancel that change as soon as they got power. What was very odd to me was the incredible closeness of election after election – in my view, parties should shrink and grow as their policies showed successes or failures. But it seemed like despite the course changes, only the rich were benefiting in quality of life; the poor were having to make do with promises, excuses, and spiritual victories.

Eventually, I had to start looking at this. As a scientist, I looked for when things changed. That was not hard. The Pew "Trust in Government" polls showed a classic scientific change – just after JFK's assassination.

Why was Kennedy assassinated? What I read claimed only

that Oswald seemed to have no discernible reason to kill Kennedy other than some vague "lone nut" or "ego drive." At the same time, I mistrusted any idea of a conspiracy because it would, in my view, be extremely hard to build a secret group around the idea of shooting the most popular man in the World. And then, keeping secrets would require everyone involved to be absolute cowards when I knew that a lot of people are definitely NOT cowards and would come forward despite any intimidation. I like to think I'd be one of them, for example.

I got the Zapruder film as a fuzzy VHS tape, but I could single-step it and look. Having done my Ph. D. in the study of low-level brain operations, I knew something that many did not: the audio startle reflex is mostly bilateral: when Zapruder heard a rifle shot, he would "jump" and his camera lens would move up and down. That jump might not be huge, but if he otherwise was moving his aim horizontally, as when tracking a car, then the audio startle jumps should be easily detected. I spent a weekend single-stepping and measuring where he pointed his camera. Bingo. I found the first inspiration for this book.

What was even more interesting: I could use bullet flight times, sound times and response times to build a "map" of who reacted as the sound reached them. That map allowed me to confirm that only a person near Oswald could fire the shots – that is, Oswald was very likely the killer.

What was stunning: I could use my vertical audio startle jumps to say almost precisely when Oswald pulled the trigger. I could then work backward to see what he saw through his telescopic sight when he pulled his trigger.

That was the biggest surprise of all.

This book is not a discussion of theories and testimonies. It is not a rehash of Bugliosi's impressive Lone Gunman work (Bugliosi, 2007) or of Case Closed (Posner, 1993), nor is it focused on disproving conspiracies. It depends on hard evidence to calculate what Oswald was aiming at. It turns the "kaleidoscope of evidence" until a new, clear pattern emerges. We can know with confidence why Oswald was shooting. We can then look back at the mountains of evidence to see how Oswald's motive originated and why he behaved as he did after his shooting.

This book is intended to be a companion piece with an explanation of why JFK's death was so destructive to America. It led to the paralyzing polarization that has grown to strangle America ever since Oswald shot JFK.

Understanding how the ego of one man caused this disaster does not fix it – but perhaps it can help break the cycle of knee-jerk mistrust and end our crippling polarization.

# 1

## JACKIE TOLD US

Jackie scowled just once in front of Dallas cameras: by scowling, she inadvertently told us who shot John Kennedy and why he shot.

Moments before, Jackie had been all smiles, as usual. And why not? Jackie Kennedy anticipated an improving marriage with the most popular man in the World.

Their dark blue presidential limousine had turned onto Houston Street into what became the infamous Dealey Plaza. The Texas School Book Depository loomed ahead, just another building to her. Her husband leaned towards her to be heard over the cheering. She wouldn't remember exactly what he said.

That weekend in Texas was Jackie's first campaign trip for JFK's 1964 re-election bid. Jack had launched his campaign without her the week before. He had braved potential violence in front of dangerously disenchanted Cuban exiles in Miami, but his trip had gone smoothly. Kennedy's 1964 victory would have been much easier if he could flip Florida and hold Texas. The Dallas right wing had recently abused other Democrats, but Kennedy was certain that Jackie's magical presence would smooth his trip. Kennedy had cajoled Jackie into joining him not just to smooth the crowds: she could rebuild his public family image, and she could recover from the devastating loss of their baby, Patrick, only three months before.

Jackie insisted she disliked campaigning. JFK's energetic 1960 run had been awkward for her. Jackie had retired early from that exciting 1960 campaign: she had been increasingly pregnant with John Junior. Yet Jackie had sparkled. The first direct sound documentary ever filmed, Drew Associates' *Primary* (Associates, 1960, 1961, 1963), captured it. She discovered that she was tough, charismatic, and liked despite her inner nerves. Jackie saw most of that 1960 effort from her home, protecting her unborn baby from a miscarriage. She was able to help JFK by writing a newspaper column, 'Campaign Wife,' explaining and marketing JFK's campaign while mixing in friendly personal stories of motherhood. Jackie had been happy to stay in her private world with her children, occasionally stepping out to do television campaigning. Once in the White House, she was often in the press but remained disarmingly shy.

She was surprising herself in Texas. Campaigning at Jack's side was a thrill. Times had changed. Kennedy was not an unknown, unproven Catholic "whippersnapper." He was now a world figure whom everyone knew and almost everyone respected. He was the bringer of peace and prosperity. The streets of San Antonio, Houston, Fort Worth, and now Dallas were lined with friendly, cheering faces.

Jackie was also an immensely popular world figure. Her charisma amplified her husband's. She heard friends joking that she and her husband had to be careful to look in opposite directions from their car seat; if they both happened to look at the same person, it might kill them with joy.

Their limousine swung onto Elm Street. At that moment, Abraham Zapruder pushed "record" on his state-of-the-art Bell & Howell movie camera. Zapruder recorded at full zoom from his precarious perch atop a short column 300 feet down Elm Street. His is now the most studied film in history. Its frame numbers define every moment of the next 26 seconds. Jackie's limousine first shows in Zapruder's 133<sup>rd</sup> frame – known simply as F133.

The crowd was finally thinning. Nellie Connally turned back in her little jump seat, saying, "Mr. President, you can't say Dallas doesn't love you!" At Jackie's right, President Kennedy enthused, "No, you certainly can't." Soon, they would accelerate away to their next engagement, where her husband expected to enthrall another crowd. Jackie smiled at the few people to her left. At that moment, F138 spectator Phil Willis took this slide (#6) of her last smile:

*Phil Willis Collection © The Sixth Floor Museum at Dealey Plaza*

Jackie heard a loud bang that she thought was a motorcycle backfire. Jackie gave a brief glare back over her left shoulder towards a trailing motorcycle. Jackie hated the loud Harleys and their backfires; she had asked her husband to keep motorcycles away from her side of the car. Bob Croft, another bystander, snapped this picture of Jackie's sudden scowl at F160 (1.2 seconds later):

Jackie remembered that "everything was really slow then." She swiveled to her right, looking at her husband – perhaps she intended to complain about that backfire. She recalled hearing Governor Connally yelling. Otherwise, the next few seconds were a traumatic blur for her. She had first thought there were three shots but changed her mind to only two shots after she read that a single bullet had hit both Jack and Connally. She remembered seeing him with his left hand raised towards his neck, with a "quizzical look on his face." Then she remembered seeing a flesh-colored piece of his skull. She remembered thinking, "he just looked like he had a slight headache... no blood or anything." Then, "he sort of put his hand to his forehead and fell in my lap."

She remembered falling on her husband and crying out in agony: "Oh, no, no, no ... Oh, my God, they have shot my husband ... I love you, Jack."

Jackie did not remember "climbing out on the back of the car." Everyone else remembered that iconic foray. Why didn't Jackie?

Jackie's vague memories are a microcosm of the problems that impede understanding that day in Dallas. Unlike any other crime scene, hundreds of witnesses were interviewed. But as we've seen with Jackie, memories simply are not reliable. She was the closest witness to the disaster. She did not discuss the tragedy with anyone and actively avoided reliving it through media stories. She should have been the best witness, yet we know she was wrong – films prove it.

Memories are not indelible films. They are formed, mysteriously, from millions of jumbled inputs from eyes, ears, other senses, and our previous experiences. Our eyes, for example, constantly jerk about in what are called saccadic movements, yet our brains somehow stabilize that view. Our retina cells blast out seemingly random sets of pulses that only vaguely correspond to their tiny part of the retinal image. Those eye pulses don't go directly into our cortex but go through primitive nerve centers that can cause actions: target tracking, parallax eye motion, protective blinks and startles - faster than our conscious brain can understand. The same is true of ear nerve pulses, which can cause audio startles, or touch nerve pulses, which can cause reflex startles. Although science still can't explain how Jackie made her memories, we know that her brain was slower than a movie camera. Not all of us have the same memory powers – 2.5% are prosopagnosics who can't easily remember faces, for example. Memories change over time. Perhaps most unsettling, "putting pictures into words always makes our memory for those pictures worse!" (Shaw, 2016)

In contrast to frail human memory, the Zapruder film and many other Dealey Plaza films and pictures captured a blurry truth. We can see enough immediate unthinking reactions of Jackie and others to piece together what we should have seen decades ago.

Jackie's head turn and frown tell us when the first shot rang out: they are involuntary, immediate responses to a loud noise. Scientists have studied such head turns: they take about 300ms (milliseconds) to begin (Nijhuis and Janssen, 2007). Jackie's partial head rotation takes about 150ms. Since Jackie was fully turned at F160-F161, the sound must have arrived at her ears at least 450ms before (at 18.3 frames per second (fps), that's about 8 frames). Therefore, the sound of the first shot arrived at least 8 frames before F160: no later than F152. By a closer examination of the Zapruder film, we can see when she moves her head: between F133 and F157 her head is at about the same angle; then she turns her head quickly to her left. That would put the shot sound reaching Jackie at about 300ms (5.5 frames) before F157. The shot itself happened between F149.5 and F152. An overview of nerve actions is presented later in **Chapter 10: Nerve Responses and Startles.**

A sound "reaching" Jackie is not the same as her consciously "hearing" that sound. Jackie's ears had to turn the sound into a barrage of nerve impulses, which then traversed brain elements that began her involuntary head turn, and which eventually were cascaded into Jackie's cortex where it recognized a loud bang; her conscious mind eventually misidentified and remembered the bang as a motorcycle backfire. Jackie "heard" what she thought was a backfire about 150ms to

200ms after the noise reached her – that identification is what added a scowl to her head turn.

Jackie inadvertently told the world about when the first shot sound reached her. By itself, it does not say exactly where or when that shot was fired or what kind of bullet was fired. We do know it did not reach the car, so it must have been deflected by something.

To narrow down where and when the shot was fired, we can find other reflex reactions. Fortunately, there is one person whose reactions are easily and nearly exactly seen: Zapruder's (Hartmann, 1978). Others have noted this but did not realize that Zapruder was panning left to right much more than up and down. Therefore, film blurs are dominated by panning motions. To find his audio startles, we focus exclusively on up-and-down motions, not blurs.

Zapruder had an "audio startle" at each shot, bumping his camera. His camera recorded those bumps in each frame's aim point, just like a seismograph. Zapruder's audio startle motions are fast and mostly bilateral – meaning they affect both sides of his body equally: his eyes blinked at 3ms; his head ducked at 8ms; his shoulders hunched at 12ms; his arms and hands flexed at 15ms. The timing of audio startles is accurate within hundredths of a second. We can see the resulting vertical camera motion by tracking where the background stationary objects show in each frame, as detailed in **Chapter 11: Measuring Camera Movement.**

Zapruder clearly startled vertically at 3 and only 3 frames: F155, F227 and F318.

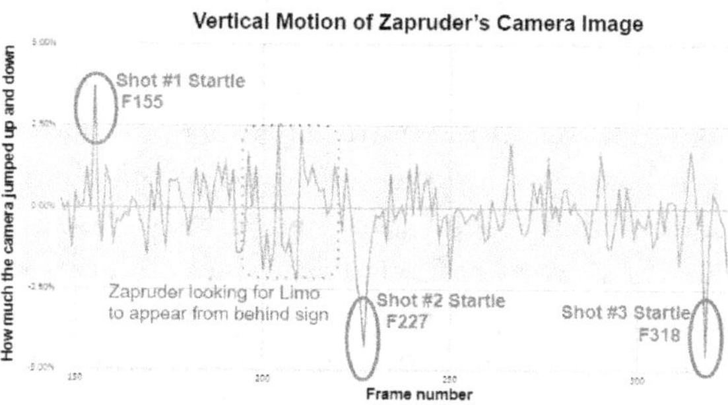

Two of these frames correspond to known shots – they will fit with crowd reactions, such as Jackie's, to tell us where the shots came from. The first startle, at F155, will add to Jackie's head turn to tell us what happened to that first bullet.

More importantly, the startle at F155 will tell us Oswald's motive and why this was the worst accident in America's history.

The first shot startles "upwards" because Zapruder had his eye on his camera and hit it with his head "duck." The first shot's muzzle blast reached Zapruder between 0.06 and 0.12 seconds before he jumped at F155: between F153 and F154. Because Jackie heard the noise slightly before Zapruder, we can calculate that the shooter must have been between 60 and 170 feet farther from Zapruder than from Jackie. Graphing will tell us where the shooter might have been: in particular, the sixth-floor eastmost window of the Texas School Book Depository (TSBD) is about 100 feet farther. See **Chapter 13: Details of the First Shot**. The noises of his next two shots also tell us the shooter was somewhere within 50 feet of the TSBD sniper's nest.

This book is not about arguing whether Oswald did the shooting. This book is about why Oswald was shooting and why it is easy to misunderstand the disaster.

A mountain of other circumstantial and direct evidence supports the Warren Commission's finding: Oswald was at the TSBD and was seen on the sixth floor before the shooting, eyewitnesses saw someone like him actually shooting, he owned the murder rifle, he snuck it into the TSBD, he fled and killed a policeman, he tried to kill another policeman, he lied under questioning, and he had no alibi for either murder. This startle analysis further cements Oswald's guilt. Ballistics and wound calculations presented in this book are all consistent with the Warren Commission basic finding: Oswald killed Kennedy from his sixth-floor TSBD "sniper's nest." Further, they are all in some ways inconsistent with other shooting site. While each bit of evidence can be questioned with conspiracy suppositions, together, they are compelling.

For the rest of this analysis, we regard lone assassin Oswald as the shooter of three shots.

We can tell, within a half-frame, when the trigger was pulled for each shot: F149, F220, and F311. Oswald shot three times from the TSBD sniper's nest in 8.85 seconds. The second shot hit JFK and Connally. The third shot hit and killed JFK.

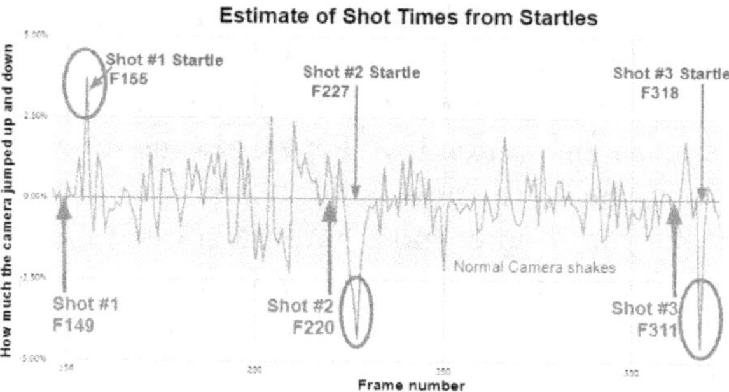


We will use the Zapruder film to discover Oswald's motive. We will show that Oswald was motivated by politics and his place in the history of politics. We will show that Oswald would never intentionally shoot Kennedy because Kennedy was doing the things that Oswald's politics demanded. We will show that Oswald intended to shoot Governor Connally, ironically, to protect Kennedy's reelection.

How can we know? Because we can scientifically deduce from Oswald's first shot:

- when Oswald shot
- what Oswald expected to hit
- where Oswald's bullet went

The Result: Oswald's first shot hit a tree branch that **could only have been blocking Connally.**

Oswald would not have known what that first bullet had done. It should have hit the car, at least, but that car had disappeared behind trees. Oswald's second shot would also not have given him a clear result. Up until his fatal third bullet, Oswald could not have been sure what his shots had done. Only after the third shot could he begin to realize his horrible mistake.

We will trace how Oswald tried to shoot Connally, expecting to become a hero in the eyes of his wife, his children, his few friends, and the World's Ultra Left Wing. Oswald was not a lone nut. He was a lone gunman blind to the possibilities of collateral damage.

In the hour before his arrest, Oswald realized that he had killed Kennedy. He attempted to die by police fire. Once arrested, Oswald tried to minimize his disaster. He repeatedly claimed that "Kennedy's death didn't matter: the new president would do about the same." But if he thought JFK and LBJ were "about the same," then why kill JFK? He obviously did not intend to kill Kennedy.

# 2

# WHY OSWALD LIKED KENNEDY

When Oswald fled to the Soviet "worker's paradise" in 1959, he had cited three reasons that he wanted to leave the USA:

1. Racial discrimination plagued the US.
2. The downtrodden were often exploited in the US.
3. Inter-factional hate wracked and paralyzed the world with nuclear war approaching.

Kennedy was a senator in 1959, little known to Oswald.

Kennedy first became important in Oswald's world when he ran and won the presidency in 1960. Self-taught Marxist Lee Harvey Oswald was beginning his second year in the Soviet Union. The Russian people and Oswald got only restricted news – but what they saw created enthusiasm. The charismatic Kennedy won the hearts of Russians. Oswald, who had come to Russia complaining about his homeland, soon spoke more favorably about the US.

Russian press started talking about the impending US-managed invasion of Cuba in late 1960. Back in April 1960, Eisenhower had approved an exile guerilla infiltration to fight Castro; by late summer 1960, the CIA evolved the plan into a full invasion – supposedly following Eisenhower's directive that "the hand of the US should not show." The CIA recruited exiles and set up training camps, largely in Guatemala, with "ghost" B-26 bombers, ships, and equipment; Guatemala was itself run by a repressive junta installed by a CIA-corporate 1954 coup. In theory, all was to be cleaned of American connections. By JFK's inauguration, the Russians and Oswald knew that Eisenhower had left JFK a ticking bomb – Eisenhower lied about the state of the program at that point, assuring JFK that it was going very well and JFK had the responsibility to bring to a successful conclusion. It blew up in Kennedy's face in mid-April 1960. Kennedy took the blame for the failure.

Some Russians around Oswald were amazed. Why hadn't Kennedy led his powerful military to squash Castro's Cuba? Kennedy had refused to authorize US attacks on a sovereign nation. Russians compared JFK's humanity with what the Russians had done in, for example, Hungary (technically, the Soviet "aid" to Hungary was at the request of the Hungarian puppet government). Kennedy had swallowed his pride and done the peaceful thing – that took a great man. Other Russians gave Kennedy even more credit for putting an end to an Eisenhower-designed excuse for a US invasion of a sovereign nation.

In June 1961, Khrushchev demanded that all armed forces leave Berlin. Rumors came to Minsk that Kennedy had called up nearly one million reserves and was moving nuclear weapons "forward positions." No shots were fired. Khrushchev decided to build the "Berlin Wall" to keep dissatisfied from fleeing west. Oswald saw that Kennedy had resolved the conflict without violence - and that many people were dissatisfied with living in the East.

In October 1961, the Soviets exploded history's most powerful H-bomb, their 50-megaton "Tsar Bomba." Soviet newspapers bragged about their space program. Oswald could see that big missiles could deliver big bombs. Tensions were building. Oswald's writings discuss his fear that nuclear war was coming. Armed radicals would enslave any survivors, he wrote.

In 1962, the Cuban missile crisis brought the world to the brink of nuclear war. By then, Oswald was back in Ft Worth with his Soviet wife and baby June. Oswald was amazed that JFK engineered a peaceful solution - winning worldwide renown for resisting the Hawks. But to the conservative Texans around Oswald, Kennedy was a wild liberal, a traitor to capitalism, a man too cowardly to launch war on the communists. Kennedy started towards nuclear disarmament with his nuclear test ban treaty. Ultra-right Texans declared that Communist-loving Kennedy had to be stopped.

Outside Dallas, by June 10, 1963, John F. Kennedy was the world's most popular man: his "Peace Speech" announced his plan to limit nuclear weapons. People everywhere realized their families might not end under mushroom clouds. Kennedy was leading the world away from nuclear Armageddon.

The next day, Kennedy launched his plan to end racial discrimination. His "Report to the American People on Civil Rights" announced comprehensive civil rights efforts. "We preach freedom around the world, and we mean it ... but are we to say to the world, and, much more importantly to each other, that this is the land of the free except for the Negroes?" Kennedy declared that civil equity was a moral issue that was the responsibility of all Americans. "This is not a sectional issue... Difficulties over segregation and discrimination exist in every city, in every State of the Union, producing in many cities a rising tide of discontent that threatens the public safety."

He proposed what became the Civil Rights Act of 1964 and the Voting Rights Act of 1965, in theory ending discrimination and providing equal treatment to all before the law. He decried lagging education, lagging employment, lagging pay, lagging lifespan. "Law alone cannot make man see right" to end institutional racism. It is "a moral crisis... that must be solved in the homes of every American in every community across our country." Kennedy intended to lead his country to better race relations both legally and interpersonally.

His speech on civil rights was forceful and timely. Governor George Wallace had just stood in the door of the University of Alabama to deny registration for two qualified Black students. Kennedy wanted the federal government to prevent this kind of state-local tyranny – but he needed Civil Rights laws to provide a legal basis.

Oswald's oral and written history discuss his conviction that America's wealthy had enslaved America's poor. He was particularly concerned with the abuse of Black Americans. Kennedy's civil rights speech struck exactly the chord of Oswald's own thoughts on racism. Kennedy's smaller initiatives raised the minimum wage, improved education, and generally pushed Federal "small-scale" Socialism to improve life for the poor. Kennedy, despite his family wealth, seemed to be on the people's side. Wealthy people were not automatically evil - Cuba's Castro had come from a wealthy family, after all.

While Oswald respected the maturing Kennedy, Texas conservatives attacked him. Kennedy's attention to the disadvantaged immediately hurt his popularity. Most Americans agreed that Deep South anti-Black riots, murders, and intimidations had to be stopped, but many found the idea of Black equality threatening. Kennedy's approval ratings slid slowly from 64% down to stabilize at 58%, still high, but a long way from his 83% high and his near 70% average. Disproval was strident in the South, where Oswald lived. Places like New Orleans and Dallas printed hate-filled pamphlets and barely less virulent editorials.

Oswald checked out Mansfield's *The Portrait of a President [John F. Kennedy]* from his local New Orleans library. Oswald's wife, Marina, recalled that he read this book slowly and with concentration. It is a book that "adores" JFK. Oswald voiced no bitter sarcasms during his reading or thereafter – he was impressed.

Oswald told Marina he saw parallels between himself and Kennedy. Like Oswald, Kennedy was a man of ideas, a voracious reader who claimed that he "got most of his ideas from reading." Kennedy "hated to be told what to do." Kennedy remained calm, focused on key issues, was an independent thinker who could hold unpopular views, and was a man of World Peace. These were traits that Oswald imagined in himself.

Oswald began to talk to his wife about how he, too, would be a great leader someday. She laughed at him.

As he absorbed *The Portrait of a President*, Oswald admired Kennedy's acceptance of responsibility without blaming others. Oswald envied Kennedy's "total recall." Most important, Oswald was amazed at Kennedy's intense work ethic. Despite his wealthy origins, Kennedy had earned the right to be president as a liberal who would work to help everyone rather than just capitalists or just Catholics or just Irish (Manchester, 1962). Oswald followed up his Kennedy biography by reading Kennedy's Pulitzer Prize-winning *Profiles in Courage* and at least checked out one of Kennedy's recent reads, *The Blue Nile*.

Kennedy was in every magazine by this time. Marina cut out a picture of JFK and put it on their wall. Oswald patiently read her every article they found on JFK and his family - that meant a lot of translation since Marina only spoke Russian. Oswald seemed to like JFK nearly as much as Marina and read with interest and enthusiasm – this was one of the few good times in Marina's rocky marriage. Both Jackie and Marina were pregnant mothers; Oswald related to Kennedy as a father. Oswald tuned the radio to hear JFK's speeches and allowed no interruptions. Oswald expressed admiration for Kennedy as a worthy leader who was trying to steer his country and the world in positive directions.

No one ever heard Oswald say bad things about JFK.

Oswald saw Kennedy as transforming from a rich politician to a leader that could make America better for all Americans. Kennedy was doing what Oswald wanted done. As Oswald heard and read more, it became clear that Kennedy was working to fix his very problems:

1. Racial discrimination plagued the US.
2. The downtrodden were often exploited in the US.
3. Inter-factional hate in the US and the World.

JFK said he would do much more after his 1964 reelection.
Why, then, did Oswald kill Kennedy?
It was an accident.

Oswald hoped to hurt Connally, to give himself a courtroom platform to expose and impede what he thought was a looming ultra-conservative takeover of the USA. Connally was a rising conservative star who Dallas newspapers said might dethrone Kennedy. To Oswald, Connally was the dangerous antithesis of Kennedy:

1. Connally would perpetuate segregation and racial discrimination.
2. Connally would aid corporations in exploiting the downtrodden.
3. Connally would fan political hatred and further divide America.

Oswald did not "hate" Connally and never showed personal animosity towards him.

Oswald wanted to save America from "a second Hitler." He imagined the imminent birth of an ultra-right revolution for racism and classism. He imagined his subsequent trial would allow him to explain why he had killed Connally. He would declare that he had saved Kennedy's America from that ultra-right threat.

Oswald hoped to be a hero. His wife, his few friends, his two children, even the greats, including Kennedy himself, would respect him for exposing the Ultra-Right. Instead, Oswald accidentally killed the man sitting just behind Connally. Oswald extinguished America's best progressive hope, changing history in exactly the opposite direction from his intent.

## 3

# STOPPING ANOTHER HITLER

Oswald lived his life as a political firebrand who never could light a fire. His intense political views, his powerlessness, and the ridicule of his wife and friend are the accelerants that drove him to murder.

The Kennedy assassination is the most studied murder in history. In the beginning, it seemed simple. Hundreds of policemen and agents swarmed the area, initially trampling the area in searching for an active shooter but eventually gathering evidence and testimonies. Within fifteen minutes of the assassination, authorities put out a very rough description of their man. Within two hours, Oswald was in custody for murdering a policeman then tied to Kennedy's death. Within six hours, Oswald's irritating smirk was on the World's TVs, generating thousands of death threats.

Oswald never admitted anything. If he just wanted any place in history, he certainly had a strange way of claiming it. His odd behavior makes sense – if he had killed the wrong man.

. . .

We can prove beyond reasonable doubt that Oswald was aiming at Connally with his first shot.

Zapruder's camera aim point provides the key.

- Zapruder startled at the sound of the first shot, at Zapruder frame F155.
- Given the speed of sound was 1125 feet per second, Oswald's muzzle blast took .24 seconds (4.4 frames) to reach Zapruder.
- Zapruder's head-duck startle reaction took about .09 seconds (1.6 frames) to make his camera aim jump.
- Therefore, Oswald pulled the trigger about 6 frames before F155: **at F149.**

We can construct what Oswald saw when he pulled the trigger at F149. We'll use the second-by-second FBI reconstruction photos taken from the sniper's nest. The FBI published photos only at F140 and F159 and a reenactment film. We can construct the sniper's view at F149 for this Zapruder frame:

*Abraham Zapruder Film © The Sixth Floor Museum at*
*Dealey Plaza*

Zapruder's F149 locates the limo passing the lane marker – we can see that lane marker just disappearing behind the left limo tire. The front of the limo passed the near end of the lane marker at F144. The limo was traveling at about 11 mph at that point. By F149, the car would have traveled between 4.2 and 5 feet west along Elm.

The FBI *What Oswald saw* photos (CE875) is a series of photos of Elm Street, taken from the Sniper's Nest, in the TSBD sixth-floor window. Unfortunately, the FBI did not align their sparse still photos with each Zapruder frame. The nearest to F149's view are:

*About F140*

*About F159*

These pictures are just one Zapruder second apart, but the car traveled about 16.1 feet in each second. We do not have exactly the right frame picture to show what Oswald saw, but we can construct one (on the left). On the right is a similar frame from the FBI reenactment. The fatal limo had an extra bench seat, where Mr. and Mrs. Kennedy sat – the reenactment used a normal Lincoln convertible, so JFK's outline looks like he is out on the trunk while Connally's is slightly forward and left of the normal back seat.

*~F149 (FBI Telephoto)*

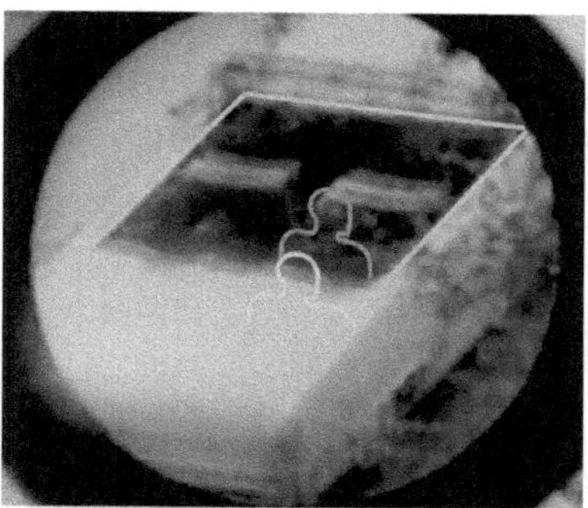

*~F150 (from reenactment)*

These stick-figure replicas of the Kennedy limo estimate where
the limo was for F149 and F150 of the Zapruder film, as seen
from Oswald's sniper's nest. The error in all calculations has
been estimated and shown as fuzzy areas: the front of the car

was in the green shaded area at F144; it moved about 4.5 feet to reach the turquoise shaded area at F150; the blue shaded area estimates where JFK was at F150; the red shaded area estimates where John Connally was.

Oswald saw a rapid-moving, smudgy, jumpy view through his cheap scope at F149:

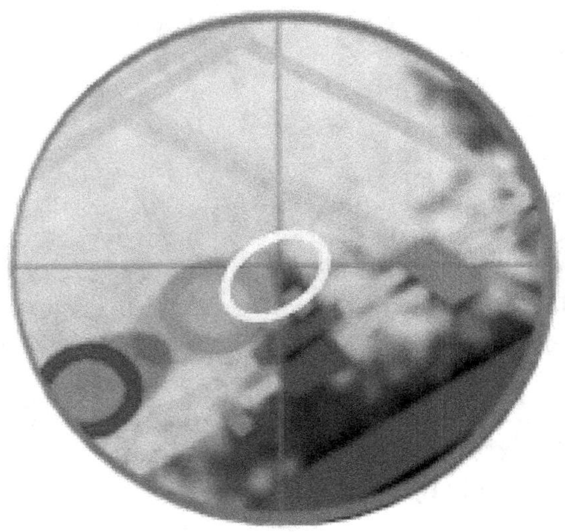

We know his first bullet did not hit the car or anyone in it. The only way that bullet vanished is by deflecting on a tree branch. There is NO tree branch between Oswald and Kennedy (the blue circle), nor would there be until about F154. The yellow area estimates where Oswald's first bullet struck. There is only one candidate branch – it was over Connally at F150.

**Conclusion:**

. . .

**Oswald's first bullet was aimed at Connally rather than Kennedy.**


## Reconstructing Oswald's Shot


Several witnesses saw Oswald in his window before the shooting. These witnesses describe Oswald as not having a rifle in his hands, standing looking out down Elm Street rather than towards Houston.


When Oswald did aim, the limo was probably just past him, going under the streetlight arm. It was moving diagonally away from him at about 16 feet per second. It was only 120 feet away, so Oswald had to swing his rifle quickly to track it. He had a very narrow view through his cheap 4x18 sniper scope. When the bulk of the tree swept into his scope view, Oswald had less than 0.3 seconds to shoot. That was just enough time for the car's motion to put Connally under the branch. Oswald missed, ahead of Connally by a few inches.


Oswald had not practiced with that kind of moving target, even as a Marine. He simply was not prepared to succeed. He knew his old life was over if he shot, yet in the end, he tried it. Probably a major factor was the embarrassment he had endured when he had missed an easy shot at General Walker. He had already convinced himself to take the shot, even if it would take a lot of luck. He had already left his wedding ring and money behind. This rushed shot is evidence that Oswald was not a brilliant assassin; he was just a little man with a blinding ego and a cheap rifle.

. . .

**Where did the first bullet go?**

Oswald's first bullet hit along that oak branch at a flat angle: the shot was aimed at about 30° down, and the branches in that area drooped about 10°, so the angle of impact was about 20°. That shallow angle caused the bullet to dig along and then skip on the tree bark - like a stone on a pond.

The bullet jacket peeled off as it spun along the rough oak bark. Pieces of that shredded jacket apparently dropped in the street or sprayed into the grass. The heavy lead core of the bullet spun on, tumbling through the air across Elm Street, striking the curb about 420 feet away near a bystander named James Tague.

Tague was hit by a fragment from the impact of Oswald's first bullet with the South side of Main Street's curb, near Tague's feet. The rest of the bullet was never found.

There is more discussion in **Chapter 13: Details of the First Shot.**

## Oswald's Second Shot Hit Both Men

Once the limo had cleared the oak trees at F210, Oswald had an unobstructed view but very little time. Oswald had no idea of the limo layout or seating; he was not aware that Connally would be in the low inboard jump seat blocked by whoever was sitting behind him. Connally's striking silvery hair and white Stetson hat made him easy to identify.

This picture was taken a few minutes before the shooting from a slightly lower angle; it shows how Connally lined up with Kennedy, given Kennedy's higher back seat and the inboard location of Connally's jump seat. It was this alignment that proved fatal for Kennedy in these two later shots.

At F220, Oswald shot again, about 3.9 seconds after his first shot and a short half-second after Connally cleared the tree. Connally was partially obscured by another rider, but Oswald took the shot anyway – he was already committed by his first shot. The downward slope of the street, the lower jump seat, the slight right-ward curve of the street, and the slight inboard position of Connally's jump seat had combined to align Kennedy and Connally from Oswald's nest.

Oswald's 6.5mm bullet hit JFK at F222. That bullet caused a temporary cavitation in Kennedy's neck tissue, like a rock dropped into a pond makes a temporary hole in the water. That cavitation compressed spinal nerve bodies at C7-T1, causing them to artificially "fire," immediately tensing all the muscles in Kennedy's shoulders, arms, hands, and some in his chest and back. This compression firing is **not** a reflex: it is an artificial action beginning after the .05 second transit down the nerve axons to muscle. That is why JFK's right arm is already up by F226 when he is again visible; his left arm, starting from a downward position, took about .6 seconds to rise to equilibrium as its muscles fought each other. The bullet missed Kennedy's vertebrae and top ribs, glanced off his trachea, pushed out his well-knit shirt, and glanced slightly off his tie knot.

Slightly slowed and slightly deflected, that second bullet hit Connally's right back somewhat sideways, making an elliptical hole through his suit, shirt and skin near his right underarm. It careened next to Connally's fifth rib. Its impact and cavitation energy broke the rib, exploding bone shards into his lung. It emerged, making a large exit hole under his nipple. Although having lost about 90% of its energy, it hit sideways and fractured his right wrist. Deflected again, it embedded slightly in his left thigh. See Failure Analysis Associates reconstruction as reported in (Posner, 1993), or as modelled for the PBS Nova documentary *Cold Case JFK* (Haag L. a., 2013).

Connally's reactions were slower than Kennedy's trauma-forced arm raises. The bullet impact and rib damage was reported by normal sensory nerve actions. Those nerve reports first alerted his solar plexus, causing his diaphragm to contract in the classic "oof" of a stomach punch, hunching him slightly forward towards the side of the car while forcing air through puffed cheeks at F226. The sensation of impact continued up to his brain, which interpreted it at about F230 as a "hard push in his back." By F230, Connally had mostly completed his turn and now faced forward so that his realization of impact was conflated with his forward vision at that point. He would remember that he got hit when he was facing forward, causing him and his world audience to forever doubt that he was hit by the same "magic bullet."

Because Kennedy and Connally were aligned from Oswald's point of view, we cannot be certain whether he was aiming for Kennedy or Connally in this second shot. Oswald was not expert enough to figure out the motion, the wind, and even the bullet speed. There was no evidence that he pre-calculated the shot or knew that there was a 12 to 17 mph wind gusting across the limo. He did not even know the speed of the car. As Oswald's Marine 1959 shooting manual says, it is difficult to hit even a target walking, so it did not teach moving target shots.

As a result of the C7-T1 ganglion trauma, Kennedy's own muscles forced him into an upright, arms-up, elbows-out rigid posture for several seconds; his hands did not touch his throat but became fists a few inches in front of his chin. Mrs. Kennedy (Jackie) saw her husband's elbows lift in about a half second in an unnatural way. She said he "looked quizzical." Jackie turned to look directly at JFK only 0.7 seconds after the impact. Then she raised her right hand, then her left, to grab JFK's raised left arm. We can tell that Jackie was pulling on his arm because Kennedy started leaning towards Jackie and because we can measure that she pulled herself up out of her seat a little. The car slowed down a bit from this point, probably because the driver turned to look back and the twist of his body lifted his right foot from the accelerator. Jackie appeared to pull herself forward to get close to her husband's face as Kennedy's arms began to relax out of his cavitation-induced elbows-up position. She was no doubt mystified.

Connally had turned sideways starting at F157 and remained twisted to his right. When he was hit at F222, he was in shock for a moment and then turned to look back at Kennedy. Sadly, Connally shouted "no, no, no!" instead of "everyone down!" or even "I'm hit!"; his ambiguous "no!" left Jackie with no clue as to what was going on. She might have pulled her husband down into her lap instead of holding him up to look into his face.

.  .  .

There is more discussion in **Chapter 14: Details of the Second Shot.**

## The Third Shot, "Back and to the Left"

When Oswald again sighted his rifle, he would have seen Connally starting to duck backwards towards his wife. Had Oswald shot at F290, he would have had a clear shot, but Connally's head was already moving towards his wife. Oswald was probably put off by Connally flopping backwards (from right to left from Oswald's perspective). Oswald finally shot just as Connally's head was eclipsed by JFK, who was stiffly upright but leaned 20° towards his left. Once again, being unpracticed at hitting moving targets, Oswald aimed at Connally's moving head, but his bullet went one inch too low. His bullet just struck Kennedy's leaning head. Only a half an inch higher and the bullet would very likely have glanced off.

Everyone agrees that a shot hit Kennedy's head fatally at F313. Zapruder's startle and the bullets' impacts indicate that Oswald took almost 5 seconds to make that fatal shot. Had Kennedy's head not been there, Oswald would have hit Connally in the head. Instead, Kennedy was brain-dead from the massive trauma of the third shot.

The bullet impact pushed Kennedy's head forward a couple of inches from F312 to F313. Then he fell back and to his left. Many believe it was due to impact(s) of shots from the knoll behind Zapruder. Here are some brief reasons why that is not the case:

- His whole head and torso move together; a head impact would move his head.
- He moved relatively slowly – not "slammed"; he moved at "sitting down" speed.

- He was already tilted left, enough so that gravity
  would assist his fall.
- Jackie was pushing on his rigid left elbow; that is the
  major accelerator back and left.

There is more discussion in **Chapter 15: Details of the Third Shot.**

Many believe that Jackie crawled onto the trunk to get a piece of JFK's head. An analysis of the ejection material shows it went primarily upward and slightly forward. Only light mist was blown to the rear to spatter the following motorcycles. No material shows on the trunk in the Zapruder film, nor does Jackie's hand appear to grasp anything. The driver, realizing too late the awful situation, stomped on the accelerator. The car jumped forward just as Jackie was standing up, instinctively away from her bloodied husband; it was that acceleration that caused Jackie to fall onto the slick trunk. Only her thighs hitting the back seat kept her gloved hands from sliding off that trunk. Fortunately, the driver saw her and stopped the acceleration, allowing her to get back to her seat. Agent Hill falsely remembered that he "saved Jackie"; in the film, it is clear that she saved herself and that Hill barely touched her elbow as she was dropping to safety. Jackie may have brought a piece of her husband's head into the hospital – but likely, she picked that piece up from the bloody mess of the back seat.

The alignment of Kennedy and Connally in shots 2 and 3 leaves us no certainty as to who Oswald intended to shoot – read *Tragic Truth: Oswald Shot Kennedy by Accident* (Pierre Sundborg, 2016) for a more in-depth analysis of why Oswald's intentions are not discernable in shots 2 and 3. Only the first shot reveals Oswald's intent.

**Regarding Conspiracy Theories**

*Jackie Scowled* is not specifically a resource for assessing conspiracy theories. This book makes its assertions on analysis of the hard evidence and discusses the ramifications of those analyses. All its analyses are relatively simple and explained in detail; anyone can reproduce them and judge error latitudes. The conclusions about Oswald's shots rest on these facts, not on the author's opinions or skills or on memories.

The Kennedy Assassination remains the most studied single-day event in history. Vast resources of all kinds and reliability are available for those interested in other opinions and analyses. This book does not suggest any other specific views, though it does depend on many others for facts, as noted in its footnotes and bibliography.

Some basic information came from these resources. *JFK Assassination Logic: How to Think About Claims of Conspiracy* (McAdams, 2011) presents ideas on how to think about conspiracies. *Conspiracy of One* (Moore, 1991), *Case Closed* (Posner, 1993), and *Beyond Reasonable Doubt* (Ayton, 2014) show Oswald as the sole killer. The most thorough treatment was done by Vincent Bugliosi in over 2500 dense pages (Bugliosi, 2007). Several books identified Connally as Oswald's target, for example, *Tragic Truth* (Pierre Sundborg, 2016) and *The Accidental Victim* (James Reston Jr, The Accidental Victim: JFK, Lee Harvey Oswald, and the Real Target in Dallas, 2013). DAVID VON PEIN's extensive JFK research and sites like https://www.youtube.com/user/assassinationforum/videos provide a great deal of information. *The JFK Myths* (Sturdivan, 2005) scientifically analyzes forensic evidence of Oswald's guilt. Litwin's *Oliver Stone's JFK: Destiny Betrayed* provides a thoroughly researched debunking of many major conspiracy theories (Litwin, 2023). More recently, consider *Tales of Deception and Imagination.* (Perry, 2021) Internet sites such as https://jfkassassination.quora.com/, is https://www.jfk-assassination.net/ and https://debunkingjfkconspiracies.quora.com/ carry on still-raging discussions. However, denying a conspiracy means accepting government assertions, whether from FBI, Dallas police, CIA, and so forth.

. . .

As for conspiracy thought, there are literally thousands of books and notes. There are flaws in every reference, for example, in *Case Closed* (Weisberg, Case Open: The Omissions, Distortions and Falsifications of Case Closed, 1994). More are discussed in **Chapter 9: Conspiracy Theories Had Fertile Grounds.**

*Jackie Scowled* tries to present only facts and fact-based history for its framework. In some cases, there is not enough fact basis to make determinations, yet it is important to suggest likelihoods; *Jackie Scowled* tries to mark such passages as "Speculation." In a few cases, *Jackie Scowled* even suggests its own conspiracies – yes, people did collude to protect themselves from the judgements of history and, in doing so, changed their future and ours.

**4**

# THE MAKING OF AN ASSASSIN

Oswald's life has been examined and dissected by many, starting with Appendix 13 of the Warren Commission Report. This book does not provide an exhaustive history of Oswald, but it does extract and emphasize the events that motivated Oswald's shots at Connally. This is not intended to be a cherry-picking distortion – it focuses on Oswald's political development.

From his teens, Oswald had almost no friends in his life in the USA and had little contact with his working mother or much older brothers. He had lived in 17 different places during his youth and so had no long-term connections. His character was shaped by his inner drive and by the material he read. Unfortunately, his inner drive was for attention from others, and when he did not get it, he devolved into a humorless loner, wanting no friends, suspicious and defiant of authority, contemptuous of societal norms, overly sensitive, with "paranoid ideas of grandiosity" and "self-vindication by shocking others." That was the analysis of a certified psychiatrist looking at Oswald at age 13. Oswald had "given up hope of being understood." Young Oswald expected rejection and frustration.

Oswald's earliest IQ testing indicated an IQ of 103 (118 in later testing). He was apparently dyslexic but became skilled at reading. He had been forced to 11 different schools in Texas,

Louisiana and New York before 9th grade. Increasingly, Oswald skipped school.

Oswald got comfort from reading books. His early life encouraged him towards anti-capitalism, shaped by his mother's crushing poverty, her broken family, and her depressing need to be working most of the time.

Living in the Bronx in 1953, truant Oswald was given a pamphlet on Marxism and saving the Rosenbergs. This pamphlet had a lasting effect on Oswald: thereafter, he occupied some time he should have been in school with doing his own reading on Communism. Oswald read library books by Marx and Lenin. He apparently had no one with whom to discuss these difficult subjects, so Oswald, wading through *Das Kapital* and the like on his own, wandered off into his own interpretations. People who knew him then described him as "interacting with no one," "shifting for himself," a child who "made his own meals" in an empty house as a 13-year-old latchkey kid in a big, impersonal city.

In his short life, he read political books, but also spy novels, some comic books, some science fiction, and eventually several Communist newspapers. In less than four months in his 1963 New Orleans summer, he read 10 political books, 10 science fiction books, 5 spy books, 4 history/philosophy books, and three other books – almost a book every three days. His readings those months included mostly respected titles: *Portrait of a President: JFK* and *Portrait of a Revolutionary: Mao, One Day in the Life of Ivan Denisovich* and *Hornblower and the Hotspur, What We Should Know About Communism* and *The Berlin Wall, From Russia With Love* and *Moonraker, Sixth Galaxy Reader* and *Nine Tomorrows*, and even *Ape And Essence* and *Brave New World*. In younger years, we know he read on wide topics, including Darwin, Norman V. Peale, various Jack London, and *The Idiot* by Dostoevsky. In later years, Marina would complain that Oswald stayed up late into the night to read, neglecting her.

But it was muddling through Communist "classics" that shaped him from an early, receptive age and was his pride. His reading focused on the trials of the downtrodden. His life with his mother was a case in point. The McCarthy-led abuse of Communists was another example. The treatment of Black people in New York, in the South, and beyond was yet another.

One of Oswald's few childhood friends recalled Oswald's claim to have been involved in the nationally reported Mansfield Crisis. In 1956, a federal appeals court had ruled to desegregate a high school, as required by 1954's Brown v. Board of Education. Local Black kids had been forced to attend a run-down all-Black school. The Texas Rangers were deployed to prevent integration amid strong anti-Black demonstrations. Ultimately, Black kids were bused 20 miles to Terrell High School, only three miles away from Oswald's own High School. The nearly 17-year-old Oswald had just moved to Fort Worth and was enrolled to repeat 10th grade at nearby Arlington High School. It is likely that Oswald at least watched ugly anti-integration demonstrations. Mansfield remained segregated throughout Oswald's remaining life.

## Oswald Wanted to Be a Marine

Peers reported that he resented school back in New York as early as 1952. At age 13, he had been ridiculed for his Texas drawl, for his poor-person clothes, and for his learning disabilities. He became withdrawn and temperamental. His brother, Robert, had left to join the Marines. Oswald had been proud to wear his brother's Marine ring, probably his only "cool" thing. He cut school over half the time. His truancy earned him weeks in Youth House, a "boys home," where a psychiatrist evaluated him as "disturbed," suffering from "emotional isolation and deprivation, lack of affection, absence of family life and rejection by a self-involved and conflicted mother." His confidential recommendation: Oswald should be committed to an institution to "save" him; that recommendation was ignored - or his mother heard of it and left town.

His mother moved them back to New Orleans to start 8th grade. Oswald had somewhat better attendance but was bored and often fought his classmates. Although his grades were below average, his achievement tests were above average for his start in high school. After one month in high school, and only 15, he tried to follow his brother Robert into the Marines: He forged a letter to his school, asking that copies of ID papers be given to him "becaus (sic) we are moving to San Diego," forging his mother's name. He briefly joined the Civil Air Patrol and attended a few meetings. He tried again to enlist in the Marines on his 16th birthday but was rejected. Oswald then quit school and spent some time reading more about Communism and Socialism at the local library while doing some delivery-boy jobs. His friend at the time said Oswald read trash novels and did not speak of ideologies.

He and his mother moved back to Fort Worth in August of 1956. Oswald reentered high school, meeting some of his old peers from 6th grade. Unfortunately for him, he had transitioned from a tallest 6th-grade "leader" to a "nobody" who was repeating 10th grade. Oswald told his mother when he dropped out of high school that he would enlist. She was upset. Since Oswald was still only 16, he repeatedly asked his mother to alter the birth year on his documents; she repeatedly refused. He wrote to the "Socialist Party of America," describing himself as a Marxist and asking for membership in their youth league. Before getting an answer from the socialists, Oswald turned 17, and convinced his mother to allow him to enlist. In October 1956, Oswald enlisted for a three-year tour. His five years older brother Robert Jr., already a Marine and Oswald's idol, was required to sign as his legal guardian.

After basic and specialty training, he was posted to Japan as a radar operator with a Confidential clearance, directing Marine planes while tracking and intercepting foreign aircraft. He taught himself to read Russian, and even to speak it a little. He flaunted his Communist books, magazines, and knowledge to his fellow Marines. Not surprisingly, he had troubles, including two court-martials. The first, over a personal derringer that fell and shot him in the arm, caused a suspended sentence. The second court martial was over challenging an NCO, resulting in 45 days of hard labor in a Marine brig. Oswald emerged from prison as a bitter loner, reading and complaining - and with a secret plan to defect to Russia. He was transferred back to the US at El Toro in November 1958.

His Communist literature also told him that Khrushchev had relaxed visa requirements to enter the USSR; much was made of thirty thousand young foreigners who enjoyed the "Socialist Carnival" in Moscow. In March 1959, he began executing a plan to get to Russia. He applied to several European colleges, and was accepted at Albert Schweitzer College in Switzerland, even paying a $25 holding fee. In June, his mother said a work-related injury prevented her from working; she had exhausted her savings with six months in bed. In July, the Soviets announced that visas could be given to anyone with a valid passport in Helsinki, so Oswald would no longer need to reside in Switzerland. On July 8, 1959, Oswald sent a special delivery letter that explained exactly what his mother needed to do to try to get Oswald an early discharge. He included $40 for her – a donation required for a hardship discharge. His mother followed instructions, increasing her pleading with "progressive arthritis had set in" and she had trouble caring for herself. Using his mother's letters and affidavits, Oswald applied for and got a "hardship discharge" honorable exit from the Marines three months early. A few days before his discharge took effect, still-active Marine Oswald applied for a passport that allowed him to attend school in Switzerland and Finland and to travel as a tourist to several countries, including Cuba and the USSR. He got that passport the day before he was discharged, probably using his school start date to encourage expediency.

Oswald stayed with his mom for just three days, then snuck off, leaving her $100 but taking the bulk of his savings. In homage to the newly popular James Bond, Oswald gave his occupation as a "shipping export agent" for his voyage. He reached Helsinki in three weeks, probably using the Military Air Transport Service from the UK. He heard, probably from the American Consulate, that he could arrange his visit with Intourist and get a one-week Soviet visa immediately from Russian consul Golub - because of Khrushchev's relaxed visa requirements - in fact, Khrushchev had just been visiting Eisenhower in the US. Oswald bought $300 in Soviet vouchers and arrived by train in Moscow on October 16, 1959, met by his Intourist guide.

Oswald had been planning this exit to Moscow for a year and had saved about half his Marine pay (~$1600) to pay for his defection trip, unknown to his mother or anyone else. It is typical of Oswald that he executed his entire defection plan without discussing his ideas or plans with anyone, even his mother and brothers. It shows that Oswald made big plans for abnormal goals in total secrecy. When his mother eventually learned of his attempted defection via a Ft. Worth newspaper report, she said, "I know nothing of Lee's activities because Lee doesn't confide."

The CIA apparently knew about Oswald through Finland Intelligence – but Finland would insist that their involvement be redacted until 2022; the Finns had a special agreement with their huge neighbor, which required them to tell the KGB about any spying, an example of why the CIA redacts documents. At least five State Department notes about Oswald's defection and later Minsk life were routed for CIA inspection but apparently did not trigger interest. The CIA did not create a "personality" 201 file on Oswald until 12/9/1960, and then only because in late October 1960, the US State Department requested information on all 14 "defectors" then in the USSR; the CIA may have lost data for Oswald's first year in the USSR. The CIA was later unable to explain their seeming negligence.


**In the USSR**

Oswald's time in the USSR was not as he hoped. The first bureaucrat he met tried to persuade him to go back to the USA. "USSR only great in Literature!" In response, Oswald attempted suicide by slitting his wrists. Out of the hospital, he attempted to renounce his US citizenship and threatened to tell Marine radar secrets to the Soviets; this threat later caused the Marines to change his discharge status from "honorable" to "undesirable," as well as to change any active codes and frequencies that Oswald might have revealed (given his low-security clearance, no changes were apparently needed). The US Embassy tried to change his mind by lining up reporters, then multiple phone calls from his brother and mother. Oswald had tried his defection just when Khrushchev was trying to better relations with the West, so the Soviets were very careful with him.

Oswald explained his defection to his brother Robert: "I came for freedom, to at last be with my own people," and that he "owed nothing to the US." He gave his three reasons for leaving America: racial discrimination, poor treatment of the underdog, and a climate of hate. Oswald spoke to Aline Mosby of the UPI about his defection. That story came out in Texas as "Fort Worth Defector Confirms Red Beliefs." The UPI reporter said that [Oswald] "seemed full of confidence, often showing a 'small smile, more like a smirk,' and that he talked almost 'non-stop.'" In 1964, she said, "he (Oswald) struck me as being a rather mixed-up young man of not great intellectual capacity or training, and somebody that the Soviet Union certainly wouldn't be much interested in ... a young boy full of bitterness and hate ...not brilliant...extremely superficial, very immature and very misinformed."

As it turned out, that reporter was right: the Soviets were not much interested in "developing" Oswald. However, unknown to Oswald, the KGB opened an espionage file on him on December 21, 1959, empowering covert surveillance of him throughout his stay. The KGB was the equivalent of the US's FBI, plus the CIA, plus Homeland Security, with a bit of NSA thrown in; further, the KGB was unconstrained by citizen's rights if it saw any hints of disloyalty to the USSR. The KGB was puzzled by the odd Oswald and watched from afar to see if he was a CIA plant.

Oswald spent two weeks with dysentery and then seven weeks studying Russian for eight hours a day on his own. In January 1960, the Soviet bureaucrats sent Oswald "out of Russia" to Minsk, the capital of Belorussia. He wrote to his mother and brother to "end" his family relationships. He lived "Russian-well" in Minsk: an allowance from the Red Cross doubled his pay to "Director level," plus an above-average rent-free apartment and an easy job as a lathe operator at the Gorizont Electronics (Radio) Factory.

As an exotic American who could teach English, he easily fell into friendships; compared to any other time in his life, Oswald had numerous social activities that kept him busy during off hours. Oswald was assigned to work with Pavel Golovachev to trade English for Russian language skills. Pavel became Oswald's good friend, helping him move in and get into some Minsk social activities. Oswald dated several girls – unaware that some were KGB. Pavel, in late 1960, told Oswald that the KGB had been interviewing and pushing him to probe Oswald. The KGB files on Oswald remained uneventful.

Work did not go as well. His department head was an Argentinian immigrant who told Oswald he would be better off going back to the US: the Argentine had a long list of complaints. Oswald, shaken, gradually became disillusioned with the USSR. He had drab work, long hours, mass gymnastics, compulsory farm work, no paid vacations, expensive shoddy goods, irritating party hacks, bad unchanging food, and boring compulsory propaganda meetings.

Oswald bought a simple Soviet camera, a Smena-2. He already had a camera from his time in the Marine Corps. He also bought a cheap Soviet two-band radio. Pavel reported that Oswald was not mechanically inclined, either with electronics or with his camera: Oswald had to get Pavel's help to make either work.

In November 1960, Oswald became friends with Ernst Titovets, a medical student who used Oswald to improve his English skills. Titovets wrote a book (Titovets, 2020) describing Oswald's *Russian Episode*, bringing together recollections of those who knew Oswald, as well as some information from old KGB files. Some of his insights were unknown to the Warren Commission and most researchers. His observations include:

- Oswald was self-centered, crude, uncultured, unaware, and blamed others.
- He was quiet with new people, then overconfident with young women.

- He liked parties, girls, dancing, opera, and talking with Titovets about politics.
- He loved Voice of America radio, starving for USA news.
- His little Russian transistor radio was weak; he used Titovets'.

[Note: His mother sent Texas news; Oswald could follow John Connally, JFK, the Minutemen, and the John Birchers as Dallas saw them.]

- He agreed with local Russians that JFK would be/was a good leader.
- He came to defend USA capitalism versus Soviet bureaucratic "enslaving."
- He complained about propaganda, after-work lectures, meetings, and exercises.
- He complained that Soviets jammed Voice of America instead of providing electricity to their people.
- He pushed for improvements at work, even staging a one-man 3-day strike.

Oswald was only 21 years old; Titovets overlooked Oswald's idiosyncrasies and had fun as Oswald's friend (Titovets, 2020).

While Oswald's Russian was improved with his casual work with Pavel, it was not good enough for his Minsk radio factory. They assigned physics researcher Stanislau Shushkevich to help Oswald improve his Russian (or maybe improve Shushkevich's English). Astoundingly, Shushkevich was in 1991 the first head of Belarus!! Apparently, the CIA was unaware of this Oswald connection until 1992.

Titovets became more engrossed in his own studies, spending less time with Oswald. Oswald wrote that it was altogether a lonely and dull life. Oswald apparently used his new radio to pick up Western broadcasts, which may have made him homesick: he wrote a letter asking for his passport and a return to the US. Unbeknownst to Oswald, his letter was intercepted by the KGB and inadvertently filed instead of sent on, so nothing happened.

As the Russian winter closed in, Oswald had a few desultory affairs. He proposed to a factory co-worker, Ella, twice, unsuccessfully in January 1961. According to Oswald's diary, he became despondent over Ella's refusals. After that, he really started dwelling on the downsides of Soviet life.

He turned down the offer of a Soviet Citizenship path about January 3, 1961. He had never returned to the US embassy to formally renounce his American citizenship. On February 1st, 1961, Oswald again asked for his US passport back if any charges would be dropped. Thereafter, he lived "in a state of expectation about going back to the US."

In March of 1961, Oswald met a vivacious 19-year-old pharmacology student named Marina. Six weeks later, they were married – a whirlwind courtship, especially given that Oswald spent two of those weeks in hospital for ear infections. In Oswald's diary of his Soviet Life, he said that he had "married Marina to spite Ella, but was coming to love Marina." Marina said she married Oswald because he was an exotic 24-year-old American "outsider" who accepted her illegitimate orphan status; he was clean and neat, he had chosen her, and he had an apartment. She did not know till later that he had lied: he was 21 rather than 24, his mother lived so he was not an orphan, and he had chosen another girl but had been rejected. Marina, too, had issues beyond being lazy, fatuous, and untidy: at 19, she drank, smoked, swore, flirted, and partied – including sexual liaisons that her compatriots said she continued after marrying Oswald (Titovets, 2020).

Oswald became convinced that his apartment was bugged by the KGB. He turned out to be right, as KGB records eventually revealed. At one point, Titovets visited to find Oswald fiddling with two odd metal devices – Oswald claimed he had stolen them from his Radio Factory Research area and was turning them into "hand grenades" to deter KGB action. Oswald may have intended to give stolen Soviet microwave radar parts to the US embassy to get back in good graces; he apparently gave up – his "grenades" disappeared (Titovets, 2020).

In July of 1961, Oswald asked the Soviets for an exit visa for himself and Marina. The visa was delayed, but Oswald's salary was reduced to the level of Russian coworkers – about in half. Oswald's diary showed: "Russians cruel, crude, always spying." The Soviets tried to persuade Marina not to go to the US. Nevertheless, the pair eventually did get their Soviet exit visas - on Christmas day - and surprisingly easily. Marina had only a trade school education, was apolitical, did not know anything sensitive, and carried no weight in the unlikely event that she criticized the USSR once in the US. She was married to an American citizen who had asked to return to the US even before he had met Marina.

CIA interest in Oswald increased when they heard of his intent to repatriate. On Aug 7, 1961, they put him on the secret HT-Lingual WATCH LIST, reading his mail to and from the USSR; only about 300 other people got that kind of attention at that point. (Oswald was taken off that list after ten months when he returned to the USA.) The CIA also did some investigation of Marina, adding a little background to Oswald's 201.

Oswald, on the other hand, was listening to Western radio. On September 25, Oswald strained to catch every word of Kennedy's speech to the UN. When Marina asked what it was about, Oswald replied, "War and peace," and provided quotes from JFK. A few days later, Oswald angrily defended JFK in an argument with Marina's uncle. Oswald saw that the Soviet newspapers had distorted what Kennedy had said. The uncle and Oswald only agreed on JFK's peaceful handling of the Bay of Pigs.

Oswald's Minsk acquaintances remembered him as a good husband, caring for Marina and June while in Minsk. Many described Oswald, when not with Marina, as reserved, unemotional, unathletic, and a little boring, yet a person who craved attention. His factory co-workers called him diligent, not too smart, hard to correct, and incurious. The Russians remembered that when Oswald saw Kennedy on Russian TV, Oswald said he liked him. Oswald generally spoke proudly of America and of Kennedy's accomplishments. No one in Russia thought that he would be an assassin, least of all of Kennedy.

Marina was not a loving wife, at least according to Minsk acquaintances. KGB surveillance transcripts show angry marital arguments. Later, in the 1964 Warren Commission hearings, his wife Marina was one of Oswald's harshest critics. She said she married Oswald out of pity, as he had no friends - "Everybody hated him, even in Russia." At other times, Marina said Oswald was never happier than when he was in the Soviet Union with her and that he had friends there. Marina's inconsistency in testimony should be remembered in any evaluations.

In mid-February of 1962, Marina bore a daughter, June. Oswald again asked for a US visa. The USSR was no longer held in Stalin's iron grip; under Khrushchev and Kennedy's influences, there was a softening that might have helped Oswald and Marina get their visas. It is another bitter irony that JFK's work to open the USSR might have helped let his assassin back into the USA.

Oswald tried to raise money for his family, from the US government and from the Red Cross – he did reject his mother's idea of publicizing his need to collect donations in Fort Worth. The US State Department gave them a "stranded American" repatriation loan of $435.71 (over $3700 in 2020 dollars). Such loans are supplied, based only on "destitution," for temporary subsistence and transportation to a U.S. port of entry. (Oswald repaid it within nine months.)

In May 1962, the Oswald family of three emigrated. On the boat back to the US, Oswald prepared responses to questions he guessed might be asked during any upcoming FBI interrogations or news interviews. He wrote two sets of answers, one as an American patriot and one as a Communist. His actual text and a direct transliteration are available as Warren Commission CE100. Below, they are rearranged so the answers are paired for better understanding Oswald.

1. Why did you go to the USSR.?

[Marxist Oswald:] I went as a mark of disgust and protest against American political policies in foreign countries; my personal sign of discontent and horror at the misguided line of reasoning of the US Government.

[Patriot Oswald:] I went as a citizen of the US (as a tourist) residing in a foreign country, which I have a perfect right to do. I went there to see the land, the people and how their system works.

2.A What about those letters?

[Marxist Oswald:] I made several letters in which I expressed my above feeling to the American Embassy when, in Oct 1959, I went there to legally liquidate my American citizenship and was refused this legal right.

[Patriot Oswald:] I made no letters deriding the US!! In correspondence with the US Embassy, I made no anti-American statements, any criticism I might have had was of policies, not our government.

2.B Did you make statements against the US there?

[Marxist Oswald:] yes.

[Patriot Oswald:] no.

2.C What about that tape recording?

[Marxist Oswald:] I made a recording for Radio Moscow, which was broadcast the following Sunday in which I spoke about the beautiful capital of the Socialist work and all its progress.

[Patriot Oswald:] I made a recording for Fadie the Moscow Tourist Radio travel log, in which I spoke about sight-seeing and what I had seen in Moscow tourist circles. I expressed delight in all the interesting places. I mentioned in this respect the University, Museum of Art, Red Square, and the Kremlin. I remember I closed this 2-minute recording by saying I hoped our peoples would live in peace and friendship.

3. Did you break laws by residing or taking work in the USSR?

[Marxist Oswald:] I did, in that I took an oath of allegiance to the USSR.

[Patriot Oswald:] Under US law a person may lose the protection of the US, by voting or serving in the armed forces of a foreign state or taking an oath of allegiance to that state. I did none of these.

4. Isn't all work in the USSR considered State work?

[Marxist Oswald:] Yes, of course and in that respect, I also broke US Law in accepting work under a foreign state.

[Patriot Oswald:] No. Technically, only plants working directly for the State, usually defense, all other plants are owned by the workers who work in them.

5. What about statements you made to UPI[United Press International] agent Miss Mosby?

[Marxist Oswald:] I was approached by Miss Mosby and other reporters just after I had formally requested the American Embassy to legally liquidate my US citizenship, for a story, they were notified by the US Embassy, not by me. I answered questions and made statements to Miss Mosby in regard to my reasons for coming to the USSR, her story was warped by her later, but in barest essence, it is possible to say she had the truth printed.

[Patriot Oswald:] I was approached just after I had formally notified the US Embassy in Moscow of my future residence in the USSR by the newspaper agencies in Moscow, including UPI, API and Time Inc., who were notified by the Embassy. I did not call them. I answered questions and gave statements to Miss Mosby of UPI. I requested her to let me OK [her story.] She sent her story before she released it, which is the polite and usual thing. I saw her version of what I said just after she sent it. I immediately called her to complain about this, at which time she apologized but said her editor [had not let her and had] added several things. She said London was very excited about the story (that is how I deduced that she had already sent it), so there wasn't much else I could do about it. And I didn't realize that the story was even more blown out of shape once it got to the USA. I'm afraid the printed story was fabricated sensationalism.

6. Why did you remain in the USSR for so long if you only wanted a look?

[Marxist Oswald:] I resided in the USSR from Oct 16, 1959 to the spring of 1961, a period of 2 1/2 years. I did so because I was living quite comfortably. I had plenty of money, an rent-free apartment, lots of girls, etc. Why should I leave all that?

[Patriot Oswald:] I resided in the USSR until February [1961] when I wrote the Embassy stating that I would like to go back (My passport was at the Embassy, for safekeeping.), they invited me to Moscow for this purpose. However, it took me almost 1/2 year to get a permit to leave the city of Minsk for Moscow. In this connection, I had to use a letter from the head consular to the Russian authorities in Minsk (the Russians are very bureaucratic and slow about letting foreigners travel about the country, hence the visa). When I did get to Moscow, the Embassy immediately gave me back my passport and advised me on how to get an exit visa from the Russians for myself and my Russian wife. This long and arduous process took months, from July 1961 until ----- ____ 1962. Therefore, you see, almost 1 year was spent trying to leave the country. That's why I was there so long. Not out of desire!

7A Are you a communist?

[Marxist Oswald:] Yes, basically, although I hate the USSR and socialist system. I still think Marxism can work under different circumstances.

[Patriot Oswald:] No, of course not. I have never even known a Communist outside of the ones in the USSR, but you can't help that.

7B. Have you ever known a communist?

[Marxist Oswald:] Not in the USA.

8. What are the outstanding differences between the USSR and the USA?

[Marxist Oswald:] None, except in the US the living standard is a little higher, freedoms are about the same, medical aid and the educational system in the USSR is better than in the USA.

[Patriot Oswald:] freedom of speech and travel, freedom of outspoken opposition to unpopular policies, freedom to believe in god.

[Newspapers, Oswald imagines:] Thank you, sir, you are a real patriot!!

In addition to Q&A preparation, Oswald also spent travel time writing down a kind of position paper on his views of

Capitalism versus Communism. It is available as Warren Commission CE25. Some salient points:

- In America, radical elements like anarchists, communists and fascists talk of "saving" their country, but their movements will destroy everything by hating everything.
- Patriotic groups like Freedom Foundation are sellouts to wealthy patrons.
- Having lived in each system, both Communism and Capitalism are fatally flawed.
- Automation will bring new hardships to the masses.
- The biggest fault in our era is the fight for markets: wars, crises, and oppressive frictions.
- The biggest fault in Communism: the state (bureaucracy) does NOT wither away but grows ever stronger; attempts to kill a department make several new departments.
- Democracy also requires a centralized state, which continually grows so that true democracy only works at the local level.
- An Atomic War is expected. The Minutemen [a militant arm of the John Birch Society founded in 1961] are preparing to simply defend the present system and reinstate its influence after the mutual defeat.
- The armed Minutemen will survive as a hard core of fanatical American capitalist supporters. Armed groups will also survive in Communist countries.
- Post-Atomic War, the majority will want a new alternative to Capitalism and Communism.
- [Oswald intends to] put forward just such an alternative system.
- What is needed is a constructive and practical group of people desiring peace but steadfastly opposed to the revival of Cold War systems.
- "I despise the representatives of both systems whether they be socialist or Christian democrats,

> whether they be labor or conservative - they are all
> products of the two systems."
> - [Oswald excused his taking] money from
>   government agencies to survive, and to not appear
>   "crackpot": "After all [what sane person] would
>   refuse money?!?"

Oswald's shipboard manifesto was hand-written, with terrible spelling and punctuation: it shows his pessimism of a coming atomic war, his wide reading, his private-world planning, and his arrogance in thinking he would lead the rebuilding of a new alternative world system.

Oswald described his "alternative system" much later (available as CE98). [He may have written CE98 on March 20, 1963, just before he attempted an assassination of General Walker, as a way of explaining his radical anti-fascism – and why he was killing Walker.]

His alternative system is "not Capitalism" because he advocates collective production and distribution, ownership by equal worker-investors, and equal sharing of all post-tax profits. His alternative is "not Communism" because individuals (and small businesses) would be guaranteed freedom of private property, speculation, employment, and remuneration as long a profit is shared; only the means of production is owned collectively. He notes that the Soviets had committed horrific crimes against their own peoples, mass exterminations and repressions far beyond their capitalist counterparts. American Capitalism is no alternative: Oswald says it is decadent and dying from within in a mass of poverty.

He calls this not-Communist, not-Capitalist system his "Athean System":  no centralized state, with local Democracy instead. Fascism, nationalism, racism, discrimination, weapons of mass destruction, war mongering, handguns, monopolizing, and dismissal without cause are outlawed. Freedom of religion, speech, travel, shotguns, and press are guaranteed. He imagined it would be funded by 30%-90% profit taxes and some fees. Police and similar services would be provided, as would education to age 18, healthcare, and welfare for the incapable and aged.

He was thinking of something "best of both" capitalism and communism that would be looked upon as evolutionary rather than revolutionary, to be designed by "a constructive and practical group of persons." He rejected the basic tenet of Soviet (Stalinist) Marxism: Capitalism transitions to Marxist socialism only by violent revolution. In some ways, Oswald seemed pragmatic about human behaviors, preferring a committee-reasoned evolution to a revolution that would spin out of control, commandeered, personalized, and bureaucratized by aggressive radicals. Oswald had learned the terrifying cult effects of the "Great Historical Man" Stalin.

Oswald wrote one other major work: a 50-page essay describing the life of Russian workers [WC Exhibit 92]. This draft manuscript is impressive and worthy of publication (after edits) at the time. His first-hand observations, together with statistics and views from others, describe how workers live and how they resolve management, domestic, social, and political problems under the Soviet system. His Minsk friend calls it "a painstaking study of contemporary Soviet-style Socialism that qualifies Oswald to be viewed as a serious researcher on the subject" (Titovets, 2020).

## Back in the USA

FBI agent Fain twice interviewed Oswald on his return to Texas; Oswald was impatient, arrogant, and unwilling to talk about his Soviet adventure – it was his private business. He said he was not connected with any intelligence services. He agreed to report any contacts from foreign agencies.

The CIA's apparently unproductive HT-Lingual mail surveillance concluded on June 22, 1962, noting that Oswald, Marina and baby June had returned to the USA. Oswald settled back in Fort Worth. We have a wealth of information about his activities from the Warren Commission and others. Many books have been written about this period; only a brief review will be given here.

Oswald first spent the little money his mother and brother gave him to hire a stenographer for his CE92 *Russian Life* book. Oswald had his manuscript typed and wrote a "forward" and "about the author." He did not have the connections to arrange its publication.

Oswald then tried to get Russian translator jobs via Paul Gregory, who taught Russian at the library. A Russian émigré, Gregory hired Marina to teach his son, Paul, Russian. Paul visited Oswald's threadbare apartment and remembered only one non-essential item: a January 1962 Time magazine with JFK as Man of the Year on its cover.

Gregory and the Dallas-area Russian émigré community stepped in to help Oswald and Marina. They were suspicious of how easily Oswald and Marina had gotten out of the USSR: the other emigres had real horror stories in that regard. The émigrés agreed that Oswald was not smart enough to be a spy, but they figured the FBI would continue tracking him. The émigrés decided it was safe to help Oswald, Marina, and June in small ways. Marina was given nice dresses, food, medicine, baby things, rides, shopping, occasional money, and human interaction in Russian. Oswald was not comfortable accepting anything.

Oswald had gotten a job as a sheet metal worker but quit within three months, complaining that the job was hard, hot, and dirty. He did not get along with his co-workers. He told Marina he had been fired, but that was a lie: he was rated "satisfactory" but left of his own accord. He and Marina fought, and she ran out into the night with baby June to live with émigrés temporarily.

Oswald moved alone to Dallas the next day and interviewed with a Texas Employment Commission clerk. She tested him and found that his "verbal" and "clerical" skills were quite high. Oswald, however, had trouble landing a job until the émigrés put in a good word for him. Two days later, he was working at a commercial advertising photography company in Dallas as a photoprint trainee.

JFK announced the Cuban Missile Crisis a week after Oswald joined that company. Oswald got into arguments with co-workers over Cuba: he was "churlish and rude" to the brink of fighting. It did not help that Oswald had subscriptions to several Communist magazines, some of which he brought to work: *The Militant* (weekly newspaper of the Stalinist-leaning Socialist Workers Party of the US) and *The Worker* (a competing newspaper of the Trotskyist-leaning Communist Party of the US). He also continued receiving Soviet magazines in Russian: *Komkrin Inc.*, *Agitator*, *Ogonyok*, *Belowsi*, and *Krockill*. His subscription to *The Worker* was noted by the FBI.

The émigrés also irritated Oswald, with their politics, their support of segregation, and their capitalist successes. Continued émigré attentions to Marina drove a wedge into their marriage – they supported Marina's growing fear of Oswald's Marxism. Oswald fought with Marina and became physically abusive. Several times Marina fled to, or was rescued by, the émigré community. However, against the advice of many, she refused to initiate divorce; by 1963 most of the émigrés dropped her because she stayed with Oswald.

Marina missed her Russian life. She had enjoyed her life in the USSR more than her stressful poverty in the US, especially when Oswald denied her the chance to "party" with makeup, dresses, drinking and smoking. Yet she was not ready to leave Oswald.

One émigré couple, George and Jeanne De Mohrenschildt, stayed friends with Oswald and Marina. At age 51, George was described as handsome, tanned, tall, a world adventurer, an oil geologist, a womanizer, a provocateur, an atheist, loud, unpredictable, and contrary. He was a son of a Byelorussian noble. (Marina Oswald had also grown up in Minsk, Byelorussia.) He earned a Doctor of Science degree in international commerce in Belgium. In 1938, he joined his brother, an OSS employee, in New York. George worked as a perfume salesman and agent for French Intelligence, collecting information about pro-Germans. Remarkably, he became friends with the Bouvier family, including the 10-year-old future Jackie Kennedy, who called him "Uncle George" and sat on his knee. After trying insurance sales and movie production, George wandered the world in the oil business. On the way he was married four times, Jeanne being his fourth. Jeanne was exotic in her own right – born in China, fleeing, dancing, and finding success as a dress-designer in Dallas. After George's son died of Cystic Fibrosis, George and Jeanne created a Cystic Fibrosis Foundation with Jackie Kennedy as honorary chairman. Still despondent, they dropped their careers and spent their savings on a year-long walking trek through Latin America. George had some CIA contacts, from his foreign business dealings, and gave the CIA reports and films of his walk. When George and Jeane returned, they had become almost childlike in their carefree determination to live life without constraints, aggressively unconventional – but apparently fun to be around.

George, like the other émigrés, had been curious about how Oswald had gotten out of the USSR so easily. George used his CIA contacts, asking agent J. Walton Moore if it was "safe to associate with [Oswald]." George recalled that Agent Moore replied, "He's OK, he is just a harmless lunatic." (Mohrenschildt, Lee Harvey Oswald as I Knew Him, 2014) CIA Agent Moore denied that he ever spoke to George about Oswald. Moore's CIA files showed many contacts with George, who several times provided non-clandestine reports to Moore's Domestic Contacts Division concerning George's trips abroad – as did many business travelers.

Given his worldly background, why did George De Mohrenschildt become "Lee Harvey Oswald's best and only friend" from December 1962 to April 1963? In 1960, George's child had died, breaking his heart. George had made himself poor in 1961, with his year-long walk in Latin America, and had broken his career track; he and Jeanne were therefore pinned by poverty, awaiting his delayed Haiti geology contract; he had free time for little amusements like the Oswalds. George himself said that he and Jeanne pitied the Oswald family, but that there was "something charming" about Oswald. Yet George was instrumental in extracting Marina, June, and all their belongings out of Oswald's abusive clutches to move them in with an Emigre family - while Oswald screamed threats. George said that Oswald's threats did not concern him because Oswald "was small, a rather puny individual, and indeed he submitted to the inevitable, and even helped to carry everything out." In his memoir, George remembered that extraction as calmer, but it was still a forced separation – and one that George would never have allowed done to himself. Oswald got over it, maintaining George as his "best friend" till April when George left for Haiti.

As Oswald's "best American friend," George was interviewed repeatedly by many assassination investigators. He had a lot to say about Oswald and his family, most of which aligned with other acquaintances:

- Oswald and Marina were destitute in the US.
- They had a strained, violent relationship; neighbors overheard arguments.
- In public, Oswald seemed indifferent to Marina, she "bitched" at him.
- Marina made fun of Oswald's political talk.
- Marina complained publicly about his inadequacies as a lover. Note: There is no evidence that debonaire George had any untoward relationship with young, attractive, and vocally sex-starved Marina– though it certainly seems like a possible explanation of George's interests. The FBI's James Hosty later described Marina as "a pretty young brunette with beautiful green eyes." George's first three marriages were to much younger women – and both he and Jeane were "unconstrained." Again, there is no evidence one way or the other.
- Oswald wanted people to be interested in him, not in Marina.
- Oswald wouldn't let Marina smoke, drink, wear makeup, or learn English.
- Marina, pregnant again, was diagnosed as undernourished in this period.
- Oswald "was clinging to me [George]. He would call me."
- Oswald was "a forlorn individual, groping for something" ... "Utopia."

- Oswald was too outspoken, crude, and sincere to be an agent for anyone.
- Oswald "was a semi-educated hillbilly. You cannot take such a person seriously."
- Oswald read rather advanced books...[perhaps] without understanding them.
- Oswald hated his jobs and governments. "He was always disappointed."
- Oswald liked kids, dogs, animals, and walking, especially in woods.
- Oswald liked Kennedy as a world peacemaker and anti-segregation leader.
- Oswald "hoped for Kennedy's détente and for friendship [between US and USSR]."
- Oswald had declared "Kennedy is an excellent President, young, full of energy, full of good ideas."
- Oswald was a ferocious advocate of integration, and admired Kennedy for his stand.
- Oswald knew that Jackie had bounced on George's knee.
- Oswald knew that Jackie was the honorary chairman of George and Jeanne's Cystic Fibrosis Foundation – for which he admired her.
- Oswald hated the FBI, the KGB, religion, and bureaucrats in both the US and the USSR.
- Oswald was a nonconformist contrarian who disliked all political parties.
- Oswald defended the US against the Soviets and defended the USSR against Americans.
- Oswald "was above all an individualist, an idealist who hoped to change the world."

**George Goads Oswald**

George appears to have played a key role in turning Oswald into an assassin. It began with Oswald's talk of General Edwin Walker – "the next Hitler," according to Oswald's *The Worker* Communist newspaper. Walker was supported by financial backers like local oil billionaire H. L. Hunt. Dallas, according to

*The Worker*, was the headquarters of America's violent right wing.

General Walker had gained fame as a leader of the "Devil's Brigade," a Canadian-American WW2 early Special Forces group in Italy and Southern France. He became disillusioned when he concluded that Roosevelt had given up Eastern Europe and later the UN "kept the US from winning the Korean War." He had found common cause with the John Birch Society (JBS) and become its "hero" by 1960. JFK had reassigned him for indoctrinating his NATO troops with Bircher "Blue Book" propaganda, and Walker had resigned. Back in Dallas, Walker spoke for the ultra-right: no UN, no liberals, no integration, and no compromise with Cuba. Newsweek Magazine had put him on their cover, as "Thunder from the Right." Time magazine reported that Walker and the JBS had well-organized ultraconservative citizen activists appearing all over the United States.

Just before the Missile Crisis, Walker had been arrested by the Federal Government for inciting murderous anti-integration riots against enrolling James Meredith in "Ole Miss." Dallas radio, TV and print quoted him saying "desegregation is a Communist plot" (as per John Birchers). He called Kennedy a "Red," demanding his removal from office along with all the other Communists in the government and in America. Kennedy's younger brother Robert (RFK), serving as Attorney General, tried to have Walker committed to a mental institution, but a landslide of infuriated ultra-right letters, and ironically the ACLU, quickly extracted him. Walker returned to Dallas amid waving flags – both American and Confederate. JFK's fights with Walker raised Kennedy in Oswald's eyes: JFK was fighting "the next Hitler."

George spent surprising amounts of time talking to Oswald. Some say that he was toying with Oswald, getting him to make amusingly wild political statements. Oswald clearly wanted to impress George, with "smart observations" and "bold ideas." George took Oswald and Marina out to some parties, as well as providing support for Marina.

In December, the book *Seven Days in May* became a #1 bestseller. It was based on General Walker's persona, describing an attempted coup by a Walker-type general. Oswald may have read it, but certainly heard much of the plot and its connection with Walker. Between that book and Walker's ongoing fight with the "Red JFK" reported by the Dallas press, Oswald saw Walker as a clear danger to JFK. Oswald made remarks that someone should stop Walker, again saying Walker could be an American Hitler. The press queried Texas Governor-elect John Connally about the plausibility of a military coup against JFK; Connally's coup comments might have been heard and remembered by Oswald (Clarke, 2013). George De Mohrenschildt appears to have encouraged Oswald to "do something."

In January, Martin Luther King visited Dallas, giving a speech on "America's dream." A bomb threat hoax delayed his speech, and some picketers showed up, though King's visit remained peaceful. MLK said: "Segregation is wrong, there is no superior or inferior race, and the idea of white supremacy must come to an end now and evermore." He said Kennedy had done some impressive things for civil rights, especially when compared to previous administrations. Walker loudly disparaged MLK and civil rights. Excited by the Walker-MLK "fight" and his own Communist literature, Oswald repeatedly argued with his co-workers.

Oswald's still-steady job allowed him to get some money together. On January 25, 1963, he paid off his two outstanding loans: the $212 remaining on his US State Department repatriation loan, and a $200 personal loan from his brother Robert.

Two days later Oswald used $29.95 (about $300 in 2022) to buy a mail-order Smith & Wesson .38 Special revolver, using the alias A.J. Hidell and forging "D. F. Drittal" as his witness. As it turned out, that pistol did not arrive for two months.

Why did Oswald buy a relatively expensive pistol, under an alias, at this point? True, there were some recent violent political actions in Dallas, sparked by the MLK visit and the John Birch Society ultra-right, but it did not seem unusually serious nor personally threatening to Oswald. He does not appear to have carried that pistol until November 22. Oswald seems to have bought the gun because of De Mohrenschildt's goading, in combination with Walker's all-white jury acquittal for his Oxford MS insurrection. Walker also claimed he would be taking on Cuba next. Although the self-serving De Mohrenschildt did not admit to provoking Oswald, he did say that he and his wife Jeanne saw a lot of Oswald and Marina during this time, even having them for dinner. And George liked to talk about the rising fascism of the ultra-right and General Walker. In any case, Oswald ordered that pistol.

Just a week after ordering the pistol, on February 13th, Oswald went to another émigré party with George. There Oswald had heated discussions with right-winger Volker Schmidt. George testified later that he was astonished when Oswald had talked so long with a right-wing "fanatic"; George said he warned Oswald of the dangers posed by "people like Schmidt." Dr. Schmidt was later deposed by the Warren Commission: he had spent two hours talking with Oswald, whom he described as a man "desperate to make an impression on history" and who harped on General Walker as "a kind of Nazi" (Walker had been supported by the American Nazi Party.) Dr. Schmidt told the Warren Commission that their argument might have "instigated [Oswald] to take a potshot at [Walker]." Schmidt told George that Oswald "appeared to be a violent person."

Marina later reported that evening's conversations as a turning point in Oswald's life, cementing his belief that US fascism was a real and present danger that should be stopped at any cost. Oswald began listing "fascist organizations" in his reasons to dislike the US of 1963. George certainly made no secret of his dislike for fascists, the John Birch Society and General Walker. Several witnesses remembered that at one point George told Oswald that "knocking off Walker would be doing society a favor." Oswald greatly admired George, and no doubt paid a lot of attention to whatever he said.

A couple of days later, Dallas newspapers reported that General Walker would go on a five-week speaking tour with the famed Billy James Hargis. Hargis was the anti-communist leader of the Christian Crusade, and a pioneering televangelist. His fervent group of 100,000 paying followers was based in

Tulsa, Oklahoma. He could ask them for donations and collect tens of thousands of dollars in an afternoon. He had written speeches for Senator McCarthy, published a weekly newsletter, a monthly magazine, tape recordings, and occasional albums. He was doing daily broadcasts carried by 250 television stations and over 500 radio stations across the country. A $25 donation got you a free copy of his record album, *The United Nations Hoax*. Hargis and Walker rallied their faithful against Kennedy, Washington liberals, and desegregation.

Walker demanded that Kennedy assassinate Castro. Anyone listening to "talk radio" at that point would likely hear them on the right-wing programs like H. L. Hunt's *Life Line* program - where Walker was already a common fixture. Oswald still had his little Soviet portable radio at the time of his arrest.


**Oswald Attempted to "Kill Hitler"**

By this point, Oswald had certainly changed course. For one, he wrote to his Trotskyite Communist "Militant" magazine complaining about the exploitation of renters by Dallas land-lords, signed "LH" (That letter was published in the March issue, a month later). For another, Oswald started forcing Marina to write to the Soviet embassy asking to allow her to return to the USSR without him; Marina obviously disliked many things about her life with Oswald, but she had begun to like living in the US. Oswald insisted that "he loved her, but she would be better off in Russia"; he did not explain why. They quarreled about that, and Marina remembered that Oswald hit her again.

On March 5th the Dallas Times Herald quoted General Walker: "the US Military should liquidate the Communists in Cuba." Oswald started planning the assassination of General Walker in a legal-sized notebook, becoming secretive with Marina. He went to Walker's house, photographed it, watched its traffic, and studied bus schedules. Oswald realized a rifle might be a better killing weapon, given Walker would be in his house. Most assassination movies in Oswald's adulthood did involve rifles: *The Manchurian Candidate* (1962), *Three Came to*

*Kill* (1960), *Thunder Island* (1963), and Sinatra's *Suddenly* (1954). Besides, his pistol had still not been delivered (it was not even shipped until March 20.

On March 11, the leader of the failed attempt to assassinate French President Charles De Gaulle was executed by firing squad. This man recruited 17 members of his far-right terrorist OAS ("Secret Army Organization") to spray the De Gaulle's car with 187 machine gun bullets, back on August 22, 1962. Remarkably only a bystander was injured. The event and the execution were serious news, world-wide, and Oswald would have been aware. That attempt showed that it is hard to hit a moving target, even with many shooters at close range. Apparently, Oswald was not dissuaded either by execution or by difficulty.

On March 12th Oswald mail-ordered the Carcano rifle and scope, using his alias "A. Hidell," for $21.45 - cheaper than his pistol. "A. Hidell" received that rifle (C2766) at Oswald's PO Box 2915 in the Dallas Post Office on March 25th. At some point, Oswald had used his photo-printer job to forge a new Selective Service card and "honorable" discharge card in the alias name "Alek James Hidell," the name he used in picking up his weapons. (At this time, Oswald had no driver's license – he had not learned to drive. In his own name, he had a Social Security card and his 1939 birth documents, which he used as ID.)

On March 17, Marina sent back a questionnaire to the Soviet Embassy. Again, she asked that she be allowed permanent residence in the USSR, and that Oswald would not return with her. About this time, Oswald took time to write down his proposed "alternative system between Capitalism and Communism" [CE98 above], probably as a way of ensuring his ideas would get publicity in the furor he expected over Walker's assassination. Oswald discussed the issues with Micheal Paine: American capitalist exploitation of workers was unforgiveable, even if it improved on Soviet twisted-communism's enslavement of workers. Oddly, Oswald said little when asked about Walker.

Jeanne De Mohrenschildt visited Marina in this period and saw Oswald's rifle sitting in a closet. Marina complained

"Oswald is such an idiot - he buys a rifle instead of food."
Jeanne noted the telescopic sight and later told George about it.

By March 31, Oswald had picked up his pistol and holster.
He had Marina take pictures of him, holding his "Militant"
magazine containing his recently published article, and
festooned with his new rifle and pistol. [Two days after the
assassination, some of these "backyard photos" were found in
the Paine garage. In 1977 another surfaced at De Mohrenschildt's suicide: at its bottom Oswald had inscribed "For my
friend George from Lee Oswald" with the date April 5 written
Russian-style as "5/IV/63"; at its top in Marina-like Russian was
printed "Hunter of fascists - Ha-Ha-Ha!!!" with a tiny sketch of
Jeanne's dog breed. Marina did not recall adding that sarcastic
caption when she was asked 14 years later.]

Also by March 31, Oswald's photo-print employer quietly
told him he would be let go. Oswald claimed he quit on April 1
and gave one week's notice. His employer later described him
as "inefficient, rude, inconsiderate, and inept," and likely to be
fired soon anyway. Oswald was sloppy, much of his work had to
be redone, he was argumentative, and he again flaunted his
Communist magazines at the office. Oswald did not tell Marina
about his job issues or his quitting.

About this time, Oswald had time to practice with his new
rifle. He bused and walked to the Trinity River bottom and tried
some shots. His Marine Corp training had taught him to care
for a rifle, so he cleaned, oiled and worked its action repeatedly
- a habit that he maintained into the future when he could. His
bolt action 6.5 mm Carcano 91/38 was 25% lighter than his
similar Marine 7.62 mm MI. Both weapons are very accurate out
to 500 yards. The MI fires a 50% more powerful cartridge; its
gas capture system and heavier weight reduces the MI kick so
the guns are similar in recoil and barrel climb. Oswald spent
April 7 carrying his rifle to a wooded area near Walker's house,
hiding there so he would travel unencumbered to the shooting.

On April 10th Oswald attempted to assassinate General
Walker. First, he wrote an 8-point list of "things to do" for
Marina if he was killed or arrested: here's some money, the
keys, the bills, what's paid till when, etc. [CE 1]. Oswald snuck

off, perhaps poisoned a neighbor's border collie to keep it quiet, and tried a single rifle shot at Walker from a back alley. His bullet glanced off the window frame and hit the wall above Walker's head. Walker was struck only by fragments and went on TV the next day to blame the attempt on a vast hidden left-wing conspiracy. The police and FBI stalled their investigation, saying later that they thought Walker had staged the attempt to get publicity - after all, what serious assassin could miss at 50 feet? Oswald returned to Marina, amazed that he had missed, and amazed that the police did not come for him. Marina said later that she was very upset and told him so - but Oswald claimed that he was doing a good thing, like killing Hitler before real trouble began. He laughed that the police did not even come up with the right kind of rifle. After a couple of days, Oswald retrieved his buried rifle. Oswald had apparently expected to be caught, and had kept his notebook; his failure to kill left him viewing his notebook as a humiliation, so he burned it with his photos of Walker's house.

Three days after that shot at Walker, the De Mohrenschildts came by to tell the Oswalds that they were very soon moving to Haiti. George asked Oswald "by any chance, did you take a potshot at Walker?" Everyone laughed, except Oswald. George claimed later that he only knew that Jeanne had seen a rifle there, he was just joking. Marina was sure he either knew or guessed that Oswald had been the shooter. Oswald probably told himself that he would not miss, the next time. George and his wife left Texas for an oil contracting job in Haiti, seven months before the assassination. Had any of George, Jean or Marina told the police about their suspicions, JFK would have lived; but apparently each feared the inconveniences of reporting and of course had no inkling that JFK was at risk.

Having explained his job loss to Marina, Oswald applied for unemployment insurance. He also agreed to look for a job in New Orleans, where he could stay with his relatives. Unknown to Marina, he contacted the "Fair Play for Cuba" Committee (FPCC) in New York, asking for 50 of their pro-Castro pamphlets. Clearly Oswald had a new plan, again confiding in no one. The FBI watched the FPCC since June 1961 under its

COINTELPRO operations, and was informed that Oswald was parading about Dallas with a neck placard saying "Hands off Cuba ... Viva Fidel," handing out his new FPCC pamphlets.

Almost the next day, on April 21st, Oswald read the Dallas Morning News to see the headline "Nixon Calls for Decision to Force Reds Out of Cuba," a virtual call to invade Cuba. It also printed a speech by Governor Connally: "victory or death" over Cuba. Marina saw Oswald putting on his suit jacket, with his revolver in his belt. She says she confronted him, and he declared he was only going to "have a look" at Nixon. Marina claimed that she forced Oswald to stop, with the threat of turning over the Walker evidence to the police - and possibly some heroic bathroom locking. In any case, Marina is the only witness to this second threatened assassination. If Oswald had really wanted to shoot Nixon, Marina's threats seem unlikely to have stopped him. More likely he felt uncomfortable that he had no plan to do that shooting, perhaps knowing that Nixon was not even in Dallas anymore, and so was easily put off. Maybe he was just making a show for Marina.

On April 23rd, Oswald boarded a night bus to New Orleans, where he had been born only 23 years before. He moved in with an aunt while job-seeking.


## Oswald Attempted to Reach Cuba

By May 6th, Oswald had an oiler-machinist's assistant job. He continued his anti-social behaviors: surly, immature, mostly silent, and generally a poor worker. He was fired after two months. But for now, it provided the excuse to get his own apartment and to ask Marina to join him in New Orleans. Surprisingly, she did.

Oswald looked for a local FPCC and, finding none, worked to create at least the appearance of one. He renewed his membership in the national group but was told that New Orleans would not be a good area for FPCC activities as it had a lot of Cuban exiles and a strong anti-Castro mindset. Unfazed, Oswald ordered 500 FPCC applications and 300 FPCC membership cards for $13. Oswald created his own "Hands off

Cuba ..." pamphlets and spent $4 on 1000 copies. He bought a rubber stamp and marked them with a newly rented PO Box under the names A Hidell and Marina Oswald. Thus armed, Oswald went out into New Orleans, handing out pamphlets to a hostile street audience. He got few, if any, takers – perhaps because some of the pamphlets had a non-existent PO Box 30016 instead of the rented 30061.

By June 4th, Marina again wrote the Russian Embassy, asking to return to Russia. She cited homesickness, family problems, and wanting her second child to be born in the USSR. She could have added poverty, as Oswald had spent his money on his FPCC plan instead of paying for prenatal care for Marina.

On July 1st, Marina sent in her completed application for a USSR visitor visa. This time, Oswald asked to join her and provided the letter and information for a visa application of his own, adding a note: "As for my return entrance visa, please consider it separately." It is possible that Oswald had learned that a Soviet visa was needed to get a Cuba visa. He also forged a smallpox vaccination card and renewed his US passport. Apparently, he wanted to be ready to leave the US. A week later, Marina sent a letter to the Soviet Embassy again, begging for fast action on her visa. Neither Marina nor Oswald heard that the Soviets eventually denied their re-entry: on October 7, the KGB acted on Marina's stepfather's declaration that Marina was a person of loose morals who was not welcome in his family anymore and would not be allowed to return to the USSR; a couple of weeks later, the KGB declared that Oswald was a waste of time and money, who should not be allowed back into the USSR (Bugliosi, 2007).

On July 22nd, Oswald lost his job, and for the rest of his time in New Orleans picked up an unemployment check - about half the weekly money he made while employed. Money got tight for his family. Despite his problems even holding a job, Oswald began talking about himself in comparison to Kennedy. Kennedy's "Peace" speech and "Civil Rights" speeches had caused quite a stir. Oswald read *Portrait of a President*, William Manchester's mostly positive biography of

Kennedy, and Kennedy's *Profiles in Courage*. Marina reported that Oswald said he was inspired to "follow in Kennedy's footsteps." She ridiculed him, but generally enjoyed Oswald's Russian translations of the many articles on JFK and his family.

On July 27th Oswald and Marina travelled 150 miles east to Spring Hill College, where Oswald's cousin had arranged for him to speak on life in Russia to a small group of Jesuits. The Jesuits reported Oswald's speech as "Capitalism doesn't work, communism doesn't work. In the middle is socialism, and that doesn't work either." Oswald was mostly articulate, but they concluded he was a frustrated, angry malcontent. Oswald's notes are preserved in CE 102: he warned the Marine Corps could stage a coup in the US, that segregation damaged more than Communism, that US Communism is insignificant, and the US Right Wing is corrosive.

For the next month, the jobless Oswald intensified his FPCC activities, apparently trying to provoke an arrest. He handed out pamphlets, illegally, on the US Navy pier. He stirred up harassing attacks by a few Cuban exiles, and attracted interest from the police, the FBI and the CIA. He tried to "infiltrate" the rabidly anti-Castro student organization (DRE); Oswald was apparently unaware that the DRE was funded by the CIA. Rejected, Oswald returned to handing out FPCC pamphlets, was attacked, arrested, interviewed by police and FBI, and fined $10. He was written up in the newspaper. Minor notoriety got Oswald an interview with local WDSU TV. He was asked to a more extensive 37-minute WDSU radio interview on *Latin Listening Post*, where he was interrogated on a panel discussion. The FBI was given a transcript and then the original tape of these programs. Oswald held his own. He told the radio audience: "Russia has gone soft on Communism, Cuba is the only revolutionary country in 1963."

Oswald's activities led the Army Intelligence Group to open an "Oswald File," including his "A. J. Hidell" alias, as a counter-intelligence threat; this file helped quickly identify Oswald's gun purchase but was unfortunately destroyed ten years later in a routine purge of non-DoD files. The FBI started interviewing people around him. Oswald was busy compiling a "resumé file" describing the actions he had taken in support of Marxism and of Castro's Cuba. Marina later testified that, in her opinion, Oswald was never interested in recruiting members for a new FPCC chapter in New Orleans. Rather, Oswald intended to create a dossier of letters, documents and news clippings which would help him emigrate to Cuba. All his other activities that summer, Marina believed, were merely "window dressing." Indeed, Oswald wrote a "resumé" describing his revolutionary credentials – and inflating his FPCC success (WC Exhibit 93). In retrospect, his Minsk friend concluded that Oswald was trying to lay a foundation to be a political leader – to bring his "Atheian System" to life in the US; given Oswald's multiple requests to get exit visas, this seems unlikely.

Oswald's radio programs exposed him as a Marxist and near-defector. He realized his FPCC agitation was over in New Orleans. He dreamed up schemes to get them to Cuba. For a while he asked Marina to help him hijack a plane to Cuba; she declined. He sent letters to various ultra-left periodicals, asking for jobs - unsuccessfully. He worked with Marina to arrange for Marina to return to Parkland Hospital, to get free maternity service for her coming child. Oswald began making plans to go to Mexico City and from there to Cuba.

On September 22nd, Marina and toddler June returned to Fort Worth with Mrs. Paine's help. Witnesses saw Oswald sneak out of his apartment on the evening of September 24, bound for the Greyhound station. Oswald arrived in Houston late on September 25. At 2:25 am September 26, Oswald took buses from Houston to Loredo to Mexico City, where for several days he asked for a way to Cuba or Russia via Cuba at the Soviet and the Cuban Embassies. He called himself a "friend of the Cuban Revolution," showing his "resumé file" as head of the New Orleans FPCC. He ran into bureaucratic red tape, ran out of money, and had to return to Dallas in frustration. The Warren Commission apparently did not try hard to track what Oswald did for his full five days in Mexico City. Marina testified that this red tape fiasco drained Oswald's enthusiasm for the Castro regime and ended his talk of going to Cuba.

Another effect of Oswald's trip: putting the CIA back into this picture. Since Mexico City had the largest CIA and KGB stations in the hemisphere, the CIA had photo, audio and LIENVOY wiretap surveillance of the Soviet and Cuban embassies. The CIA should have had extensive records of Oswald's activities there – perhaps including his three days in Mexico City after his visa failures. The CIA may have impersonated Oswald after he dropped his visa effort. The CIA apparently downplayed their interest in and knowledge of Oswald. Immediately after the assassination, the local CIA sent a picture and audio for their wrong guess of Oswald, then claimed that other media had been erased in the 8 weeks after Oswald's visit. Conspiracy speculation and FBI anger was the natural result. The Mexico City CIA did ask the Navy's Intelligence (ONI) for a picture of Lee Henry[sic] Oswald on Oct 24 '63, but Oswald's picture did not arrive till after the initial assassination reporting. In 2018 the CIA did disclose that their tap on the Soviet Embassy revealed Oswald's attempt to get a visa. The CIA did not disclose their manipulation of the Mexican police in arresting and brutally interrogating people of interest after JFK's death. This information was, of course, secret and illegal, so in later investigations the CIA did not disclose their embassy spying to the Warren Commission. In fact, that tap of the Soviet Embassy had been part of a joint CIA-Mexico secret program which the CIA feared might bring down the Mexico government if disclosed in 1964.

## Oswald in Dallas

Back in Fort Worth, Oswald visited Marina but did not move back in with her. Instead, he got a room in Dallas, where he looked for a job. He attended a meeting of the ACLU at SMU, again hearing about the menace of the ultra-right in Dallas.

On the weekend of October 11, Oswald took some driving lessons with Marina's friend, Mrs. Paine. Later he and Marina watched a film, *We were Strangers* about revolutionaries assassinating a Cuban dictator. Marina said that Oswald was "very excited." That 1949 film was based on the actual overthrow of the Machado dictatorship in 1933 Cuba; spoiler alert: the bomber assassin dies but inspires a revolution, and the movie ends with dancing in the streets. Oswald had by this time given up on Cuba, but he did comment on the film's historic accuracy.

Dallas TV guides list a rebroadcast of *We were Strangers* that night, and it may be that Oswald watched the same film twice. It may also be that the TV Guide listed the wrong movie. Marina said she only partly watched the first show – it could be that Oswald had seen a second assassination film at another time, without her: that may have been *Suddenly*, a 1954 film featuring Frank Sinatra as a hired sniper who attempts to assassinate the President of the United States. Sinatra fails, as the members of his team crack and inform the Secret Service. In any case, Oswald later may have vaguely quoted a line from *Suddenly* while he was under arrest for the assassination, suggesting that "the assassination of the president did not matter ... his replacements would continue on."

Oswald took the General Aptitude Test Battery at a Dallas unemployment office, scoring Verbal 126 and IQ 116, but with "sub-average" hand-eye coordination; the tester commented, "you must read a lot." Oswald failed two job interviews, possibly for his unfavorable Marine discharge or possibly from reference checks. Oswald got the job at the Texas State Book Depository (TSBD) by lying that he had an honorable discharge, then via conversations among Ruth Paine, Wesley Frazier, Frazier's sister (friend of Ruth), and the TSBD manager. The TSBD had openings only because of 6th floor remodeling and the fall book rush. Oswald could have been assigned to another building – the building manager made that choice. Each step of Oswald's employment involved independent, random, unpressured choices.

Oswald established a new pattern at the TSBD: steady working. Each Monday through Thursday, after work, he walked 2.2 miles back to his room in Dallas. There, he read Westerns, ate a lot of fruit, and made sandwiches. If the shared house TV was on, he would watch for 5 minutes before going silently to his room. Each Friday night at 4:45 pm, he rode from the TSBD to Fort Worth with Mrs. Paine's neighbor and fellow TSBD worker, young Wesley Frazier. Each weekend, he stayed with Marina at Mrs. Paine's. Each Monday morning, he returned, again with Frazier, directly to work at 8 am. For the first time, Oswald made no fuss at work, had no missed days, and was a good, silent worker, filling book orders. After a couple of weeks, he began calling Marina most nights from a pay phone across the street from his boarding house.

On Friday, October 18th, Marina and Mrs. Paine surprised Oswald with a birthday cake. Oswald was emotional. He cried and apologized for mistreating Marina in the past. Two days later, Marina gave birth to Audrey Marina Rachel Oswald at Parkland Memorial Hospital, taking advantage of its free service to the poor. On Monday night, Oswald went to Parkland to see Marina and his new daughter. Marina and the baby went home the next day. A month later Kennedy and Oswald would die at that same hospital.


## The FBI Tracks Oswald

Oswald was trying to be a normal father at this point. But away from home, he was still looking at the enemies of "America" on the ultra-right. Oswald wrote General Walker's telephone number into his notebook in October 1963. Michael Paine later testified that Oswald attended ultra-right "National Indignation Conference" meetings in this period.

Governor Connally had designated October 23 as "US Day" to incite Dallas against the UN – the day before Adlai Stevenson was to speak on "UN Day." Oswald attended General Walker's ultra-right US Day speech in Dallas – "admission free!" There were 1200 rabid supporters there. No doubt they were raucous complainers echoing the John Birch Society: anti-UN, anti-integration, anti-Communist, anti-Castro, anti-CIA, anti-liberal, and anti-Kennedy. The next day, an ultra-right mob attacked Stevenson as he left his UN Day speech – all caught on national TV.

Oswald went with Michael Paine that weekend to an ACLU

meeting. They had an hour driving out to the meeting in Michael's car, where Michael tried to convince Oswald that the ACLU's slow pressure could keep the US from a right-wing dictatorship. Paine remembers Oswald saying that only violence would change anything.

Oswald was likely listening to Radio Havana at night on his little Soviet radio. Their broadcasts increasingly blamed the CIA for the terrorist acts of Cuban exiles – and blamed President Kennedy for the CIA. Such tenuous arguments did not likely impress Oswald: he was hearing from the right-wing meetings and from Dallas media in general that Kennedy was restraining the CIA and undermining the Cuban exiles.

On November 1st, Oswald wrote the Communist *The Worker*, reporting the strong left-versus-right friction in Dallas, his experience with the Walker ultra-right meeting, and his lack of faith in the ACLU. He described the Dallas ACLU as "firmly in the hands of 'liberal' professional people, but that some of those present showed marked class awareness and insight." Despite his lack of faith, Oswald paid $2 to apply for ACLU membership.

A recent Time magazine article had described Kennedy's difficult road to a '64 victory. Kennedy's primary problem was the Deep South and Texas – the two regions which LBJ had helped carry in 1960. The Time article saw no way for JFK to win in the deep south, but it did suggest that Kennedy had an even chance in Texas (Time Magazine, 1963). Governor John Connally might fight him rather than help him. If Oswald had killed Connally, then liberal Lieutenant Governor Preston Smith would take over; Smith had come up for tenant farms and had supported better farm roads, more small-town hospitals, better schools and teachers' benefits, and better funding for state colleges. Smith would undoubtably be a strong Kennedy supporter in Texas, though of unknown effectiveness. Still, if Oswald knew this, he would have seen it as a help for Kennedy's '64 chances in Texas.

During October, the FBI resumed its interest in the Oswalds, likely because CIA reports of his Mexico City trip. Hosty related these details: (Hosty, 1996)

- October 1962: FBI Agent James Hosty inherited Oswald's closed file from retiring agent Fain.

- February 1963: Hosty decided to investigate Marina as a possible KGB "sleeper" agent.

- May 63: Hosty reopened Oswald's file after discovering he lied in his 1962 entry questioning.

- late May: Hosty transferred Oswald to the New Orleans FBI office (A. J. Hidell alias noted).

- October 1: the FBI interviewed Oswald's Aunt Murret in New Orleans, probably triggered by Oswald's trip into Mexico, given CIA information.

- October 9: independent of Hosty, FBI headquarters canceled their "Wanted Notice Card" that was created when Oswald gave up his US Passport to the US Embassy in Moscow back in 1959.

- October 18: CIA reported that Oswald had argued with "Consul" Kostikov. The CIA did not reveal that Kostikov was the Mexico KGB Division 13 head, responsible for terrorism, sabotage, and assassinations. No evidence has surfaced of any manipulation of Oswald by the KGB.

- October 29: New Orleans sent Oswald's new address at the Paine's. Hosty visited the Paine's neighbors, then checked the Paine's credit record, employment, and police records: everything was in order. Hosty now had "jurisdiction" and asked New Orleans to transfer the Oswald file back to him. They failed to do that until the morning of JFK's death.

- November 1: FBI James Hosty interviewed Ruth Paine in her house; Marina walked in, was initially alarmed but was relaxed by Hosty's brief questioning and almost protective manner. Oswald returned home, this being Friday night, and became very nervous and agitated when Marina told him that FBI Agent Hosty had just left. He tensely instructed Marina to get the make, model, and license of any FBI car the next time.

- November 4: FBI Hosty got the transcript of the FBI New Orleans interview of Oswald; Hosty noted that it was filled with lies, not aligning at all with his Dallas-based information.

- November 5: FBI James Hosty saw Ruth Paine again, in her home. She repeated that Oswald worked at the TSBD, but she still did not have Oswald's address in Dallas. Hosty failed to ask Ruth for Oswald's phone number, which would have located Oswald via the phone company – Hosty's little mistake likely cost JFK's life. Oswald had rented his Dallas apartment under the name "O. H. Lee," apparently just to stymie FBI surveillance. Hosty verified Oswald's job at the TSBD and found its address on Elm Street but did not look further. During this interview, Marina did sneak out into the street to write down the make, model, and license of the FBI car, as Oswald had asked. Oswald recorded that information in his journal, a fact that later caused speculation that Oswald worked for the FBI.

- November 8: FBI headquarters sent reports to the CIA, covering Oswald's FPCC pamphleteering, his arrest and interviews, his radio appearances, and his move to Dallas.

- November 9: Oswald wrote a letter intended for the Soviet embassy in Washington DC, that he was disappointed the embassy had not helped him reach Cuba, that the FBI had told him to stop his FPCC activities, and that the FBI was snooping about in Dallas. He suggested that Marina could defect under FBI protection (CE 15). Neither Oswald nor the FBI knew that the Oswalds were on the Soviet no-entry list by then.

- November 12: Ruth Paine found a draft of Oswald's embassy letter, upsetting her and Marina; after JFK's death, Ruth gave her copy to the FBI. Independently, the FBI read Oswald's letter by intercepting it by its Soviet embassy address. Oswald's letter referenced the replacement of the Consul who had yelled at Oswald as "not a good Communist" during his visa fight; at some point, the FBI and CIA noticed that Oswald had no obvious way of learning of that replacement, a still-unanswered question. The FBI sent the letter to Hosty's office for inclusion in Hosty's Oswald file, but Hosty said it did not reach him until the morning of the assassination and then disappeared, apparently because Oswald referenced the KGB's Kostikov; Hosty was able to read Ruth's copy but still didn't connect the KGB.

- November 13: Oswald visited the Dallas FBI office, asking for agent Hosty; Hosty was out, so Oswald left a "threatening note." We have only vague notions of what that letter said: Hosty's boss told Hosty to (illegally) destroy that threatening note (and Hosty's memo about it) after Oswald died, which he did by flushing it down the toilet. Again, Hosty had missed a chance to elevate Oswald's danger factor and to locate him.

- November 15: Marina suggested Oswald not come that evening. It was the Paine daughter's birthday, and Ruth seemed upset with Oswald - probably because of Oswald's embassy letter that he wrote on her typewriter.

- November 17: Marina tried to call Oswald to make up for missing that weekend but was surprised when the landlady declared there was no Lee Harvey Oswald living there.

- November 18: Oswald called Marina, angrily explaining that he was registered as "O. H. Lee" to avoid the FBI. She was equally angry that he was still indulging in "foolishness."

Oswald was furious that the FBI was "destroying his life." He had started to repair his life with Marina, and now the FBI was upsetting her and him. He also said that the FBI might nose around his work enough that he would lose his job. He might also have been concerned that his attempted killing of General Walker might come back somehow. His threatening letter to Hosty probably looked more and more like a bad idea, though Oswald's arrogance might have suppressed such doubts.

Despite Oswald's anger with the FBI, and agent James Hosty in particular, Oswald was carrying on with his life. He was playing with his daughter, in fact, he seemed to sincerely enjoy playing with kids anywhere, as for example, the 11-year-old girl in his boarding house. The one thing that made him happily animated was talking about his daughters. He continued learning to drive, with the help of Mrs. Paine, and tried a couple of times to schedule his driver's examination. And he was still reading books and newspapers. Marina said that she begged Oswald not to go back to Russia and that he suddenly agreed, promising that Russia was done for them; he was quite loving that Veterans Day weekend.

During this period, Agent James Hosty failed to recognize the danger Oswald could pose. Oswald's file and interviews showed he physically abused his wife and that he would make wildly aggressive plans like defecting to the USSR; he threatened Hosty and the FBI, and he was a frustrated Marxist in "ultra-right Texas." Hosty was responsible for tracking politically dangerous people. Unfortunately, Hosty was deeply concerned with the known dangers posed by the Dallas ultra-right, especially since there should have been no reason for Marxist-Socialist Oswald to threaten "soft on Communism" JFK.

On Nov 5, Oswald checked out his last book: *The Shark and the Sardines*, by Juan Jose Arevalo, and published by a real FPCC member. It was overdue on Nov 22. This last library book might have influenced Oswald if he read it. It was written by President Arevalo of Guatemala (1945-51), who was elected after a popular uprising against the US-backed dictator Jorge Ubico. President Arevalo governed by "spiritual socialism," in which "individual liberty must be exercised within the limits of social order." Vaguely anti-communist but definitely anti-oligarchy, Arevalo tried to steer a middle course of democratic socialism by reforming and regulating capitalism. After surviving 25 coup attempts, mostly from the Catholics and the military, Arevalo complained to the US Congress:  "I fear the West has won [World War II], but in its blind attacks on social welfare will lose the war to fascism." After Arevalo declined re-election, his elected successor extended his policies with land reform to move Guatemala's economy from pseudo-feudalism to capitalism. By 1954, U.S. foreign companies with investments in Guatemala (especially the United Fruit Company, which owned 42% of the nation's arable land) used "anti-Communism" to enlist the aid of the CIA, who engineered a coup. Guatemala's eight-year experiment in democracy ended in a pro-Corporate-America dictatorship. Arevalo wrote *The Shark and the Sardines* to explain and condemn America's Corporate Despotism in Latin America and a super-secret plot by corporate agents to "deliver the USA" to Wall Street. In April 1963, JFK's administration had secretly helped prevent a November election that would have returned Arevalo to the presidency (Friedman & Ferreira, 2022).

Just at that time, Kennedy was making a speech in Miami about rapprochement with Cuba and his new Alliance for Progress. Given Oswald's disgust with Communist bureaucracy and life in Communist regimes, he would have appreciated Kennedy's calm and rational approach to the Cuban problem. More importantly, Kennedy's Alliance for Progress was designed exactly to remedy the horrible exploitations that he read about in *The Shark and the Sardines*. This inspired leadership would likely have been received enthusiastically by Oswald, especially as it was received very badly by the ultra-right in Dallas.

Oswald eventually read the page one story in the Dallas press: the headline screamed, "Kennedy Virtually Invites Cuban Coup." Oswald no doubt took that as right-wing fake news: the story was only that the US would help any people throw off a foreign-imposed Communism. It was, in fact, fake: Dallas editors had become so concerned over the brewing hate in their ultra-right that they decided to make JFK look more anti-Castro to defuse possible violence (Hosty, 1996).

On the morning of Tuesday, the 19th, Dallas newspapers reported that JFK would visit Dallas with a motorcade going by the TSBD.

5

# OSWALD FEARED THE ULTRA-RIGHT

How did Oswald become so filled with fear and hatred of the Ultra-Right?

In Oswald's mind, the ultra-right was dangerous to his ideal world. What was that ideal world? Oswald wrote it down sometime after he shipped back from the USSR. He refreshed his ideas when he spoke to the Jesuits in Mississippi in July of 1963. He refreshed it again when he debated Michael Paine in October and November of 1963. We know a lot more about what Oswald wanted than we know for most of the rest of us.

From the evidence, during Oswald's childhood, he saw that US Unregulated Corporatism strangled the masses under a capitalist yoke; in the USSR, he saw that Communism strangled the masses under a bureaucratic and police state yoke; after a fight at the Cuban Embassy, he saw that Cuban Communism was also mired in bureaucracy. Finally, in September of 1963, he seems to have decided that the US under JFK was the best way forward.

In Oswald's stated view, the future would be a battle between the ultra-left and the ultra-right, probably after a nuclear war. Kennedy had proven to be just the middle-of-the-road leader that America needed regarding racial issues, class issues, and radicalism – and could bring peace instead of Oswald's feared cataclysm. Oswald could contribute by exposing and decapitating Kennedy's internal enemy: the ultra-right.

Oswald saw a chance to be a "hero."

### The Dallas Ultra-Right

The ultra-right typically believed that the United States was a libertarian capitalist "white" country at its founding. Its humanist Founding Fathers forced it to separate church and state, but everyone knew it was Christian. It was "libertarian" by necessity. Likewise, it had to compromise to unify North and South – at the cost of preserving slavery.

After the Civil War, racial strife continued. Jim Crow laws and attitudes became the norm in Texas and elsewhere. D. W. Griffith's 1915 *Birth of a Nation* (originally titled *The Clansmen*) became the first "blockbuster" movie – but spread violently anti-black KKK propaganda. After World War One, the stress of the war, new automation and the flu epidemic upset the economic and social status quo: the Texas Ku Klux Klan reappeared at a 1920 Confederate Veterans parade and quickly became one of the nation's most powerful. By 1924, KKK membership claimed millions of Protestant, native-born whites. It used economic, social and vigilante terrorism to intimidate individuals, newspapers and the police. The "roaring twenties" prosperity undermined the KKK fear foundation, but KKK sympathies helped create the ultra-right.

During the Great Depression of the 1930s, the ultra-right asserted that the government should not expand to give handouts to the disadvantaged and should fight Communism at every turn. When FDR instituted the first true social safety net, the ultra-right was enraged by FDR's "embrace of Communism."

. . .

By 1930, over 600 radio stations had sprung up, with most independent of RCA's (government-backed Radio Corporation of America) NBC or its rival CBS. Most radio stations were financed by radio sales ($843m in 1929), but advertising had gained a foothold and was growing rapidly. By 1934, 60 percent of the nation's households had radios, as did 1.5 million cars. Stations wanted content that would attract listeners and, therefore, advertisers. With the depression and war approaching, politics became exciting. Both the Left and the Right joined in.

Father Charles Coughlin was one of the first political influencers to use radio to reach a mass audience: during the 1930s, an estimated 30 million listeners tuned to his weekly broadcasts. At first, he was strongly pro-Roosevelt, but by the mid-1930s, he criticized Roosevelt as a "tool of Wall Street" and big banks. Ultimately, FDR's administration shut down Father Coughlin: the Code Committee of the new National Association of Broadcasters (NAB) declared that any scripts on "controversial public issues" had to be pre-approved by the NAB, or radio stations would lose their license. Interestingly, JFK's father, Joseph Kennedy, was FDR's point man in first trying to "tame" Coughlin and then shutting him down.

Another leader of talk radio, Walter Winchell, had a pro-Roosevelt show that included a lot of name-calling, rumor-mongering, attack-humor, and sensationalism. His leftist scripts were apparently OK with the NAB. He became famous for attempting to destroy the careers of rightists, both private and public, whom he disliked. Winchell cheer-led the New Deal, pushed war against Hitler, ridiculed isolationists and conservatives and eventually attacked Father Coughlin. He also had a huge listener base. After World War II, Winchell turned rabidly anti-Communist and supported McCarthy (Both JFK and RFK also became strongly anti-communist in 1948-1952 and also initially supported McCarthy; RFK was on McCarthy's staff.) Some described Winchell as one of the most powerful voices in America.

In 1941, radio editorializing was made illegal to protect wartime enthusiasms. In 1949, editorializing was allowed, but under the new Fairness Doctrine, which declared that because radio dominated a public resource, it had public interest obligations: radio stations may present controversial issues of public importance but must be honest, equitable, and balanced - as judged by the FCC. The Fairness Doctrine did not eliminate all biases since its application was complex, but it did keep larger stations from egregious personal attacks and constant evidence-free bias. However, as TV gained national ubiquity, the FCC spent less and less time policing radio. Some radio hosts, like Fulton Lewis Jr., found TV too constraining; Lewis went back to his 16 million radio listeners to resume his right-wing opinions that he called "news." Talk radio continued as the bastion of editorial talk.

After World War II, Truman protected FDR's socialist changes, followed by Eisenhower from 1952-1960. The ultra-right was shocked when Republican Eisenhower continued this new US "Communism": Ike did NOT arrest alleged spies everywhere; he did NOT fire government liberals; he did NOT dismantle FDR's socialism; he did NOT wrestle Eastern Europe from the USSR. In fact, Republican Eisenhower attacked the ultra-right by shutting down McCarthy's rabid anti-Communism while starting desegregation of schools.

With the FCC distracted by TV, vitriolic talk radio increasingly ignored the Fairness Doctrine. Ultra-right Reverend Carl McIntire began delivering a daily 30-minute monologue in 1955. He espoused anti-Communism, anti-socialism, anti-liberal, anti-any-church-but-his, and anti-sex-education. His program claimed 600 radio stations and 12 million listeners.

Dallas' H L Hunt was considered one of the richest men in the world and a bankroll for the Dallas ultra-right. He was a "good Baptist," a secret bigamist and cheater, a clever oil tycoon, and a germaphobe. During the Korean War, he started an ultra-right radio talk show called *Facts Forum*. It ran in 1951-56. In 1958-75, it was restructured as *Life Line* and had more than 10 million listeners in 1963 - about 10% of the voters in the US.

Oswald likely heard *Life Line* on one of its 500 country-wide radio stations (Minutaglio, 2013).

In 1963, Dallas had Minutemen, but the John Birch Society was the leading ultra-right group in the Dallas area. H L Hunt supported both groups. Bircher tenets were:

- Communist spies had extensively infiltrated the US government and media.
- Truman, Eisenhower, and now Kennedy were surrounded by Communist influencers.
- FDR's, Truman's, and Eisenhower's socialist programs were destroying America.
- The UN and NATO were designed to integrate the US into a One World (Communist) Government controlled by "hidden elites."
- The civil rights movement was Communist-inspired and supported.
- The Back-to-Africa campaign had merit.
- Liberals were Communist sympathizers - the Supreme Court was liberal.
- Eastern Europe, China and Korea had been abandoned to the Communists.
- Nuclear war was a reasonable solution to Communist aggression.
- "Better dead than Red."
- The Federal Government had trampled the Constitution with overreach.
- International Communist Conspiracies were everywhere.
- Socialism is a gateway to Communism.
- For Texas only: the oil depletion allowance must be preserved.

The Bircher sales pitch was short and simple: "Unless we win against Communism, we'll be killed, and our kids will be enslaved." (Verhoeven, 2015)

. . .

Some important ultra-right leaders in Dallas included Oswald's target, General Edwin Walker, the editor of the Dallas Morning News - Ted Dealey, Dallas Mayor Earl Cabell, and the "godfather banker" of the Dallas ultra-right - H L Hunt (Minutaglio, 2013).

Oswald read Ted Dealey's Dallas Morning News editorials in the TSBD lunchroom:

The Supreme Court was the "Judicial Kremlin," run by the "Courtniks."

Washington, D.C., was the "Negro Capital of the U.S."

Good for business means good for everyone.

Choose freedom over candy-coated socialism.

NAACP are agitators for colored people, sowing trouble and ill-will between races.

The US needed a strong leader on horseback; JFK was a weak sister on a tricycle.

Oddly, the war-monger Ted Dealey had somehow missed his chance to volunteer or be drafted for service in WWI while accepting his nepotistic position in his father's paper.

### Facts Supporting the Ultra-Right

The ultra-right had grounds for some complaints. In the 1950s, rumors of the top-secret Venona counter-espionage project revealed that it had found Communist spies or sympathizers in the US. Venona was set up by math and crypto expert Gene Grabeel; her project was initially so secret that even Presidents FDR and Truman did not know of it.

A few people had sent US secrets to the USSR or sometimes carried out actions. Oswald's requested lawyer, John Abt, was listed as a possible spy since he worked with the Communist Party USA. And there were some serious spies. Agnes Smedley, for example, was a triple agent who, with Alger Hiss, helped Communist China overpower the Nationalists. After the war, Elizabeth Bently had defected, telling the FBI of nearly 150 people (including 37 federal employees) as Soviet spies, which had ended much but not all Soviet spying. From 1945 to JFK's time, there were surprisingly few spies in the US: less than 100 people were sending information to the USSR, and only a few had any important position in the government. Some informers sent bits about radar and jet aircraft data. Judith Coplon sent FBI data. Most Americans were unaware that our spying on the Soviets was extensive and fruitful, for example, saving billions of dollars in our own radar defenses. Looking back from 2020, most of the Soviet early Cold War spying had little real effect - with the huge exception of nuclear spying.

Rudolph Abel, Klaus Fuchs, George Koval, the Rosenburgs and others had sent important nuclear secrets to the USSR. The ultra-right was on firm ground in their complaints about the "atomic spies." In fact, in 2020, the 1956 records of another "atomic spy," Oscar Seborer, were disclosed: it appears that these spies were able to pass on the key design for the implosion triggers that made for practical nuclear weapons, helping the Soviets to build a big arsenal. Other than the ultra-right, American media tended to dismiss or even defend the spies - so on this important issue, the ultra-right was "right."

The ultra-right also had firm evidence that the Communist regimes were authoritarian killers of their own people. The US media had not reported the gristly extent of Stalin's purges - when that poor media coverage was discovered, it undermined trust in the media. The Communists had killed 10 million people before Hitler was even elected - in fact, that was the major reason that Hitler was elected at all. The ultra-right became justifiably contemptuous of the ignorance of American Communist sympathizers; the Left's flagship New York Times won a 1932 Pulitzer Prize for glowing reports of Stalin's government while he killed millions, for example.

**Ultra-Right Exaggerations**

As to the oft-made charges that Eastern Europe was "given away," the ultra-right was not on firm ground. US media reporting of World War II had been purposely inaccurate, downplaying the contribution and military effectiveness of the

USSR. That was partly the natural nationalism that "we won the war" and partly a foundation laid to gain popular American support for a coming "Cold War." Misleading data about the war and the collapse of the German war machine in 1945 led many Americans (e.g., Patton) to think it would have been "easy" to drive the USSR out of Eastern Europe. In fact, military and intelligence experts in early 1945 were very afraid that the huge, battle-hardened and well-equipped Soviet military would push the US off the European continent - in a matter of a few months. To block possible Soviet expansion, the conference at Tehran (1943) had Stalin pledge to invade Japan. In 1945, soon after Hitler's defeat, Stalin kept his promise: about three million Soviet soldiers and support were withdrawn from Europe and sent to invade Japan. They began invading Japanese Manchuria, Korea and the Kuril Islands on August 8th, as agreed, and likely would have subdued at least the northern home island of Japan before the US could begin its own invasion; the USSR's invasion, as much as the American atomic bombs, forced Japan's surrender. People like General Walker, who was involved in Italy and the South of France in World War II, were evidently unaware of Soviet military power. The misleading media coverage of Soviet military power made Americans in general and the ultra-right in particular unappreciative of the delicate politics of post-war Europe.

With no believable media explanation of why Eastern Europe had been "given" to the Soviets, the ultra-right more and more constructed their own alternative facts that involved rampant conspiracy: Roosevelt "gave away" Poland and Eastern Europe - therefore, Roosevelt and his advisors "must be" Communist Sympathizers or worse. When Stalin agreed to help set up the United Nations, the ultra-right rejected that body and its world peace agenda. After ruthless Soviet-directed campaigns ensured that elections returned only pro-Soviet governments in Eastern Europe, Truman launched a "cold war," but there was nothing that Truman could do: Soviet military strength was overwhelming in Eastern Europe. "Giveaway" views were nearly "mainstream" in the late 1940s: even young

John Kennedy said that a sickly Roosevelt had sold Eastern Europe to Stalin and Robert Kennedy worked for McCarthy to ferret out hidden Communists in the early 1950s; the Kennedys later changed their views when they learned more about post-war Soviet power.

The ultra-right was not convinced - although no realistic ideas were ever suggested on how the Soviets might have been dislodged without millions of further dead, and particularly more American dead than had been lost fighting Hitler. As to their airy claims of using nuclear weapons in 1945-6, they apparently had little idea of the number or effectiveness of our little reserve of fission bombs (less than 10) when used against an entrenched military rather than a paper-built Japanese city. Each A-bomb might severely damage about 3 square miles of non-hardened defense - hardly decisive, with no way to even attack a Soviet target. Nor did they explain how our airpower would survive against the Soviet's large and effective fighter corps, the force which had won air superiority over the Nazi Luftwaffe in 1943. Nevertheless, the ultra-right had a story that they believed, built around some believable facts. With McIntire's, Fulton Lewis's and Hunt's radio programs reaching five times more stations than Winchell's, the Ultra-Conservative narrative was getting hammered into a lot of heads.

In 1961, Kennedy approved the sale of F-86 fighters to Communist Yugoslavia. With training going on only 80 miles from Dallas, right-wing Texans went berserk, led by Birchers. JFK's move kept Yugoslavs from being forced into the USSR's Mig-17 camp, the Mig-17 being faster, more agile, and well-armed: the F-86 was subsonic, obsolete, and unarmed. The US had supported Yugoslavia since 1949 to keep it out of the Soviet camp, even under Ike. Still, the F-86 brouhaha rankled: a "National Indignation Conference" gathered over 100,000 to protest this travesty of pro-Communism, calling Kennedy a traitor – Oswald's target, General Walker, was an organizer.

. . .

Kennedy had asked White House counsel Myer Feldman to evaluate the ultra-right in August 1963. Feldman described it as "a formidable force [that was] well-funded by 70 foundations, 113 businesses, 25 utilities and 250 identifiable individuals" who saw "the Nation as imperiled on every front by a pro-Communist conspiracy" threatening "imminent takeover." They had elected 74% of their candidates. They broadcast daily programs on many radio stations multiple times a day. They sent out colossal weekly mailings. Kennedy observed that the ultra-right would put Goldwater in the race, although he was too radical to win the US presidency. Oswald knew nothing of this White House assessment, but the Dallas ultra-right claimed similar power.

### The Ultra-right as Seen By Oswald

After Oswald joined the Marines in 1957, he would have heard a lot of ultra-conservative talk. He responded by isolating himself and secretly planning to go to the USSR. In 1960, when Oswald was in the USSR, his mother and brother located him and started sending packages that included Dallas newspapers and magazines – most Dallas news was slanted to the ultra-right.

From the beginning of John Kennedy's presidential run, the ultra-right hated him. JFK's personality, religion and principles did not fit even with Dallas conservatives, let alone Birchers. Dallas voted against Kennedy by 2 to 1. After JFK was elected, the Dallas Morning News turned nearly every news story about JFK into a direct attack on JFK. The newspaper dwelt particularly on African Americans as a critical part of Kennedy's election, framing every appointment of a Black person as a payoff for Black voters.

In June of 1961, Kennedy relieved General Walker of command for spreading ultra-right John Birch Society (JBS) propaganda and voting directives to his 24th Infantry Division posted in Europe. JFK received massive amounts of hate mail calling him a traitor and a Communist for firing Walker, mostly from mobilized Birchers. The Dallas Morning News published "hero" articles on Walker, as did H L Hunt's *Life Line* talk radio program. Having been President for only a few weeks, Kennedy faced bigger issues: the Bay of Pigs disaster, the discovery that his "missile gap" campaign issue was evaporating, and the secret details that modern nuclear weapons might kill hundreds of millions worldwide. Meanwhile, Dallas papers were talking about how nuclear war was really the only way forward against the Communists. As Dealey said to Kennedy directly: "[You, JFK, are] a weak sister. We need a president who is willing to bomb Russia and to destroy them utterly." Kennedy responded with speeches decrying "crusades of suspicion" by extremists who recklessly cried, "treason." Kennedy enlisted Eisenhower to condemn warmongering. Oswald, in the USSR, would have heard both the Communist take and the Dallas take on Kennedy's battles with the ultra-right (via his mother-sent Dallas newspapers). Ultra-right extremism, one of Oswald's key issues, was Kennedy's target.

On February 10, 1962, Oswald would have heard the excitement of the "Bridge of Spies" exchange of U2 CIA pilot Francis Gary Powers for the atomic-secrets Soviet hero-spy William Fisher (aka Rudolph Abel). In early 1960, Eisenhower had approved the first full overflight of the USSR's ICBM sites by Powers in a U2 at 65,000 feet. The Soviets tracked the flight early and tried to shoot it down, but it was out of range. After Powers flew over ICBM bases and a plutonium factory, the Soviets knocked the U2 with a salvo of their SA-2 missiles (still in use in 2023, worldwide). The CIA had photographed that SA-2 site during a Nixon visit there in 1959 so that SA-2 site was known. Powers had to fly quite close to it to be within range at 65,000 feet – something he was probably ordered to do. In 1998, declassified documents revealed that the USAF was a joint participant; it was critical at that time to ascertain improved SA-2 performance against a high-altitude penetrating bomber. Gary Powers found out the hard way that the SA-2 was quite capable; sadly, in 1959, the SA-2 had already shot down an RB-57, but that was a Taiwanese pilot. The USAF used Powers' experience to shift American bombers from high altitudes to low altitudes. The Mach 3 XB-70 bomber was (eventually) cancelled. Instead, the F-111 Aardvark ground-hugging strategic bomber program was begun. In addition, the B-52 fleet was converted to have electronic counter measures and was retrained to perform ground-hugging (<400 foot) approaches. First-wave B-52s were repurposed with cruise missiles to destroy Soviet SA-2 sites to clear a path ahead of later waves of B-52s. The immense changes in American nuclear warfighting that followed Gary Powers' SA-2 sacrificial evaluation strongly indicate that his was a planned mission of great import.

The ultra-right knew nothing of the importance of Powers' SA-2 sacrifice, and hated the trade of Rudolph Abel for Powers. They viewed Abel as hugely valuable because he had run the Rosenberg / Cohen spy network, smuggling US atomic secrets to the USSR; after the Rosenbergs' arrest, Abel had escaped and developed another network to spy in the United Nations. In contrast, the ultra-right viewed Powers as "worthless" as he failed to either take his suicide pill or to trigger the self-destruct of his spy plane – they did not know that his U-2 was unsophisticated and had no secret tech. In the USSR, Oswald heard the ultra-right lambaste the Powers trade as evidence that Communists controlled the Federal Government.

In June of 1962, Oswald returned to Dallas/Fort Worth. John Connally was running for governor against several people, including Bircher General Walker, in the Democratic primary. The Dallas Birchers (JBS) were very active.

In Dallas, Oswald would have seen the ongoing campaign to impeach Supreme Court Justice Earl Warren:

"The Desegregation Decision, which aids and abets the Communist Conspiracy to (A) Create tension between Negroes and Whites; (B) to transform the South into a Black Soviet Republic; to legalize and encourage intermarriage between Negroes and Whites and thus mongrelize the American White Race!"

JBS members believed that "both the U.S. and Soviet governments are controlled by the same furtive conspiratorial cabal of internationalists, greedy bankers, and corrupt politicians. If left unexposed, the traitors, such as JFK, inside the U.S. government would betray the country's sovereignty to the United Nations for a collectivist New World Order, managed by a 'one-world socialist government.'"

When Oswald eventually went to right-wing meetings, he heard more detailed JBS rhetoric, such as:

- We need to free the military's atomic weapons control from the civilian bureaucracy.
- General Walker on Newsweek's cover is "the new and defiant figurehead of the radical right."
- General Walker is the famous basis for *Seven Days in May*, a bestseller!
- The Government is muzzling the military to keep them from telling "the truth."
- Kennedy is worse than a traitor: every American risks Soviet nuclear attack.
- Kennedy is paralyzed over "an exaggerated fear of atomic fallout."
- Kennedy's Medicare would give him life-or-death control over everyone.
- Government "Pinkos" are undermining America with foreign treaties, like NATO.
- Kennedy's disarmament will let Chinese troops pour across the Rio Grande.
- A Super-Elite International Conspiracy runs the world.
- The US Invisible Government is visible through the Council on Foreign Relations.
- Kennedy was a member of the Council on Foreign Relations.
- If Kennedy isn't stopped, the US will fall under their World Socialist System in '64.

For Oswald, ultra-right rhetoric was a call to action. These "mean people" really were sounding like Hitler and were talking about pushing the US towards their far-right. They spoke confidently about "winning" a nuclear war.

At the same time, when Oswald listened to JFK, he would have heard speeches that aligned with his own views:

- against Super Patriots (for example, General Walker)
- against people undermining America from within (meaning the JBS)
- for integration and equal opportunity in jobs and schools
- for peace, for disarmament and for test ban treaties
- for Medicare, Medicaid and Head Start
- for rapprochement with Cuba and the USSR (a change since 1962)
- for helping people help themselves, as with "Alliance for Progress" and Peace Corps

In early 1963, right-wing radio had encouraged a boycott of Kennedy's liberalized trade with the Communist Bloc – for example, "cured Polish hams." This call accelerated in 1963. Oswald would have seen or heard of Dallas housewives parading outside of supermarkets with signs harassing buyers of Communist products; the boycott earned Kennedy an official rebuke from Congress, as well as an end to Polish hams. In August of 1963, Kennedy discussed possible countermeasures, believing that right-wing radio was corroding his chances for legislation and re-election. Kennedy suggested that the IRS audit their tax-exempt status and that the FCC apply the Fairness Doctrine. The FCC's new Cullman Doctrine forced stations to air counterarguments for free– proving helpful in passing JFK's Nuclear Test Ban Treaty. The ultra-right was loud in their anger (Matzko, How JFK Censored Right-Wing Radio, 2020).

The Dallas ultra-right was one of the loudest voices for the radical right. Connally was what some in Dallas called an "antidote" to Kennedy who might fight him successfully for the 1964 nomination. Connally was no General Walker, but he was pro-segregation, anti-Communist, anti-Castro, and had supported the Republican in two of the last three Presidential elections. Oswald would have seen killing Connally as a heroic deed for "a better America." On the other hand, Oswald knew that killing Kennedy would hurt everything he had come to believe. He knew it would leave him reviled and friendless – Marina and George would be disgusted beyond repair, along with most of the World. Only the ultra-right would be happy, if anyone.

Oswald would have seen news of swastikas put on Jewish homes and businesses in Dallas. He would have seen daily racism against Black people. He would have seen news of UN Ambassador Adlai Stevenson being harassed, spat upon, and attacked in Dallas by Birchers screaming "traitor!" and "communist!" That attack on Stevenson was encouraged by Connally's "U. S. Day" appeasement of the JBS.

The day after Stevenson was attacked, Oswald had his last known political discussions. They occurred at an ACLU meeting to which Michael Paine had taken him. Oswald heard the liberals complaining about Connally's conservatism, and particularly that Connally had incited the attacks on Stevenson's UN day speeches by setting up a U.S. Day the day before – at the request of the JBS. Oswald also revealed that he had been to a JBS meeting on that "U.S. Day" where he had heard some nasty ultra-right talk.

Oswald spoke twice in that ACLU meeting. The first time was to object when a speaker said that the John Birch Society was not anti-Semitic; Oswald spoke loudly and clearly that he had been to a Bircher meeting two days before, and more than one speaker had said anti-Semitic claims, as well as anti-Catholic; the ACLU audience seemed to take that correction without comment. Oswald later volunteered that he thought Kennedy was doing a very good job on the civil rights issues.

.   .   .

After the meeting, Oswald got into an argument with a co-worker of Paine's: Oswald asserted, as usual, that his biggest problem with the US was that its Capitalist system forced man to exploit man; Paine's friend, a part-time entrepreneur, asserted that forming a business was a risk that deserved reward or no one would do it - without risk-takers you would not have jobs. Also, as usual, Oswald calmly stood his ground but added no rationale beyond repeating Marxist lines - while Paine's friend recited facts, seethed, and wanted to punch Oswald.

Four days before the assassination, Oswald may have heard that Alabama Governor George Wallace gave a speech at the Baker Hotel in Dallas, announcing that he would run for president against JFK on an anti-integration platform. He denounced the "flood of beatniks, sex perverts, narcotics addicts and common criminals who had invaded Alabama as so-called civil rights workers," aided and abetted by Robert Kennedy's Justice Department. General Walker attended.

Although the Warren Commission would find no direct link between the ultra-right and the Dallas "hate merchants," those extremists do deserve serious blame. As Earl Warren said at Kennedy's memorial service:

*"While few will advocate assassination, many will contribute to the climate which causes men to contemplate it."*
*Chief Justice Earl Warren, November 25, 1963*

Oswald was motivated to his extreme act to "save the United States" from the dangers of ultra-right "brown shirt" bullies.

For Oswald, anything that happened after November 20th is probably moot, barring a sudden rapprochement with his wife Marina. Oswald had already decided on his plan and was executing it. Oswald would have heard that Jackie was a huge hit in San Antonio on November 21 - that is the same Jackie who George de Mohrenschildt said, proudly, had bounced on his knee.

The morning of the 22nd, if he read the Dallas Morning News in the TSBD, he would have seen Bernard Weissman's ad "WELCOME MR. KENNEDY TO DALLAS. . ." where "we, the citizens" still have the right "to question you, to disagree with you, and to criticize you" with questions like "WHY has Gus Hall, head of the U.S. Communist Party praised almost every one of your policies and announced that the party will endorse and support your re-election in 1964?" And Oswald might have heard Hunt's right-wing talk radio saying things like "the hammer and sickle would replace our stars and stripes." The other TSBD employees might have been talking about these anti-Kennedy attacks. But in any case, Oswald was already executing his plan - and it almost certainly was **not** to kill the US Communist Party's chosen 1964 candidate, John Kennedy.

## 6

# WHY CONNALLY?

Connally was the public face of the conservative Texas Democrats. Texas Democrats were often closer to the ultra-right than to their own liberal democrats. Dallas media had been suggesting that America needed the young, rich, good-looking, conservative Connally more than they needed four more years of Northeastern Liberalism. Integration was hated, as was any rapprochement with Communists. In fact, Connally would soon change parties and become a conservative Republican. Connally's politics were exactly what Oswald saw as the major threat to America.

**Connally's Ultra-Right Tendencies**

Connally was a Democrat, but he was no Kennedy. John Connally had been the first choice of only 27% of the Texans (49% of Democrats voted against him in the runoff), but as a conservative Democrat, Connally was acceptable to 74% of Texans and won the general election for governor in 1962. Conservative Dallas, in particular, styled him as a competitor to Kennedy, both ideologically and as the 1964 presidential candidate.

A creature of Lyndon Johnson ("closer to LBJ than his wife," it was quipped) and big oil, Connally was regarded as witty and elegant, a "Texan worthy of Camelot." The 27.5% oil depletion allowance, the sacred cow of Texas Big Oil, was his talisman. In protecting oil, he had fought liberals and labor unions, who were the bedrock of the Northern Democrats. Maybe as a reward, he'd also been bequeathed $1.2m on the death of one of his big oil benefactors ($12.3m in 2023).

"Lyndon's boy" Connally had been appointed Secretary of the Navy and had accepted that post on behalf of Texas Big Oil: the Navy was the largest buyer of oil in the world and had huge reserves under its control. It helped that Connally was a decorated Navy veteran of World War II, having spent a year as a superlative fighter director and eventual fleet CIC director. He earned two bronze stars for directing the anti-kamikaze fights, mostly for the "fightingest ship in the Navy," the Essex aircraft carrier.

But Connally had been tarred with scandals. In 1948 he was accused of being involved in a voting scandal when 200 votes for LBJ arrived a week late, electing Johnson to his first seat in the Senate – by 87 votes. In 1952, Connally had supported the Republican Eisenhower over the Democrat Stevenson because Stevenson threatened the Oil Depletion Allowance. In 1954, Connally was embroiled in the Boys, Inc. tax scam for questionable charitable contributions. Oswald was aware in 1956 when Connally had assisted LBJ in purging the liberal wing of the Democratic Party out of any power in the 1956 election - making Connally the "implacable foe of liberals in Texas." Oswald was also in Texas when Connally spearheaded LBJ's run as a Democratic favorite son to split the Democratic vote - and thus helped get Eisenhower his second term. Even in the USSR, Oswald might have heard the disgust as Connally orchestrated an attempt to use Kennedy's Addison's disease to undermine him in the primaries against LBJ in 1960; Connally's "sleazy tactic" boomeranged against LBJ. Kennedy won the nomination.

In the 1962 Texas gubernatorial election, Connally "stood with the wealthy and glamorous white businessmen." Oswald was back in Texas by this time and would not have liked it. Oswald probably also heard fallout from Connally's earlier fight against Kennedy's plan to reduce racist assignments in the Navy. By the summer of 1963, Connally was drawing a direct contrast between himself and Kennedy on integration. On July 19, 1963, Connally spoke at the governor's conference, saying, "[integration laws] in my judgement would strike at the very foundation of one of our most cherished freedoms: the right to own and manage private property." Connally sided with Wallace against allowing the MLK march on Washington. Integration was one of Oswald's key issues.

Texas, in mid-1963, had huge oil wealth, yet that wealth was invisible to most Texans. JFK's proposal to tighten oil depletion rules had little chance of passing, but to Kennedy, those rules were the epitome of taking from the poor and giving to the rich. Texas was 1st in number of poor, 33rd in per capita income, 44th in adult literacy, and dead last in per-capita spending on child welfare. Black people and Latinos made up 25% of the Texas population, but only 2% of Black people attended integrated schools. 75% of Texans had recently said they did not want more integration in schools or otherwise. Texas public education was low-rated in any case at that time. Connally had done nothing about these issues in his first months as Governor except start several commissions to generate and retain more Texas Ph. D. graduates. "Smart people generate businesses." Meanwhile, Connally's speeches denounced Kennedy's proposed civil rights actions. Dallas had real rumblings that Connally could unseat Kennedy for the presidential nomination or, at the very least, make the primary season so messy with anti-Communism that Goldwater could steal the presidency for segregation.

## Connally as a Threat to JFK

Connally had something that the more militant General Wallker did not: electability.

At least in the Dallas "bubble," Connally was seen as a better leader than Kennedy. Further, if JFK were reelected, the door would swing wide open of a Northeastern Liberal

Kennedy Dynasty with RFK. Dallas echoed with reasons to push Kennedy out and bring in their favorite son.

While Connally was not the most extreme of the right wing, he was a real and electable threat to Kennedy and his agenda. What Oswald saw:

1. Connally was anti-segregation.
2. Connally was anti-Castro and against softening the US-Cuba stance.
3. Connally supported and was supported by "big oil" in Texas.
4. Connally had not moved to support Kennedy's agendas.
5. Connally had helped the rich, not the disadvantaged.
6. Connally was causing trouble in the Texas Democratic party.
7. Connally had supported Republicans in recent elections.
8. Connally worked against democratic liberals, like Texas Senator Yarborough.
9. Connally worked with Earl Cabell, mayor of Dallas (CIA asset and Bircher).
10. Connally had tried to undermine Kennedy in 1960, especially over health.
11. Connally spoke at and was well-received by ultra-right groups.
12. Connally had created "US Day" to rile up Texans against Adlai Stevenson.
13. Connally had made it a crime to display the United Nations flag in Texas.

While Connally did not wear a John Birch Society button, he was a fellow traveler. Oswald was probably planning to wound or kill Connally, then play a "heroic role" of exposing Connally's "extremist views" in courtroom harangues.

The book *Tragic Truth* compares Oswald's political positions with Kennedy's and Connally's, rightly concluding that Oswald had little reason to shoot at Kennedy. Oswald sometimes made negative comments about Connally. *Tragic Truth* counts 10 people who remembered Oswald as unfavorable to Connally. Only Marina remembered a slightly positive impression: Oswald "was favorable towards Connally while in Russia. There is a possibility that he changed his mind." (Pierre Sundborg, 2016)

*Tragic Truth* dismisses political motivation as "ancillary" compared with Oswald's feelings of "terrible injustice" of his "undesirable discharge," distantly assisted by Connally. This book disagrees – Connally had only a small role in signing Oswald's defection-triggered undesirable discharge reclassification. There is no evidence that he blamed Connally for his Marine discharge. Historically, Oswald did not seem interested in personal grudges. Oswald was interested in making a big contribution to "The World's Future."

7

# OSWALD'S LAST PLAN

All Tuesday (November 19), the TSBD employees were excited that JFK would be travelling right under their windows. If Oswald planned to shoot JFK, he had a full day to get more ammunition for his gun, or prepare an escape plan, or write up explanations - as he had done before trying to shoot Walker. Instead, he did nothing.

On November 20, newspapers reported that Governor Connally would also be in the motorcade. Oswald got this news, probably, on the afternoon of the 20th after reading discarded papers. It would not have caused much excitement at the TSBD compared to JFK's appearance. But it was on the afternoon of the 20th that Oswald suddenly sprang into action.

*Tragic Truth: Oswald Shot Kennedy by Accident* assesses this lag: had Oswald intended to shoot Kennedy, he would likely have begun preparations immediately – on that Tuesday. Instead, he began only on Wednesday afternoon. As Sundborg points out, his delayed action meant he didn't have time to make preparations like getting a full clip of ammunition; he only had four bullets left in his seven-bullet rifle (Pierre Sundborg, 2016).

Right-wing propaganda and insults pilloried Kennedy that week. Dallas TV, radio, street posters, and a blizzard of pamphlets would have reached Oswald. On the 20th the afternoon Dallas Times Herald ran A. C. Greene's column: "Why do so Many People Hate the Kennedys?"

On the 21st, General Walker's ultra-right group passed out 5000 pamphlets:

*"Wanted for Treason"*

*This man [JFK pictured] is wanted for treasonous activities against the United States*

- *Betraying the Constitution which he swore to uphold. He is turning the sovereignty of the United States over to the Communists controlled United Nations. He is betraying our friends, Cuba, Katonga, Portugal, and befriending our enemies, Russia, Yugoslavia, Poland.*
- *He has been wrong on innumerable issues affecting the security of the United States. United Nations, Berlin Wall, missile removal, Cuba, wheat deals, Test Ban Treaty, Etc.*
- *He has been lax in enforcing Communist registration laws.*
- *He has given support and encouragement to the Communist-inspired racial riots.*
- *He has illegally invaded a sovereign state with federal troops.*
- *He has consistently appointed anti-Christians to federal office: Upholds the Supreme Court in its anti-Christian rulings. Aliens and known Communists abound in federal offices.*
- *He has been caught in fantastic LIES to the American people, including personal ones like his previous marriage and divorce.*

The fusillade of anti-Kennedy propaganda no doubt helped

steel Oswald's resolve. Walker's missive reads like a list of reasons for Oswald to help Kennedy.

By the 21st of November, Oswald had made his simple plan. He would get his rifle, hiding it in a homemade paper bag. He had a sniper's nest, already mostly there from boxes moved for the flooring project on the sixth floor. He had John Connally going right under his sniper's nest. Oswald sensed he would soon take his place amongst the few people who have really made a difference. He would not only stop Connally as a threat, but he could have a world stage to denounce the ultra-right threat in America. That was the kind of attention and achievement that Oswald had dreamed of his entire miserable life, the kind that would make Marina and George De Mohrenschildt respect him. It would make "his place in history." His daughters would be proud.

**Reconstructing Oswald's Shooting**

We cannot know exactly what happened. The following speculation fits the available evidence.

Oswald's behavior changed starting that Wednesday: on the evening of November 20, Oswald washed his clothes at Reno's Speed Wash, one block north of his apartment, until midnight. It was unusual for him to spend money instead of washing at Marina's. It was unusual for him to stay up late. It was as though he wanted to be arrested in clean clothes – people listen to a clean-cut spokesman, as they had for his New Orleans media appearance.

On the morning of the 21st, he left his pistol at home – as expected if he wished to survive to make speeches. Oswald treated himself to a nice breakfast at Dobbs House restaurant – also unusual for a poor man. He walked 2.2 miles to the TSBD from his room. That walk took less than 40 minutes, about the same time as commuting with Frazier from Marina's apartment.

At work on the 21st, Oswald saw his ride, Wesley Frazier,

and asked him for a special ride to Marina's that evening. He had never gone home on a Thursday, but Frazier had given him an open invitation to get a ride home any day at 4:45 pm. Frazier asked if Oswald would ride back to Marina on Friday afternoon and was surprised when Oswald answered simply, "No." That evening, the normally silent Oswald told Frazier that he would be bringing a package of curtain rods to work the next morning. He also cobbled together a long "bag" of wrapping paper and tape using TSBD materials (CE 142).

At 4:45, Oswald met Frazier and got his ride home. Frazier did not notice the empty bag. Oswald may have kept it under his shirt, as he had when he smuggled his manuscripts out of the USSR. Oswald, for the first time, had not phoned Marina before coming home - normally, after a bad weekend such as the previous one, Oswald would have asked Marina if his coming home would be OK with her and the Paines. This time, he surprised them. Marina was still angry about his boarding house 'alias' and his anger with her. She gave him the cold shoulder, refusing three kisses, and didn't warm to him even when he suggested that they move and focus on their family. He offered a washing machine despite his former complaints of her bourgeois materialistic demands. She did not soften. Oswald responded gently to her rebuffs, which was also unusual. Instead, he enjoyed an extended nice time playing with his daughters, June and the baby. Days later, Marina said that it was almost like he was saying goodbye to them.

He told Marina he was going to bed at 9 pm, an hour early. Ruth Paine testified that Oswald was "doing something in her garage and left the light on": He was taking the rifle from its blanket hiding place, disassembling it and putting it into his homemade bag. The Dallas Police and FBI later found fibers from the homemade bag and the blanket on the rifle, along with Oswald's partial prints on the bag and on the rifle. The rifle had to have been disassembled when those prints were laid down.

Marina said he slept poorly that night.

On the morning of the 22nd, Oswald slept through the alarm at 7 am. All might have been different if Marina had let him sleep, but she woke him. Marina went back to sleep. Oswald came in just before he left. He told her he had left some money for her to buy whatever she needed for herself and the kids. That was, of course, very unusual. She did not catch him before he walked out. Astoundingly, he had left $170 - almost everything he had. For the first time, Oswald had not kissed Marina goodbye, she said. Later, she found he had left his wedding ring, too.

Oswald walked 1/2 block and, for the first time, showed up outside Frazier's window 10 minutes early, at 7:15 am. Frazier's sister, Linnie Mae Randle, said she saw Oswald through the small kitchen window. She told the Commission that he was carrying a package in a sort of heavy brown bag, which had the top sort of folded down; He was grabbing it with his right hand at the top of the package and she thought the package almost touched the ground. Frazier hurried to finish his breakfast, brush his teeth, and grab his lunch. When he came out, Oswald was standing, waiting - he had already put his package in the back of Frazier's car. For the first time, Oswald was not carrying a lunch bag. When Frazier asked, Oswald said he was going to buy his lunch that day.

Frazier remembered that ride to the TSBD as uneventful. Oswald was quiet, which was normal, and responded with a chuckle about his daughters. About 30 minutes later, they parked behind the TSBD as usual. Frazier stayed in the car briefly to recharge his car battery, as usual. Oswald waited only briefly, holding his package, but instead of walking with Frazier, he took off quickly, alone. He was at least 50 feet ahead when he disappeared into the TSBD back door and was gone when Frazier got to that door. Frazier said later that he thought that Oswald's bag was only a couple of feet long and that Oswald carried it under his jacket with the end cupped in his right hand. The Carcano model 91/38, disassembled, was about 35" long, so it would have stuck about six to eight inches above his shoulder if he was carrying it vertically. Frazier admitted he only glanced at Oswald and so was not sure. His unsure glance later became one of the foundations of conspiracy theories: that Oswald's bag was too small to hold his rifle. The actual bag was found in the TSBD later – it was big enough for the rifle. No one could explain where any curtain rods had disappeared to or where they were to go since Oswald's boarding house room already had curtains.

When Frazier passed through the outer and inner doors into the TSBD, Oswald was not visible. He had gone up the stairs or elevators because when Frazier went immediately downstairs to put away his coat and lunch, Oswald was not there. Oswald went to the sixth floor and put his package in amongst boxes, probably hidden in his pre-built sniper's nest. He then went about his morning. Some said he filled book orders as usual; others said Oswald did no orders that morning.

At about noon, the workers in the building headed down for lunch. Oswald was heard and seen on the fifth or sixth floor at that time, for example, by Charles Givens. When everybody left for lunch and to see Kennedy, Oswald headed to his sniper's nest and unwrapped his rifle. Five flat head screws later, that rifle was ready to load and fire. Oswald's Marine training and a lot of practice served him well. He generally kept that weapon's action well-oiled. He pushed in his only bullet clip, with only four bullets. He practiced his motions in his head: stand for the first shot, sit and use the rest box for the rest of his shots as the car rolled west. Ready. Now, he just had to wait.

Then, the unplanned happened. One of the floor-layers, Bonnie Ray Williams, came up to the sixth floor on the elevator. Oswald heard him walk over and plop down less than thirty feet away on the other side of the box wall that Oswald was using for his nest. He could hear Williams as he ate his chicken sandwich, crunched his way through his bag of Cheetos, and swilled down his little Dr. Pepper. Minutes ticked by. Oswald probably thought he could shoot anyway, as it would only take a few seconds. But still... Suddenly, Williams stood up with a curse and stomped back to the elevator. Unknown to Oswald, the entire team of six-floor layers had agreed they would meet on the sixth floor to watch the president come by. Only Williams had shown up, and now he went down to the fifth floor to join his friends Harold Norman and James Jarman. The picture CE480 and the blowup CE482 show Norman and Jarman and a very faint view of Oswald himself a few minutes before the shooting started. They were only 10 vertical feet away from Oswald, immediately below him.

At about 12:20, Oswald walked down to the fifth floor and opened the elevator door. That would prevent anyone from coming up in it. He took the stairs back to the sixth floor.

Oswald stood back in the sniper's nest window, watching down Houston. There was quite a crowd. Some people were looking up towards him. Feeling suddenly exposed, he moved back to his left so he was facing more towards Elm, hidden from the eyes of the Houston Street crowd. He would stay back away from the window frame and take his first shot standing up at Elm Street just below him.

Seconds slowly turned to minutes. Oswald could hear cheering and motorcycles as the motorcade made its way down Main Street. He picked up his rifle, standing behind the left window frame. A Dallas Police pilot car came by, leading the motorcade by a quarter mile. The noise built towards a crescendo as the six lead Harley Davidson motorcycles blatted loudly onto Houston and came almost directly towards Oswald. An unmarked Dallas police vehicle swung onto Houston.

Connally came next, cheered on in a big convertible limo. Oswald peaked around the window frame. Connally's silvery hair and the big white Stetson made him instantly recognizable.

Houston Street would appear to be a perfect place to shoot Kennedy, as was observed first in *Whitewash* (Weisberg, 1965). Kennedy was fully exposed for over 20 seconds and coming in a straight line towards Oswald. Yet Oswald did not shoot Kennedy at that obvious point. *Tragic Truth: Oswald Shot Kennedy by Accident* (Pierre Sundborg, 2016) devotes a very worthwhile chapter to answer this problem: "The Shot Not Taken." Sundborg agrees that there was no better time to shoot Kennedy. But it was a bad time to shoot Connally. Governor

Connally, on his short jump seat, was crammed against the driver partition. At first, he was hidden by the glare of the windshield. As the car rolled forward, Connally's face was hidden behind the six-inch chrome of the roof support bar; this structure looks like a rollbar but held roof pieces while providing a steadying handhold for anyone standing up in the limo. Sundborg shows that Oswald could not see Connally well enough to shoot at him until the limo turned onto Elm Street. The short movie by Elsie Dorman confirms that while JFK was a very visible target on Huston Street, Connally is completely obscured (Dorman, 1963). Oswald may have remained hidden while the cars approached on Houston – never seeing the Kennedys. Oswald's first look at the car might have been through his little telescopic sight as the car swung beneath his window. Multiple analyses of the Hughes film have shown no human figure or motion in that sixth-floor window as the limo turned onto Elm.

Crouching, Oswald brought his rifle to his eye and pointed down to the street to let his target move into his sights. The four-power telescopic sight made his picture narrow. He saw the hood of the limo, then the driver's seat. And there, just behind the hand-rest bar, was John Connally, holding his big white Stetson. Connally seemed to be moving very fast, as seen through that telescopic sight. Oswald pressured the trigger, tracking a few inches ahead of Connally's head, compensating for the car's motion. Suddenly, the tree branches rushed into the bottom of Oswald's field of view, and he knew it was then or never. He squeezed the trigger.

Quickly racking the bolt out and in, Oswald didn't notice the tinny tinkling of the spent shell ejected away. But immediately below him, three men heard the boom, the bolt and the shell and sawdust coming down from their ceiling. That blast had happened right above them. A flock of pigeons exploded off the roof of the TSBD, just above Oswald.

Oswald settled onto his box, resting his barrel in the crease of his rest box. The limo emerged from behind the oak trees, less than 190 feet away. Nothing appeared to have happened, but Connally had half turned to look towards the TSBD.

Connally's head lined up in the cross hairs again, this time with much less relative motion as the car was moving almost directly away from Oswald. 3.8 seconds after the first shot and only a half-second after the tree cleared, boom.

Again, Oswald racked that bolt and sent another casing spinning off the boxes. Again, he lined up the scope. Connally was turning to his right, definitely hit, but just at that moment, he seemed to fall backwards towards his wife on the left side of the limo. Oswald tracked Connally's fall to his left, squeezed and 4.92 seconds after his second shot, a third boom.

A final time Oswald racked his bolt and sent a third casing into the boxes. When he looked through the scope again, he didn't see Connally. He saw a Secret Service man running, trying to jump on the back of the limo. And he saw a woman in a pink dress and pink pillbox hat on the polished trunk of the limo. As the Secret Service man gained the rear deck, the limo accelerated away, disappearing behind trees.

Oswald felt adrenaline coursing through his body... but also a tremendous sudden fear. Who was that woman in pink? It looked an awful lot like Jackie Kennedy.

Oswald stayed with his plan, conceived in the arrogance that police never expected a shooter to walk calmly away - after all, that was why he got clean away with shooting at Walker. On autopilot, Oswald strode quickly towards the back stairs. There, he paused and dropped the rifle into a hiding place down among boxes by the stairs. Then he hurried down four floors of stairs.

He heard people coming up from the first floor and dodged into the second-floor lunchroom. Suddenly, a yell told him to stop, and he did, turning around to face a Dallas policeman and his drawn revolver. Motorcycle policeman Marion Baker had been in the motorcade, about 300 feet behind the limo. Baker had identified the sounds as rifle shots, saw the pigeons fly off the TSBD, and immediately rode his cycle to the TSBD main entrance stairs. The building manager joined him as he questioned his way through that first floor, and they ran to the back elevators. Nothing happened when they pushed the button nor when they called up to get help. They went up the stairs. Baker saw Oswald walking away from him through the lunchroom door and called out.


Oswald turned and walked back towards Baker, saying nothing and showing no emotion, apparently unimpressed by Baker's pistol pointing at him - Oswald had accepted that he might be caught at gunpoint immediately. If he was an innocent man, he should have been shocked at this sudden confrontation. Baker asked the building manager if that man was known to him. The building manager recognized Oswald and said yes, so Baker and the manager charged off up the stairs.

Oswald bought a Coke from the lunchroom machine; he was nervous - he habitually drank Dr. Pepper (Moore, 1991). Having been lucky and calm enough to pass one gun-toting policeman, he had to move quickly. The police would surely cover the back exit. He crossed through the building to the front stairs and calmly walked through the milling crowd out the front entrance. NBC reporter Robert MacNeil may have asked where he could get a phone to report the shooting; he said Oswald replied, "You better ask inside." The air was filled with incredible screams and wailing. Oswald walked east on Elm Street, away from the TSBD and its pandemonium. He walked nearly three-quarters of a mile. He heard excited talk of Kennedy being hit. He had some time to think about what might have happened. He had definitely hit Connally. He might have hit a man sitting behind Connally, next to that woman in pink. He had to admit that it was Mrs. Kennedy. He might have hit President Kennedy. Oswald began to sweat.

He saw a bus and pounded on the side, at mid-block, to board. Incredibly, the lady in the front seat recognized Oswald as an unacceptable renter from a couple of months previous. She testified he "looked like a maniac, shirt undone, dirty, he looked so bad in the face, his face was so distorted." Evidently, Oswald had lost his characteristic cool sometime on his 12-

minute walk. Why was this formerly calm assassin looking like a maniac and banging his way onto a bus in a traffic jam?

After a couple of minutes of slow crawl, the bus stopped completely. The man driving the car in front of the bus got out, walked back, and told the bus driver that the traffic was completely blocked because the President had been shot. Oswald stood up, asked for a transfer, and got off the bus.

Oswald walked a couple of blocks to the Greyhound station. He had left almost all the money he had with Marina that morning, and he had not pre-bought any transportation. Very shortly the police would be checking everyone at any station. They may already have been checking at the Greyhound station. He grabbed a cab - maybe the first Texas cab of his life. The ride was interrupted by police cars, sirens wailing, speeding everywhere. The cabbie asked Oswald if he knew what was happening. Oswald said nothing.

Oswald had given an address several blocks past his boarding house so he could check it for police. He walked back in five minutes, then hurried into his room, passing the housekeeper without a word and left a couple of minutes later. He had his pistol tucked in his waistband, extra ammo loose in a pocket, and had donned a concealing jacket despite that warm afternoon.

Some have suggested that Oswald went to get his pistol to "make good his escape." That seems possible: he could carjack a passing cab or car since he had no money or friends or preparation – but that required a lot of luck. His 20 shots from a handgun were not going to let him shoot his way out. Perhaps Oswald never intended to escape. Oswald originally intended to shoot Connally, to make the Dallas Police and FBI look silly with his walking escape, then to get cleaned up at his apartment and get ready for his inevitable TV appearances and eventual trial. Oswald intended to take every opportunity to expose his views on the dangerous ultra-right and how he had saved the USA. That was his path to fame: saving the USA from Connally and the neo-Nazis.

.  .  .

Oswald's actions make sense – but only if he had intended to kill Connally. Instead, he had killed his respected President Kennedy. Oh, that was bad. Bad, bad, bad. He had no future. His plans for fame to impress his wife, his few friends, and the world – all of these had exploded with Kennedy's head.

He suspected that the DPD would be after him. Several witnesses had seen him shooting, though as always, witness reports were contradictory; even so, Oswald fit the vague and contradictory witness statements better than any others seen in the TSBD, and he had access to the sixth floor. A vague witness description was soon refined towards Oswald's since he had left the TSBD immediately after his already suspicious, unemotional gunpoint confrontation with Baker.

Unknown to Oswald, DPD Officer Tippit had been ordered to patrol the Oak Cliff area. His channel one radio told him that the killer had likely shot from the TSBD. At about 12:45, he heard the Howard Brennan's description of the killer: "Dispatcher: Attention all squads. At Elm and Houston, reported to be an unknown white male, approximately 30, slender build, height 5 feet 10 Inches, 165 pounds - reported to be armed with what is believed to be a 30-caliber rifle." Multiple witnesses saw Tippit between 12:45 and 1:00, sitting in his police car at the Gloco gas station, where he could see anyone coming into the Oak Cliff area from the TSBD area. Suddenly, at about 1 pm, he went "tearing off down Lancaster at high speed." There was no police radio order for this.

Speculation: Tippit normally patrolled Oak Cliff. Up to eight times a week, the fit, ex-Marine, walk-loving, poor Oswald would have walked about 2.1 miles to and from the TSBD. Although there was a bus route from his Beckley room to the TSBD, it cost about $0.15 per ride; Oswald did not have money for an extra $1.20 per week, but he did have plenty of time, more than the 30-35 minutes he needed for the walk. The housekeeper said he left at 6:30 to 7 am for work each day, plenty of time to walk; she said he returned at "something around 5" pm, but his TSBD day ended at 4:45, a possible bus ride or a possible inaccurate time. Walking the mile-long Houston Street Viaduct was unusual – one of those days, a patrolling Officer Tippit might have stopped Oswald on his walk and questioned him. The ever-abrasive Oswald might likely have complained about Fascist police harassment and mentioned his Marxist views. Tippit would have remembered "youngish white male Commie working at the TSBD." As Tippit sat in the Gloco station, he could have put two and two together and "torn off" to look for Oswald. It is also possible that Tippit saw Oswald go by in a cab. A possible corroboration: a local worker, James Andrews, said he was driving west on West 10th Street a little after 1 pm when a police car passed him and forced him to stop; an agitated Tippit jumped out, ran back to Andrews' car, looked in Andrews' seats, then drove rapidly off without a word. Tippit's few known behaviors from reliable witnesses do suggest that Tippit somehow guessed Oswald was the possible assassin and that it cost him his life.

Oswald left his rooming house on foot at about 1:03, armed with his mail-order .38 and a handful of mismatched ammunition. According to his housekeeper, he checked his local bus stop at Beckley and Zhang. With nothing coming, he strode south. His housekeeper was busy trying to get a picture on the house TV so she could see the assassination reports and may not be reliable.

Speculation: We do not know what Oswald did from his Beckley room at 1:03 down to his killing of Tippit at about 1:15. If Tippit was hunting Oswald, then a scenario might be: Officer Tippit thought he saw Oswald walking south on Beckley at about 1:07; Oswald saw his police car, and quickly turned east on Davis. Tippit moved to follow, seeing Oswald again dodge, this time onto N. Crawford. Tippit should have reported this to Dispatch.


Some believe that Tippit tried to call dispatch at 1:08 – but almost immediately said, "Please disregard"; the old audio is very noisy. He did not jot any notes in his police notebook. He eventually slowed to walking speed behind Oswald - who turned East on 10th at about 1:12-1:13. Officer Tippit was seen following slowly on 10th. At about 1:14, Oswald turned around, perhaps at Tippit's request. They had a brief (unknown) conversation. Oswald apparently did not use his calm persuasion to satisfy Tippit. It is possible that Tippit asked him about his TSBD job or something that convinced Oswald to shoot. Witnesses say Tippit got out of his car at about 1:16 and started around its front, towards Oswald, perhaps drawing his gun. Oswald drew his revolver and shot the officer three times. The wounds suggest that Oswald leaned over and shot the prostrate man once more in the head. Witnesses reported the killing at about 1:18, using Tippit's radio.


Oswald trotted through lots, reloading his pistol, not caring that numerous witnesses saw him. He dodged into the Texas Theater, sneaking quickly by its distracted ticket attendant. A local merchant, alerted by the barrage of sirens, noticed Oswald's furtive movements and had the attendant call the police. They arrived quickly, angered by their fellow officer's death. With theater lights blazing, fifteen police approached Oswald from all sides. Oswald said something like, "Well, it's all over now!" and raised his gun to shoot the nearest policeman. That policeman acted quickly to grab Oswald's revolver, preventing the hammer from firing a bullet - a misfire and a lucky policeman. Had Oswald succeeded in shooting that policeman, he would have died right there in a hail of furious police return fire. Since he could not possibly anticipate that the policeman could force a misfire, Oswald must have expected to die right there. He failed suicide-by-cop, screwing up again.

So:

- Was Oswald a good enough shot to hit a moving target?   Answer: Yes and no.
- Was Oswald ready to take credit for his act? Answer: Not for killing JFK.
- Was Oswald ready to make an escape?
Answer: No.
- Was Oswald happy with his result?   Answer: No.

Oswald's horrible mistake would haunt his remaining hours and explain some of his bizarre behavior after his arrest.

# 8

# OSWALD IN JAIL

After the assassination, Oswald behaved in a manner consistent with someone who had just made a colossal mistake. He wanted to die but failed. Now, he had to live on.

Oswald's arrest in the Texas Theater was nearly bloodless, considering that he tried to shoot a policeman and was already suspected of killing Officer Tippit. Several of the police had considered shooting Oswald during the arrest but said they were afraid of hitting other police or innocents. He had walked out of the theater yelling, "I protest this police brutality!" and "I am not resisting arrest!" to the crowd of 60 people that had gathered. The crowd responded with shouts. "We ought to kill him." "String him up."

A photo captured that instant (Hearings Vol XX p156) when Oswald was taken out from the theater through the crowd. Oswald, the killer of Tippit, was yelling stock phrases heard during 1963 race conflicts at Birmingham, at Cambridge, and at the famed March on Washington, where Martin Luther King said, "I have a Dream." Oswald may have been thinking of attracting an ACLU lawyer for his defense. After the excitement of attempted suicide-by-police, Oswald may have switched to autopilot, yelling the things he had planned to say in a less-dangerous arrest after killing Connally.

Handcuffed in the back of a police car, Oswald refused to

answer most questions, including his name or address. When accused of killing Officer Tippit, he said something fatalistic, like, "Well, you fry for that." He also stated his only crime was "having a pistol in a movie." He was "real calm," "not a bit excited or nervous or anything," and talked very little. During the ride to the station, the car police asked about his wallet's two IDs: "Hidell" and "Oswald." Oswald did not explain.

At about 2 pm, Oswald was taken into the Dallas Police Headquarters.

At about 2:15, came the news that the person of interest in the Kennedy assassination was Lee Harvey Oswald. Captain Will Fritz of the homicide bureau took charge - the killing of the President had no special legal status at that time, so it was to be treated as would any other murder by the Texas police. Oswald was repeatedly given Texas "Miranda-like" rights of lawyer representation and warning about self-incrimination - Texas was ahead of the Supreme Court in this area.

Captain Fritz took Oswald to the "glass all around" room 317, on the third floor, and then into his own office. With several other officers, Fritz led an initial interrogation. Unfortunately, no one kept contemporaneous notes, and no one had a tape recorder. Fritz did write brief notes hours or days later. Fritz admitted that he could not remember exactly when Oswald was asked any particular question, but he did say he could remember the questions and answers. FBI agents James Bookhout and James Hosty also jotted some notes reviewing their attendance (James Bookhout, FBI, 1963).

Fritz again made sure that Oswald understood his Texas rights. Oswald then asked to be represented by Mr. Abt, a New York City attorney who was chief counsel to the Communist Party USA. Oswald knew that Abt had represented some people accused of the violent overthrow of the U.S. government. Fritz said that would be fine, but neither he nor Oswald made a move to get Abt at that time. Oswald asking specifically for Abt suggests that although Oswald was not yet questioned or charged with JFK's murder, Oswald knew his crimes would justify getting the top "outsider" lawyer in the world for his defense. He probably realized that asking for such a lawyer was like admitting guilt at this point. In any case, he made no attempt to use his "free time" and collect-call privileges in the first 24 hours.

Fritz later described interrogation conditions as "bad": a huge crowd shouting questions and comments at Oswald, always upsetting him. Fritz was disgusted that his requests for a department tape recorder had been ignored over the last year; it is, however, surprising that Fritz did not ask to borrow tape recorders from the hundreds of reporters in the area. According to the Postal Inspector Harry Holmes, he and Fritz preferred interrogations by memory because Texas laws required that all their notes would be sent to the defense team before trial. In any case, no investigator made an immediate record of Oswald's responses – astounding, given the historic import and the certain interest from the FBI.

Fritz started with general questions to get acquainted. The interrogation was chaotic because people kept coming in and out - "violating every principle of interrogation," admitted Chief Curry. Further, Fritz was often called away as new evidence or witnesses arrived. The floor soon filled up with onlookers: the local, national, and soon international press, other policemen, people from the Secret Service, the FBI, and even random people just interested in a moment in history. A police-friendly nightclub owner called Jack Ruby is seen in films, for example. In general, there was no security in the building. Some quotes from visitors:

"No one attempted to stop me or ask for any identification at that time."

"There were no guards on elevators or stairs to the third floor for a number of hours."

At least some people got in without even being challenged for IDs.

Later, security was just as haphazard, with some people just walking out of the elevators.

Despite the turmoil, Oswald generally stayed calm. Several people commented that Oswald seemed to pride himself on staying calm no matter what, even with people inches away screaming threats. Oswald had always espoused and defended unpopular and confronting ideas and had practiced staying in control.

For people who knew Oswald, his calm was not surprising. But they found it very surprising that he was relatively quiet. Oswald, were he innocent, would have taken every opportunity to proclaim that innocence loudly to the World's Press. Further, Oswald could be expected to bring up the wonders of Marxism and the deficiencies of capitalism. Yet here was Oswald wasting his once-in-a-lifetime chance to tell the World where it was wrong. His wife said that Oswald's failure to speak out was his surest admission of guilt.

Fritz asked only questions about Officer Tippit's murder at this point. Oswald would not answer any question that seemed remotely self-incriminating. Often, he answered a question with another question, or he simply lied, even for statements that were easily checked. Most reported that he was a maddening personality, sarcastic, insolent and arrogant. Fritz had a reputation for remaining calm, but many wanted to "beat the sh*t" out of Oswald.

Oswald was treated with a lot of care because the International Press was right outside the door. Still, death threats were flooding in.

FBI Agent James Hosty entered the room soon after the questioning began. Oswald had never met him but quickly guessed who he was. When Hosty asked if Oswald had been to Russia and more recently, Mexico City, Oswald became very upset, screaming at Hosty, "I know you!" "You accosted my wife on two occasions!" Fritz asked for clarification and Oswald declared that Hosty had "implied she could be deported," intimidating her. Fritz described Oswald's reaction as a "fist-banging tantrum." Oswald admitted that he had been to Russia but denied Hosty's claim that he'd been in Mexico. They were interrupted just when Oswald was starting to talk.

Thereafter, the priority of the investigation became "Who were Oswald's accomplices, if any?" This line of questioning assumed great importance given Oswald's known background as a Marxist, a Soviet defector, and a Castro sympathizer. Was there an International Conspiracy? Unfortunately, at that point, the FBI agents were told that Hoover (and likely LBJ) did not want the FBI to give any data about Oswald's international interests (Hosty, 1996).

The interrogation remained awkward. Several times, Oswald refused to talk or suddenly demanded his lawyer, Abt. Then, after a while, he would start talking again. And Fritz, too, was often called out, and other people asked Oswald (unrecorded) questions till Fritz returned. Oswald often lied or changed his answers. For example:

- He eventually admitted his name.
- He eventually admitted living at 1026 Beckley.
- He denied registering as O. H. Lee: "The landlady must have written it wrong."
- He denied owning a rifle (he did admit he owned the revolver that killed Tippit).
- He admitted working at the TSBD.
- He said he left the TSBD because he thought work would stop after the shots.

(He was not asked how he was able to ignore the excitement or to leave so quickly without talking to anyone or what was so important at the movies.)

- He said he ate a cheese sandwich and apple that day and saw two TSBD employees (neither agreed with him).
- He denied going to Mexico City.
- He didn't know about any "Hidell" (despite his "Hidell" ID card)
- He denied taking any package into the TSBD that morning; he said the huge paper bag contained his lunch; he said he'd "thrown it in the back seat" at Frazier's request.
- His Marine discharge status had not changed to "undesirable."
- He got his revolver to go to a movie, joining it mid-plot.

- He denied shooting Officer Tippit.
- He denied shooting President Kennedy.
- He refused to take a polygraph test.

Oswald was relatively subdued at first but became sarcastic, arrogant, and cocky over time. His trademark "smirk" and "smugness" made it seem as though he were enjoying the situation. It made people around him want to pummel him. Fritz could not let Oswald go into any general detention or even be near other prisoners (for example, in a lineup) for fear that he would "accidentally" be killed by them. Feelings ran high, especially amongst the Dallas disadvantaged, who loved Kennedy. Anger was high amongst the Dallas Police: their own Officer Tippit had been brutally ripped from his wife and two children.

When Fritz started talking about Kennedy, Oswald denied shooting, but then he added that Kennedy's death would not make much difference: "Well, I think that the Vice President has about the same views as the President has" ... "he will probably do about the same thing that President Kennedy will do."

One of the federal officers asked Oswald if he thought Cuba would be better off since the President was assassinated. Oswald replied, in paraphrase, "Since the President was killed that someone else would take his place, perhaps Vice-president Johnson and that his views would probably be largely the same as those of President Kennedy." Oswald did not seem to know for sure who the new president would be.

In effect, Oswald was absolving himself of his mistake, saying that it really wouldn't make a difference to the world. It is eerily similar to a quote from Frank Sinatra's movie "Suddenly" (1954), in which Frank Sinatra was hired to assassinate the US President by a rifle shot. It is possible that Oswald had watched that movie about five weeks before. Sinatra heard about the quote and asked United Artists to withdraw his movie from circulation. In any case, Oswald was trying to convince himself that his killing JFK was not as terrible as he had thought at first.

As hours went by, Oswald considered his choices: he could

delay until he had Abt or ACLU representation; or he could admit he was an ineffective idiot who had horribly damaged his own cause; or he could brazen it out and enjoy the world's attention. No matter his strategy, Kennedy was dead. No matter his strategy, he would have a platform to spout his warning about the Ultra-Right. No matter his strategy, he had lost his few friends: Kennedy's death would end any support from his wife and from George De Mohrenschildt. He would have the hollow triumph of having made an indelible mark on history – and having earned the ignominy as the most hated man in history.

Oswald delayed making a choice. He continued to say little of consequence. He smoothly answered or parried easy questions but deftly avoided any serious questions.

Hoover and LBJ also had a choice to make. The killing of a man by another man was not a federal crime. But a conspiracy of two or more people to prevent a government official from doing his duty WAS a federal crime. Hoover and Johnson could have declared Oswald a possible conspirator and moved the investigation under Attorney General RFK and the Department of Justice. The FBI could have arrested Oswald as a saboteur or spy. Or, they could have declared the assassination as a possible threat to national security to be handled under military secrecy rules, as per FDR's infamous Executive Order 9066, which interred not one man but any Japanese. Instead, they chose to let the investigation continue as a Texas murder case – and asked for complete cooperation with the DPD.

The Dallas police first pressed Oswald for killing one of their own. Oswald was repeatedly identified in (somewhat biased) lineups as the man who killed Officer Tippit. He became even more sarcastic and impudent. He was arraigned for Officer Tippit's murder at about 7 pm. Oswald demanded to know if it was a real judge, and other flippancies. He was told to "shut up."

On the way back through the press-crowded hall, Oswald made the statement that he probably is most responsible for launching the JFK Conspiracy Industry. He was responding to shouted questions with his usual lies and sarcasm, and then this, immortalized on film:

"I'd like some legal representation. These police officers have not allowed me to have any. I don't know what this is all about."

[Were you at the Book Depository?]

"I work in that building, yes."

[Were you in that building at the time?]

"Naturally if I work in that building."

[Did you shoot the president?]

"No. They've taken me in because I lived in the Soviet Union. I'm just a patsy."

But if Oswald really believed that he was a patsy, why did he not repeat this claim? And a patsy for what crime – he had only been charged with killing Tippit. He tossed out this "I'm just a patsy" comment one time, in relation to his Soviet sojourn. He connected it to his attempted defection rather than a murder. He said it while being led through a mob of shouting reporters in a hallway on his way to be formally accused of the Tippit murder – he had not been accused of killing JFK yet. He had many other opportunities to develop his "patsy" claim, but he never did. In fact, as Marina noted later, why did he not protest his arrest and demand to be freed? Why did the normally argumentative Oswald content himself with brief sarcastic or flippant responses?

Oswald spent the rest of Friday evening in fingerprinting, paraffin tests, questioning and another lineup for Officer Tippit's murder. As Fritz said, the cheek paraffin test was unlikely to show much, given the bolt action that blocked gas discharge toward his face. The FBI later reproduced this negative paraffin test result after they had other people shoot with Oswald's rifle. Gunpowder showed on his hands from his revolver. The rifle fingerprints were re-examined in 1993 and found to match Oswald (Ayton, 2014).

The DPD tracked down and arrested Wesley Frazier. Frazier was treated as a potential conspirator: he had been part of the group that got Oswald a job at the TSBD, had transported Oswald around the city, and had carried Oswald's rifle to the assassination. His Enfield hunting rifle was brought in with him. Word leaked out. Frazier was soon to receive death threats. It was a hard and frightening night; he feared for his life in an angry Dallas. Frazier may have, at that point, decided that Oswald's paper rifle bag must have looked too short – as a way of insulating himself from blame. He passed a lie-detector test about Oswald's curtain rod story.

This first evening, media reports suggested that Oswald would be charged as part of an international conspiracy. White House aide Cliff Carter, representing President Johnson, apparently called officials overseeing the investigation: Dallas County District Attorney Henry Wade, Texas Attorney General Carr, and Dallas Police Chief Jesse Curry. Carter passed on LBJ's warning that any word of an international conspiracy might result in nuclear war and 40 million Americans dead. Fritz was summoned for a brief private talk, probably with Carr. There is no transcript of these calls.

At 11:26 pm Friday, Captain Fritz signed the complaint charging Oswald with the murder of John F. Kennedy.

Chief Curry then ordered a press conference. Fritz wanted measures to protect Oswald, such as putting him where he could be easily extracted if there was trouble. Chief Curry said "no," that Oswald should be placed "right out in front." Fritz did not attend, but there was a crush of press, police, and anyone else who happened to walk in - there was no security. No one was searched for a weapon. No guards were posted. Jack Ruby was apparently there.

The news people had not expected to see Oswald. Curry volunteered to "show" him. Oswald was paraded out and was exposed in front for about 10 minutes. Oswald mostly could not talk over the din but did assert, "I haven't killed anyone, and no one has even mentioned to me anything about the President except you people." Curry soon ordered that Oswald be taken back, saying that the crowd was getting too aggressive with questions.

He was arraigned for the murder of President Kennedy at 1:35 am. His flip comment going in: "Well, I guess this is the trial." No one recorded his reaction when he was told, "No, you are being arraigned on a different charge." Oswald was then moved to a maximum-security cell on the fifth floor, with the cells on either side kept empty.

**Saturday, November 23**

Oswald was allowed to sleep in and have breakfast.

At 10:25 am, polite "interrogations" resumed. There was little new. When shown the bus transfer taken from his pocket, he admitted to taking a bus. When confronted by the cab driver and bus driver, he admitted taking a cab to "near" his boarding-house. Oswald said Kennedy had a nice family, that he admired. There was no further questioning about accomplices – which seems odd, given the many loose ends that might support a conspiracy.

Marina visited Oswald with his mother, Marguerite. Marina said that Oswald's eyes betrayed his guilt.

Oswald announced he would stop talking until he could confer with his chosen lawyer, Abt. Fritz helped him figure out how to get Abt's address and phone number in New York and how to call him "collect." Abt was not home. Later that after-noon, Oswald again tried to reach Abt and failed. Oswald then called Ruth Paine and virtually demanded that she call Abt. Oddly, he called Ruth again a few minutes later and repeated the same demand. Why didn't he call his mother or brother? Ruth Paine was quite upset that this irritating murderer was so demanding, but she did try calling Abt a few times, also without success. Abt was camping, as it turned out.

Lawyers across the nation heard Oswald complain he was not represented. The president of the Dallas County Bar Asso-ciation, H. Louis Nichols, braved the raucous jailhouse crowd to meet with Oswald. Oswald rejected his offer for representation, declaring that Abt and the ACLU would represent him. Four ACLU lawyers had already visited the station late the previous night, as it turned out, and had been turned down. Oswald was clearly not interested in representation at that point.

After hearing that Oswald claimed he was an ACLU member, the president of the Dallas ACLU called the national ACLU office about Oswald. After searching, the national office replied that Oswald was not a member of the ACLU. They issued a press release to that effect the next day (Sunday), calling Oswald a liar who was unrelated to the ACLU. Two days later, they issued another press release, saying that they had tracked down Oswald's application and his $2 fee, apologizing that they had not yet processed his membership.

Oswald, on his way to a lineup with two cab drivers, showed his handcuffs and complained about not having a shower. It is likely that many in the room would have been happy to shower him - with bullets. By this point, death threats were coming from everywhere. Yet once again, there had been little or no security, no identifying, and no frisking of the packed crowd. Fritz clearly expected trouble and repeatedly asked Chief Curry to protect Oswald, but to no avail.

The police had found the "backyard photos" of Oswald with rifle and pistol among materials taken from the Paine house the day before. Marina had burned the copies that she knew about, but Oswald had other copies stuck in books. When Oswald was confronted with copies of these photos, he claimed that they were fake, and that he knew that because he was an expert in photography. The pictures were of a proud man holding an assassination weapon; it was odd that Oswald, after killing JFK, took no pride in his accomplishment – at all. Subsequent analysis has verified the pictures as valid.

After this incident, Oswald again insisted that he would not answer any more questions. This time, he apparently meant it. They returned him to his maximum-security cell at 7:15 pm.

Chief Curry then told the assembled press that Oswald would be transferred via the basement at 10 am the next day. Earlier, Chief Curry had asked if Captain Fritz would be ready to let Oswald be transferred immediately, but Fritz said his team was still gathering information for interrogations. Later, Curry asked if the transfer could happen at 10 am Sunday and Fritz said yes, he could probably be ready. Curry was later faulted for telling the press about the transfer time.

An officer asked Fritz what to do about security, especially about any transfer. Fritz recalled telling him: "There has been no security setup, and the Chief has something to do with this transfer, so you had better call him." J. Edgar Hoover claimed that he called Curry to suggest that Oswald be moved in secret at night, but in any case, to make sure that he was "sufficiently protected." Fritz argued against night transfer because it gave cover to attackers.

## Sunday, November 24

On Sunday, November 24, at 9:30 am, Fritz's polite interrogation continued.

- What do you think of religion?   Oswald: "doesn't think much of it."
- Do you believe in God?        Oswald: <no answer>
- Politics?                 Oswald: a Marxist, not a Marxist-Leninist; likes Cuba
- Repeated questions...        Oswald: denies Hidell, rifle, Neely Apartment, backyard pictures
- Curtain rods?            Oswald: denies bringing the rifle, bringing the rifle bag, or curtain rods
- Shootings?              Oswald: denies shooting JFK or Connally

So, nothing new from further investigations, apart from quizzing about Oswald's various PO boxes. It did take longer than expected, so instead of Oswald transferring at 10 am, they didn't get ready until 11 am.

Fritz was impressed with Oswald's ability to defeat interrogation. As long as questions were not too important, Oswald chatted easily. As soon as a question headed somewhere important, he would clam up. Fritz thought he was so good at it that he asked if he'd been trained. Oswald said the FBI had interrogated him when he had returned from Russia (twice by Agent Fain), and he had learned a lot.

At 11:15, the transfer party left Fritz's office but was delayed when Oswald asked for a sweater. At 11:21, Oswald was shot by Jack Ruby, carried into the jail office and put on the floor there. At 1:07 pm, Oswald was declared dead at Parkland Hospital, just 48 hours after his accidental victim, President John F. Kennedy.

Fritz said that he did not believe Oswald was afraid at all. "I think he was a person who had his mind made up what to do and I think he was like a person just dedicated to a cause. And I think he was above average for intelligence. I know a lot of people call him a nut all the time but he didn't talk like a nut. He knew exactly when to quit talking."

With Jack Ruby's help, Oswald had quit talking forever.


## Jack Ruby Defeated Chief Curry's "Security"

Throughout the hours that the public knew of Lee Harvey Oswald, the bureaucracy of Dallas was bombarded with death threats on Oswald. Dallas, Texas, was one of the most heavily armed cities in the US. Yet Chief Curry took little or no action to protect Oswald. Even after the Director of the FBI, Hoover himself, claimed to have told Curry to protect Oswald. That is a brave move, doing something really stupid in direct defiance of the head of the FBI – assuming Hoover really said that.

Captain Fritz said he never got instructions to take extra care of Oswald – so Hoover was lying? During Oswald's custody, there was never any serious ID checking done in the station; people could walk to the third floor without being stopped, let alone registered or searched for weapons. We do not have a list of the hundreds of visitors who crowded around Oswald in hallways and at press conferences. How many guns were out there? How many fingers itched to wipe that smirk off Oswald's face?

Chief Curry consistently made decisions to put Oswald in even greater jeopardy. There was no requirement that Oswald be "shown" at press conferences, yet Curry insisted on it. There was no requirement that the press and hangers-on should be allowed to crowd hallways into almost immobility, yet Curry allowed it. There was no reason to let the crowd turn every appearance into a circus, yet Curry requested this "freedom of the press" against the advice of seasoned men like Captain Fritz.

When Chief Curry testified at the WC Hearings, he said that he wanted to show the world that Oswald was not being mistreated. He said the press "demanded" to see Oswald, although no one in the press claims to have made such a demand. He said that the press was not to yell questions at Oswald. Well, they did.

It was as though Curry was daring one of those thousands of death-threat authors to come out and give it a try. Early Sunday morning, the DPD, Sheriff's, and FBI offices all got the same threatening call: "There are 100 of us, who've just voted to kill Oswald soon." That particular threat apparently had no substance, but at least one person was serious.

Curry did not know that he would be responsible for Oswald's transfer and so had not arranged anything. Curry and his wife had kept their phone off the hook so their sleep would not be disturbed by more late-night reporter calls. He called the County Jail's Sheriff Decker at about 9 am - it was only then that Curry learned he was to handle Oswald's transfer; the Sheriff's Department handled 90% of transfers but did not have enough personnel for Oswald's security. The only security in that basement was set up by Captain Talbert on his own initiative. Curry made no contribution except to relax security: Talbert testified that he was clearing the basement and exit of all "unaccredited people" but that Curry allowed the 70 unmanageable news people to stay. Curry admitted he never assigned anyone as overall director of the transfer.

Curry's suggested armored truck arrived late and jammed up one ramp. At the last minute of Oswald's transfer, Captain Fritz proposed having Oswald transferred by car while the armored truck became a decoy. Curry had the street police force move to guard Fritz's route, ruining the decoy's secrecy. Fritz then suggested that he could take Oswald out the first floor to a car waiting on Main Street and thus avoid the basement throngs. Curry refused, again insisting on parading Oswald in harm's way by staying with the publicized plan. Fritz's changes reached the basement too late: the crowd there prevented the transfer cars from moving into position. No car was ready for Oswald.

Curry later said his "security plan" was aimed at stopping the rumored mob action, not at stopping a lone killer like Ruby. He said he did try to put only stable officers in the plan to guard against an emotional police officer killing Oswald. No one asked why he allowed an unexamined mob into his building. No one asked why he discounted the hundreds of death threats suggesting an attack by a lone gunman in his "shows," or his halls, or during his transfers.

City Manager Crull, who was Chief Curry's boss, also went out of touch until after Oswald's death. He was on his boat on Saturday morning, through until Sunday afternoon. Crull testified that neither he nor Mayor Cabell gave any instructions or pressure to Curry about Oswald's transfer or the treatment of the press.

Captain Fritz was quite disturbed by Curry's entire lack-of-plan transfer. After the fact, Fritz was asked how he would have done Oswald's transfer. He replied that the very next day, he was responsible for transferring Jack Ruby to the county jail. "[paraphrased for clarity] We had about the same threats on [Ruby] that we did with Oswald. I had two of my officers pick me up away from the office. We drove by the county jail, checking that the driveway was open. I went back to the station told three officers to mark Ruby 'transferred temporarily,' which means going somewhere within that office [e. g. fingerprinting]. Then, without telling anyone even in the office where they were going, they brought Ruby down the jail elevator and stayed in the elevator with Ruby until our car was flush with their door. Then they hustled Ruby right through those cameras and put him in the back seat. Photographers didn't even get pictures. Then we had Ruby lie down on the back seat and two officers leaned back over him. We drove him straight up that same street, turned to the left down Main Street, and ran him into the jail entrance and put him in the jail. We didn't even tell the jailer we were coming."

As it was, Fritz said, "I was transferring Oswald like [Chief Curry] told me to transfer him. I asked the chief and he said that security was all set up." Fritz had asked Curry to have the news people moved away from the transfer path. But that did not happen. Fritz testified: "As we started to leave, Curry told me that the people were moved across the street, and the other people were back of the railing, and I think he thought they were. I think someone must have changed his order down there...I thought there would be nobody on the jail side of the rail and nobody on the main ramp. Instead, the crowd surged forward around us and blocked our path."

Oswald was shot once in the abdomen. It had a good chance of not being fatal had it not damaged both Oswald's aorta and his superior vena cava: it was fatal - but by a fraction of an inch.

At the time, the first thought of most police was that Oswald had likely been shot by another Dallas policeman. The police were extremely upset that Oswald had shot fellow Officer Tippit. But they soon recognized Jack Ruby.

Who was the shooter, Jack Ruby? He apparently was just an unstable, upset guy with a gun who liked to hang around the police station. He was one of many thousands who said he'd like to kill Oswald. Ruby had left his apartment at about 11 am, an hour **after** Oswald was to be transferred. He'd brought his gun to guard money he was sending to an employee. He bought a money order at 11:17 am at the Western Union office a block from the station. Already an hour late, Oswald should have been gone by then - but he had delayed to get his sweater. At 11:20, Ruby strolled down the basement ramp, past the sole guard who was busy getting the crowd out of the way so a "decoy" car could get out. When Ruby reached the ramp bottom, he should have been blocked by the actual transfer car, but due to the uncontrolled crowd, it was not in the right location. Ruby walked up just as Oswald was coming into the basement.

Ruby was no hired gun. He was Jack Rubenstein, owner of a struggling strip club that catered to the occasional policeman. Jack Ruby schmoozed the police to get them into his club and was known in the station. Jack Ruby, like many other Americans, had been very upset by Kennedy's death, Jackie's widowing, and that two small children were fatherless, and he was uniquely upset with the full-page advertisement that had run in the Dallas Morning News of November 22. The Dallas John Birchers implied that JFK was in league with Communists:

"WELCOME MR. KENNEDY"

Why is Latin America going anti-American or Communist?

Why is there no freedom in Cuba?

Why are you allowing the sale of American grains to the Communists?

Why did you host, salute and entertain Communist Tito?

Why do you help Communists more than you help anti-Communists?

Why has Cambodia kicked the US out despite $400m in aid?

Why has the head of the US Communist Party endorsed you for 1964?

Why are you showing the un-American film "Operation Abolition" on US bases?

Why do you let your brother, Attorney General Bobbie, go soft on Communism?

Why do you send aid to Argentina, who just seized $400m in American assets?

Why is the CIA helping overthrow anti-Communists?

Why have you scraped the Monroe Doctrine for "Spirit of Moscow"?

Ruby was not surprised. The Dallas Daily News had been editorializing in similar veins for years. What upset Ruby was that it was signed by Bernard Weissman, a fellow Jew. Ruby was complaining about that ad at the newspaper office just when the news of the assassination arrived. The killing of Kennedy, possibly spurred on by a crazy "Weissman" ad, stunned Ruby. Oswald may not have seen that ad – it would have made JFK more of a hero in his eyes since every JBS critique was an Oswald goal. But Ruby said then, and later, that he was thinking of "righting the wrong done by this Weissman" that "reflected badly on all Jews."

Ruby testified that he had been at the Saturday press conference and had carried his gun into the room. He had seen Oswald there, and he did not like what he saw. He also heard about the 10 am transfer; after his money order chore at 11 am, he saw and came to investigate the crowd at the DPD, He described his Sunday morning shot at Oswald as a chance in a million. Right after the shooting, he said to his police escort: "I hope I killed the son of a bitch. It will save you guys a lot of trouble."

In his own trial for the murder of Oswald, Ruby gave two motives. First, to show that Jews could be bold and brave and aggressive. Second, he did not want Jackie Kennedy to suffer through Oswald's trial or possibly be called as a witness herself. Both motives aligned with his statements and actions before and after killing Oswald. No believable connection was ever found to a conspirator. Ruby, like Oswald, wanted a place in history and saw a target of opportunity.

9

# IGNORING OSWALD'S MOTIVE

The subject of Oswald's motive was gradually submerged under the vague rubric "lone nut."

If Connally was Oswald's "natural target," why was that possibility never investigated? Ultimately, the investigation was set up by two men: President Johnson and FBI Director Hoover.

Johnson and Hoover were both soon aware of Oswald's arrest. For two days, they did not have the benefit of an in-depth analysis of the Zapruder film or other hard evidence. They received conflicting reports as various discoveries were made. They did not expect to get an accurate, complete, and consistent picture and were probably surprised at the ease with which evidence piled up against Oswald. They were no doubt concerned with public reactions to Oswald's Marxism, his trip to the USSR, his Soviet wife, and his one-man street campaign for Castro.

Both Johnson and Hoover would first think to protect the country from a coordinated Soviet attack. Johnson and Hoover must have quickly agreed to avoid having the Texas police dig for conspiracies. It makes some sense, given that (1) Oswald was a Marxist, had visited Russia, and had been agitating for Cuban sympathy, (2) Dallas had a vocal extreme right that would want to pin the crimes on Commies, and (3) no one could know what would crawl out from under rocks. The American people could easily have been stirred to war mode had the Texas police emphasized Oswald's past as a Russian/Cuban conspiracy. By avoiding an onslaught of semi-true speculation and especially given that there was no perfect information on Oswald, LBJ and Hoover probably did a good thing to stop initial runaway speculation.

An aide of newly-president Johnson had called District Attorney Wade, Texas Attorney General Carr, and Dallas Police Chief Curry to warn against loose talk of conspiracies, citing the danger of American stampede to nuclear war. Hoover had told his FBI to back away from sharing international data. Oswald's chief interrogator, Homicide Captain Fritz, was apparently summoned by Dallas County Sheriff Decker to receive a message before he could start questioning; it is unknown what was discussed, as the Warren Commission did not investigate. It is likely that Decker told Fritz not to dig for any international conspiracy around Oswald and especially to avoid any speculations of Soviet or Cuban involvement, despite Oswald's background.

For whatever reason, Fritz then interrogated Oswald very softly, took no immediate notes, did not involve any stenographer, and did not ask any reporter for their tape recorder, nor was one immediately purchased. Oswald was not encouraged to get council. As Chief Curry admitted, "We were violating every principle of interrogation."

As Oswald's personal history was reported, no one said he hated Kennedy. In fact, Oswald was reported to have respected Kennedy. The person who knew Oswald best – his wife Marina – immediately thought Oswald had intended to shoot Connally.

The new President Johnson spoke with J. Edgar Hoover in a recorded call to set up what became the Warren Commission. Johnson almost immediately asked Hoover if all three shots were aimed at JFK, and Hoover assured him with the FBI analysis of that day: there were three shots, "the first and third hit JFK and the second hit, Connally," but that "they were aiming directly at the President, there is no question about that...this telescopic lens, which I have looked through, brings a person as close to you as though they were sitting right beside you." Johnson followed up: "How did Connally happen to get hit?" Hoover replied, "Connally happened to turn and got hit." Then Hoover volunteered that "if Connally hadn't got in the way, Kennedy would have gotten hit three times." Hoover makes no sense at all, given the already available Zapruder film. It is also odd that this is the only call between Johnson and Hoover that had a saved recording. The conversation is so stilted that it reads like an "alibi builder" and has raised suspicions as being deliberate. Nevertheless, it revealed that Johnson did consider Connally a possible target.

Hoover and Johnson were quick to realize that Oswald's murder would spawn a conspiracy industry. There were further calls amongst Johnson, Hoover, and others in the days after the assassination – but no recordings. The day Oswald was killed, Hoover was concerned that the public be convinced that Oswald was the lone killer. Many people report that Hoover tried to limit any further investigations of conspiracies or foreign involvements in JFK's death. Hoover clearly had a lot of leverage on all concerned. Both he and Johnson said that Oswald was the lone killer, and that the country would be better off if everyone just stopped looking further.

Although Hoover wrote a private memo castigating Dallas Police Chief Curry and complained to LBJ about Curry's failure to protect Oswald, there is the possibility that his call recording and memo were "cover." Curry "paraded Oswald to death" – a move that should have cost him his job and worse. Perhaps Johnson hoped Oswald's death would "move the American people" past the tragedy. Johnson certainly did not want his ascendance clouded by a story spewed for months by a mouthy Marxist loser or that Oswald had accidentally made him president. Hoover and Johnson did manage to stop any anger-driven nuclear war, but they also stopped any consideration of Oswald's motive and any investigation of Oswald's targeting Connally.

The idea of Connally as a target did come up as the Warren Commission built its case. It became obvious that Oswald had real enmity towards the more conservative Texans, which included Connally. Oswald was incensed about mistreatment of the downtrodden and people of color. Dallas had reverberated with hate speech about Kennedy's plans for racial equity.

On January 13, 1964, Warren Commission assistant counsel David W. Belin wrote a memo suggesting that Oswald might have been trying to kill Connally. The idea was dismissed immediately: the excuse was that Oswald would have had better opportunities to kill Connally without the complication of trying to hit a moving target surrounded by Secret Service agents and hundreds of witnesses. "Common sense," they said at the time. But this seems to ignore the known attributes of Oswald. He had no car to chase around after Connally or even Dallas resident General Walker. On November 22, Connally fell into Oswald's sights with nothing to stop a bullet except another passenger. Unlike his Walker shot, Oswald left no planning materials behind: no photos, no assassination notebook, and no explanatory note to Marina – we have no confession from Oswald.

Connally thought Kennedy was the target, but he recognized that Oswald might possibly have been shooting at him. In his testimony, he said, "I am not at all sure he was shooting at me. I think I could, with some logic, argue either way." "I think from where he was shooting, I was in the direct line of fire immediately in front of the President, so any movement on the part of the President would expose me."

Marina Oswald immediately "swore before God that [Oswald] did not intend to kill Kennedy." She testified on September 6, 1964, that she thought her husband "was shooting at Connally rather than President Kennedy." Mrs. Oswald noted Connally's connection to her husband's undesirable discharge. She could not think of any reason why Oswald would want to kill President Kennedy. Rather, Oswald had said he thought Kennedy was a good president with a nice family and deserved his job despite it coming from family wealth. Marina related that Oswald had never been shy about denouncing leaders, yet through all the books, articles, radio broadcasts, and husband-wife discussions of JFK in the months before the shooting, Oswald had said nothing critical. Marina's comments on Connally as the target were not pursued further by the Warren Commission and were not included in the final Warren Report (Warren Commission, 1964).

No witness gave much reason for Oswald to shoot Kennedy. In a very thorough work, *Tragic Truth* lists 45 people who recollected Oswald commenting favorably on Kennedy and just one unfavorable. Only Michael Paine had a slightly negative impression, recalling that Oswald "did not like anyone, but disliked Kennedy least." (Pierre Sundborg, 2016).

In 1976, Oswald's best friend George De Mohrenschildt was writing a book which he titled *"I'm a Patsy"* after Oswald's famed declaration. He discussed how the Warren Commission pressed ahead with their "lone assassin" conviction despite being unable to find any reason for Oswald to kill Kennedy. He quotes Oswald, "If [Kennedy] succeeds [in ending the Cold War], he'll be the greatest president in the history of this country." De Mohrenschildt said "Only some more logical and cynical writers mentioned the fact that there was no reason whatsoever in Lee's [killing JFK]; but they approve the thesis that Lee was aiming at Governor Connally, whom he had reasons to dislike, but being a usual flop and f*** up, he killed Kennedy instead and only wounded Connally ..." (Mohrenschildt, HSCA Volume XII: George de Mohrenschildt, 1977)

De Mohrenschildt's *"I'm a Patsy"* was later edited into readability. After mulling for years, George still did not believe that Oswald had any motive to shoot JFK, nor did any conspiracy seem plausible. As the editor says, "the most plausible answer": Oswald shot at Connally and missed; thereafter, we see "the machinations of an amoral superpower trying to conceal from its own people" and the world, its everyday unsavory alliances and actions (Mohrenschildt, Lee Harvey Oswald as I Knew Him, 2014).

In 1988, historian and journalist James Reston Jr. published a book, *The Great Expectations of John Connally*, suggesting that Connally was Oswald's real target, but with no hard evidence. In 1989, Reston published *Lone Star*, a detailed biography of Connally. Again, he suggested that Oswald had targeted Connally. He said the Warren Commission dismissed the idea of Kennedy as an accidental victim because it was "an irony too grotesque to contemplate." (James Reston Jr, The Lone Star: The Life of John Connally, 1989)

In 1993, William D. Rubinstein, a professor at the University of Wales, published an article in *History Today* that the Warren Report had raised the possibility that Oswald had meant to kill Connally but had dismissed it on 'flimsy grounds' and that the subsequent onslaught of conspiracy theories had obscured the idea. In 2007, he again suggested that circumstantial evidence pointed to Connally as the target in his book *Shadow Pasts: 'Amateur Historians' and History's Mysteries* (William D. Rubinstein, 2014).

In 2010, Professor Ernst P. Titovets, MD, Ph.D., published his book on Oswald's "Russian Episode." While a medical student in Minsk, he spent about 18 months as Oswald's closest friend in Russia, as they helped each other with English and Russian. He traded letters with Oswald until a couple of months before the assassination – though the KGB impounded those letters. He interviewed others who knew Oswald in Minsk and, in 1991, got access to KGB files on Oswald. Titovets concluded that Oswald did not seem like a killer, that Oswald was highly motivated to achieve as a political leader, that Oswald sincerely liked both JFK and the United States, and that Oswald hoped to help the USA evolve peacefully towards a better social structure (Titovets, 2020).

In 2013, James Reston Jr. published *The Accidental Victim*. Reston again questioned whether JFK was the target of Lee Harvey Oswald. He builds his circumstantial case around Oswald's lifetime behavior: Oswald was never heard to criticize Kennedy in any significant way, and in fact, was respectful of Kennedy for his stand on civil rights, for pushing arms reductions, for improving US-Soviet relations, and for stopping any war on Cuba. Oswald had several times voiced a strong dislike for Connally. Reston argues that Oswald was upset personally because Connally had signed the order that demoted Oswald's Marine discharge and because Connally had never acted to repair that damage. Oswald was upset politically because Connally was making moves to undermine civil rights progress and might compete for the 1964 nomination (James Reston Jr, The Accidental Victim: *JFK, Lee Harvey Oswald, and the Real Target in Dallas*, 2013).

Reston does an excellent job of laying out the radicalization of Oswald as a "killer of fascists." He describes Oswald's penchant for shocking others, his surprising friendship with the urbane De Mohrenschildt, his failed attempt to assassinate the ultra-right-wing General Walker, and his troubled and broken home life. Reston also points out that had Kennedy's head not gotten in the way, it is likely that Oswald's third shot would have killed Connally.


**Tragic Truth**

In 2016, *Tragic Truth: Oswald Shot Kennedy by Accident* made an emphatic declaration: Governor John Connally was Oswald's target (Pierre Sundborg, 2016). His evidence, in part, echoes the analysis done by Reston but with more detail and discernment.

Sundborg analyzed key questions of the assassination, using his engineering fact-based approach. He introduces the concept of elucidating "unknown knowns," facts that are in front of us all if we just notice and check them.

One other person considered that Oswald might have aimed to kill Connally: Jackie Kennedy. She was plagued by insomniac nights and confided to Manchester:

*What was so terrible was the thought that it might have been an accident, a freak, that an inch or two here, a moment or two there would have reversed history. – Jackie Kennedy, 1964*

**An Easy Shot to Miss**

This photo shows the "X-100" passenger seats in use at the motorcade, in a picture taken minutes before the shooting. Despite Kennedy being one "torso inch" shorter than Connally, this photo shows that his higher bench seat put him about four inches higher in the car than Connally – and directly aligned from Oswald's "nest."

. . .

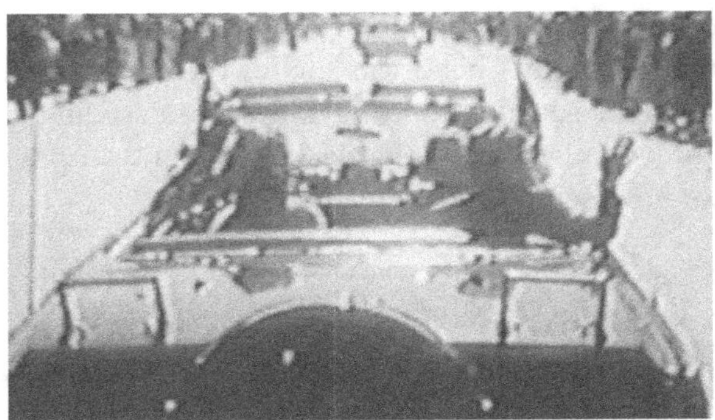

*(Dave Powers/ARRB/AP)*

Only an egomaniac would take shots where two men were so aligned. Oswald may have felt he could make an exceptional shot. More likely, he had not thought the limo would have two rows of seats and that his target would be so obscured. Ultimately, his ego dictated that carrying through his attempt was more important than worrying about accidentally hitting some guy behind Connally.

Oswald's sniper's nest was near perfect for him had the limo had no second back seat. Oswald had gotten the job at the TSBD by accident. Oswald had shot from the TSBD sixth floor because it was accidentally unattended. He was in the most eastward window because that's where the floor repairmen had moved stacks of boxes that created a basic sniper's nest. Oswald was in the best window to have the limo move almost directly away from him due to the curve of Elm Street. When Oswald was hired, there was no hint that Connally would soon take a motorcade under that window, or that he would be in the special extra-seat X-100. Events conspired to give Oswald a relatively easy shot. Too bad there was another man's head in the line of fire.

All through these shots, Oswald was likely focused on his target - Connally. Other people in the car were not his concern.

His poor scope gave only fuzzy, discolored views in its periphery – where Jackie sat. If Oswald had shot at Connally, would he have taken such unlikely and dangerous shots had he known that Kennedy's head was inches from his trajectory? In the few rushed seconds, fearing failure and seeing only the narrow, blurry view through his cheap 4x18 scope, **Oswald might not have seen Kennedy.**

**Oswald's Notebook**

After the shooting, Secret Service agent Mike Howard was ordered to be a bodyguard for Marina Oswald and the two little Oswald girls. When clothes were brought from Marina's room at Ruth Paine's, he found Oswald's little green address book. Marina said the book was hidden amongst Ruth Paine's cookbooks and overlooked during the police-warranted search of November 23rd. Agent Howard read the book and turned it over to the FBI; it is preserved in the Warren Commission Exhibits as #18. However, the Warren Commission's exhibit is missing a page (numbered 17 and 18 on the front and back sides). Howard says that Oswald had written on the 17th page, under the block capitals heading "I WILL KILL," the names of four men: the Vice President (they assumed this meant former VP Richard Nixon), FBI agent James Hosty, General Edwin Walker and Texas Gov. John Connally. Besides Connally's name, he had also drawn a bloodied dagger. Special Agent Charles Kunkel also saw and remembered that page.

Howard says that he learned only after the September 1964 publication of the 26 Volume Warren Hearings and Exhibits: this critical page had been torn from the address book.

Howard has maintained his story, even teaching about it in his college classes, ever since: Oswald was aiming at Connally. Howard suggested two possibilities to explain why the page and its obvious implications were suppressed.

- FBI director J. Edgar Hoover suppressed it, hiding the failure of James Hosty and the Dallas FBI branch to follow up on Oswald's threat against

Hosty himself, made only days before the assassination. A follow-up might have discovered this notebook and other reasons to prevent Oswald from shooting a few days later.

- Or, President Lyndon Johnson suppressed it because he did not want his close friend, Connally, to be identified as the catalyst for the shooting. Johnson, a Texan, was likely nervous about appearances if Texas was scrutinized as a political hotbed for left and right.

Howard's claim about the contents of page 17 probably cannot be verified. Howard himself spent many years after the assassination still in the Secret Service, assigned to protect Oswald's family, then members of LBJ's family, and others. He was probably reluctant, in those circumstances, to rock the Warren Report and the Johnson Presidency by complaining about a page that he could no longer prove. And he may have thought, like the Warren Commission, that it would be too tragic for America.

This incident is reported in *Tragic Truth: Oswald Shot Kennedy by Accident* (Pierre Sundborg, 2016). In personal communications, Sundborg said that he came to know Mike Howard very well through many conversations and visits. He knows Mike to be "of great memory, very thoughtful, careful and honest," and declared it "impossible that Mike and Secret Service Agent partner Chuck would invent something to have been on that page." The "I WILL KILL" note is fully in line with Oswald's psyche and his goals to protect America from his perception of the right wing.

## Kennedy Unknowingly Contributed to His Own Death

If Oswald was shooting at Connally, then Kennedy had put himself in the bullet's path. Kennedy also feared Connally and his Ultra-Right. It was no secret that Dallas was a center for the ultra-right. Several people, for example, Senator J. William

Fulbright, suggested that a trip to Dallas was not worth the risks (William Manchester, 1967).

Kennedy was becoming more concerned about his 1964 reelection. His civil rights actions had caused a deep fracture in the Democratic Party. Polls showed that his "moral obligation" launch of civil rights had taken his support down to 58%. The Southern states had been staunchly Democratic since the Civil War but were now angrily opposed to Kennedy and were already blocking all his legislation, regardless of its intent (Sabato, 2013).

Kennedy knew that he could face a difficult campaign to win in 1964, but it would become a lot more difficult if there was a primary fight in the coming summer. A leading potential adversary was John Connally, also youngish, dynamic, and well-connected to money but who was on the other side of the civil rights and Cold War issues. Kennedy feared that his trip through Dallas might create some awkward moments if Connally was cheered in his home state while he himself got the jeers and the "go home" screams that had been promised even in the newspapers of his last morning. By riding with Connally and by putting Connally in the short jump seat, Kennedy may have thought to diminish Connally's crowd presence. If there were boos, who could tell if Connally or he were the target? (James Reston Jr, The Accidental Victim: JFK, Lee Harvey Oswald, and the Real Target in Dallas, 2013)

Jackie's presence was a huge boon for JFK's popularity, but it did force a fatal circumstance. Had Jackie not come along, Kennedy would almost certainly not have used the jump seats at all. In almost all motorcades Kennedy liked to have the jump seats folded away so he could stand up in the car – he preferred having only one or two people with him in the back seat. With Jackie along, Kennedy had to either ride with just Jackie or use the jump seats.

In the morning before the motorcade, Kennedy allowed or even requested several actions that made it easier for Oswald to accidentally shoot him instead of Connally:

1. He wanted to ride with Connally instead of with, for example, LBJ.
2. He requested that the car top to be removed.
3. He put Connally in the jump seat immediately in front of him.
4. He ordered that motorcycle police ride behind the car instead of beside it.
5. He asked the car to slow to 12 mph.
6. He asked that agents not ride on the back of X-100.
7. He wore his back brace and elastic wrap, keeping him more vertical in the car.

Most of these were normal for Kennedy. Kennedy always sat in the right-side bench seat (Pierre Sundborg, 2016). Kennedy would want the top removed in clear weather and large campaign crowds. Kennedy loved to work crowds – he normally wanted his car to go slowly; Jackie was also bothered by the wind. He knew that Jackie disliked the loud Harley-Davidson exhaust noise and wanted no Harleys next to her. Kennedy always wore his back brace when in motorcades. The setup in Dallas was essentially identical to that in San Antonio the day before, right down to a slow motorcade through packed crowds among downtown buildings - some of which had windows open on upper floors.

But Connally had NOT sat in that jump seat in other Kennedy motorcades. In San Antonio the day before, leaving the airport, Connally was put on the left bench with JFK on the right - Connally's height did make him a bit more imposing. Returning to the airport, Connally was in the left jump seat, while JFK was on the right bench. Jackie and Connally's wife sorted themselves into the available seats. Had JFK allowed ANY other seating in Dallas, Oswald would have had shots at Connally without JFK in the line of fire.


**Was Oswald Hung Out for Target Practice?**
There were a lot of people who cheered at first, in their hearts and a few publicly, when Oswald was killed. There had

been many threats. And there were a lot more ordinary Americans who were very, very unhappy with Oswald, especially Oswald's televised smirk. Given the nation's emotions, it was likely that if Oswald were paraded around long enough in uncontrolled Texan crowds, someone would shoot him. Ruby just happened to be the first guy who tried - and it did not turn out to be difficult.

Seth Kantor, in his book *The Ruby Cover-up*, suggested that Ruby was let into the station, on multiple occasions, explicitly to kill Oswald. Kantor speculated that the Dallas Police wanted revenge on Oswald for killing Officer Tippit. While conceivable, it seems highly unlikely that a DPD cabal would take such an unprecedented risk in the full view of the world when they knew that once Oswald was convicted and in Texas prisons, they could enjoy a more traditional revenge process.

The World soon realized that they would never really know what had happened. The televised death of Oswald, right in the police station, with cameras rolling, was a black eye for the Dallas police, for Dallas, and for America. Worse for Curry, death threats started for him and his family. There was a general feeling that something was fishy: had Oswald been killed to shut him up?


## Did Curry Kill Oswald

The Warren Report says that Oswald was led through 20 feet of packed, unsearched spectators at least 15 times. Oswald's "news conferences" were ridiculous, as Curry demanded that no questions be asked of Oswald – they were just to look at him, and shoot him? Curry had Oswald placed outside the protective screen. The mob scene around Oswald included not only reporters but random visitors, drunks and criminals who happened to be at the station – and cranks like Ruby. That mob was extremely and overtly hostile in a city known to be heavily armed.

It is possible that Curry just did not think ahead. Perhaps he was swept away in an international spotlight and acted to let that spotlight have full access. He did not get good advice from his bosses. The FBI or Secret Service apparently did not raise any objections to parading Oswald – regardless of Hoover's alleged call to "arrange for Oswald's safety." In the absence of a rulebook for the situation, Curry said he opted for visibility. Curry did not show great judgement in Oswald's transfer. In any case, it was incompetent (or calculating) not to make sure everyone was identified and disarmed. Curry was later criticized for that incompetence - but he was not fired.

Several people claimed that Curry had been told by "someone above him," "possibly the White House," that Oswald had to be shown to the press often; however, this superior was not reported by the Warren Commission. Captain Fritz had asked Curry repeatedly about better protection for Oswald. Fritz did not remember Curry ever making a claim that a superior told him to parade Oswald.


**Speculation: Was there a Conspiracy to Kill Oswald?**

Curry did his first open-viewing unsecured press conference on the first evening - Friday night. Could he have unilaterally decided such a dangerous course that early in the process, less than twelve hours after the assassination? Did someone call Curry and suggest that he parade an unprotected Oswald amongst unsearched, angry people? Pure speculation is how we get conspiracy theories ... so ... why not try one?

No record was made during Oswald's interrogations, so we do not really know what Oswald said. Surely, Hoover should have insisted that the assassin's words should be recorded – in fact, should be echoed immediately to the FBI and CIA. What if Oswald had worked with other conspirators, foreign or domestic? Instead, Oswald's words were left unrecorded and were only paraphrased by FBI and Secret Service agents; the CIA eventually heard from the FBI.

Oswald was not ever questioned about conspirators. It made sense to hide Oswald's direct words from the public. After all, who knew what he might say? But it did not make sense to not question him about accomplices – immediately and with vigor. If there was a Soviet, or Cuban, or Mafia, or rogue CIA-FBI plot, then it should have been investigated immediately – once uncovered, Oswald would have transferred to military or FBI custody as a danger to the State, and secrecy would have been required while an appropriate reaction was developed. On the other hand, parading him about allowed Oswald to shout anything – for example, that he was part of a conspiracy with ___. If the police or FBI suspected Oswald was part of a conspiracy, then they were risking everything by letting Oswald shout to the international press. If Oswald had shouted, "The Soviets made me do it!" or "Castro made me do it!" he could launch a world war. That is too much risk. The only explanation: they knew enough about Oswald to know he could not be reasonably tied to any conspiracy – that Oswald was a big-mouthed, dissatisfied, incompetent loner in a bad marriage. Which was exactly what he was. But even that loser Oswald could spew corrosive talk to upset Americans for months, and distract Americans from LBJ, and expose mistakes by the FBI, the Secret Service, and the CIA.

Curry could not have exposed Oswald on his own initiative. Only FBI Director Hoover or President Johnson would have the authority to ask Curry to do such a thing. Hoover had a proven record of ignoring the law when he thought the law was hurting the US "security." Hoover had several calls with Johnson, only one of which was recorded; Hoover did claim to have called Curry to "arrange for Oswald's safety." Perhaps Hoover expected everyone to leap to the conclusion that he told Curry to *improve* Oswald's security, but he really arranged Oswald's repeated exposure. Curry did not "remember" that Hoover expressed concern for Oswald's safety.

Hoover and LBJ certainly had the motive, the means, and the opportunity to limit Oswald's talk and to set up Oswald for target practice. Johnson had already asked Hoover about having the FBI "take over" the investigation, and Hoover had sent 50 agents to Dallas Friday evening. There is a suspicious fourteen-minute gap in the record of a November 23rd call between LBJ and Hoover when they were discussing Oswald (Mellen, 2016).

Two key people who could have questioned Curry's

behavior (Dallas Mayor Earl Cabell and Oswald's chosen Lawyer Abt) were incommunicado. Virtually everyone else in the entire world sat glued to their TVs.

If Curry was disobeying orders from Hoover, he should have been fired, as he obviously worked hard NOT to protect Oswald. If there was a "JFK-related conspiracy" at all, this would be a likely one: Johnson, Hoover and Curry would have felt justified to protect the US (and themselves) from months or years of continued trauma from the mouth of Oswald. There is no proof other than circumstances: Curry's odd behavior, the reduced, unrecorded, and unshared interrogations of Oswald, the vague memories of unrecorded calls amongst the three, a supposedly missing notebook page, Oswald's repeated exposures, and his successful execution by the lone vigilante Ruby.

Harold Weisberg, expert on the JFK assassination, had noticed this dangerous "display" of Oswald back in the late 1960s. He also noted that Curry and others made statements to the press asserting Oswald's guilt – statements that would have precluded a "fair" trial. He wrote about it, asking how Curry could even keep his job after making such mistakes.

Prejudicial talk may have motivated Hoover and Johnson to encourage Oswald's death. They were told, by Friday evening, that Curry and the Dallas District Attorney Wade were on TV and radio with announcements that Oswald was certainly guilty. US Deputy Attorney General Katzenbach warned of the nightmare that would be likely: Oswald could be tried and found guilty but then be freed on appeal because of shoddy police actions. A similar case, Rideau vs. Louisiana 373 U. S. 723, had gone to the US Supreme Court in June 1963: the Supreme Court freed the confessed killer because prejudicial talk had biased any possible jurors in the area. Oswald's trial would have no unbiased jurors. In addition, the "active shooter" state in the TSBD trampled a lot of the evidence, bringing more possibilities for mistrials. That would truly have been a disaster for the United States.

Hoover and Johnson were good friends. They lived across the street from one another. Johnson gave Hoover one of his beagles (Pierre Sundborg, 2016). Johnson has been shown to have shady dealings – the kind of activities that Hoover loved to collect in his personal files and that could be used to pressure unwilling politicians. Johnson made Hoover "FBI Director for life" in early 1964. Hoover died while still director in 1972.

In 2017, some internal memos were finally released to the public. Hoover had written a memo castigating both Curry and Fritz immediately after Oswald's death. Hoover claimed he had told Curry directly about threats to Oswald in the hours before. Hoover had forced Curry to retract a TV interview revelation that the FBI knew a lot about Oswald, including that he was in Dallas – Curry's claims were correct but embarrassing. Certainly, Hoover wanted to protect his FBI. What better way than having Oswald die before any lengthy public trial?

There is no way that Hoover, Johnson, and Curry could be certain that a random bozo, say Ruby, would kill Oswald. As it was, Ruby's single shot was fatal only by a half-inch margin. More speculation: Hoover et al. might possibly have enlisted an agent to surreptitiously ensure Oswald's death. The attending surgeon did complain of an unidentified man in the OR with Oswald – probably FBI agent Charlie Brown, gowned and masked. Oswald's death certificate says he died from internal bleeding out; it is possible that a trusted assassin could make certain Oswald died, if necessary. For example, he could inject Oswald with an anticoagulant such as Warfarin, ensuring that any serious shot would be fatal. There would have been a certain irony to killing Oswald with rat poison. The idea of Warfarin poisoning had already been implicated in Stalin's sudden death, so it was not a conceptual leap.

This possible conspiracy involves only a small number of people. At a minimum, it involves Curry, Hoover, likely President Johnson, and possibly one trusted agent. In their minds, this conspiracy would be in the best interests of the USA: the idea that Oswald could be free on a biased venue or disallowed evidence technicality would have been a powerful motivator. Likewise, the illegality of this action would have ensured closed mouths. Finally, there is no obvious alternative – unless Oswald could die, it would have been near certain that he could make a lot of continuing trouble in the courts or out of them. Extensive

FBI (and CIA) dirt could have been exposed in Oswald's defense.

It is possible that the FBI personnel, looking at their Oswald file and hearing from Marina and the Paines, concluded that leftist Oswald was probably shooting at rightist Connally. Hoover might have explained privately to Johnson that Connally was the likely target. Those two politicians would understand that JFK's death-by-mistake might further upset the public, trigger left-right hatred, and undermine Johnson's legitimacy. It is interesting that the one **recorded** phone call between Hoover and Johnson involved a stilted conversation where Johnson asked Hoover if Connally was the real target, and Hoover insisted, without factual basis, that "no, that could not be."

The Warren Commission did not investigate Curry for conspiracy to murder Oswald by random proxy. The Warren Report contains Curry's testimony that is, at best, confused but, at worst, suggestive of deliberate actions by Curry. Whether these actions were connected to higher authorities was not investigated. That is suspicious, considering that the Oswald murder was the main reason for the creation of the Warren Commission.

## What if Oswald Had Survived

Had Oswald survived to stand trial, his defense might have attracted a capable lawyer, for example, Abt, Melvin Belli, or William Kunstler. Abt said he would not have represented Oswald, citing conflict with his CPUSA commitments. Belli and Kunstler might have taken the world-watched case – both represented Jack Ruby, for example. An alert lawyer might have shifted JFK's death to a manslaughter charge by exposing Oswald's intent to shoot at Connally. If so, then LBJ might have lost some sleep. On the other hand, no great lawyer might have stepped forward for the smirking Oswald. The ACLU would have provided a lawyer who would have focused on the process and the law.

Oswald would likely be found guilty of the murder of

Officer Tippit. It is conceivable that a jury might have hung on the assassination verdict because the case was circumstantial or because of pre-trial prejudice. While it is often claimed that much evidence against Oswald would have been thrown out because of questionable chains of custody, handling mistakes, or misrepresentations, it is likely that the judge would not "throw out" evidence completely (as, for example, the CE 399 bullet or Oswald's rifle) but instead would instruct the jury to consider evidence with care to ensure that it was reasonably honest evidence; honest circumstantial evidence is often considered more reliable than is eyewitness testimony. Regardless, there would have been a series of appeals on various technicalities.

Oswald would have eventually talked politics at his trial. He would have been ignored – unless he was able to come up with a world-shaking new story: say, that he aimed for Connally to save America from looming ultra-right fanatics. Oswald would help himself by shifting from premeditated murder of JFK to accidental manslaughter of JFK while attempting to murder Connally.

A surviving Oswald would have killed one more victim: the JFK conspiracy industry. But he didn't survive.


## Oswald as an American Patriot?

Oswald feared an ultra-right takeover of America; he spoke of it often as being "Nazi-like." Did Oswald really believe that the ultra-right was spawning a US Hitler? Certainly, Dallas was a lively place for the ultra-right.

"We had this bunch of far-right nuts here [in Dallas]. They were mean. There wasn't a big amount of them, but the mood was not pretty here."

- Hugh Aynesworth, Reporter for the Dallas Morning News who covered the crowd at the TSBD 11/22/63 (2013)

Oswald had behaved calmly until the moment he grasped that he might have killed Kennedy - probably when he saw the unmistakable Jackie on the limo trunk, magnified by 4x. He executed his TSBD escape as he had imagined, but thereafter, he lost composure, becoming suicidal. Once he was captured and under questioning, he reverted to sarcasm, arrogance and denial, with no clear purpose other than to annoy and confound authorities. After only a few hours, he was able to rationalize the death of Kennedy as unimportant: "[Johnson] will probably do about the same thing that President Kennedy would do." Oswald was saying it was a waste of his time to kill Kennedy from a political point of view. It is a strong argument that Oswald had not intended to kill Kennedy.

Other authors, notably (James Reston Jr, 2013) and (Pierre Sundborg, 2016), have concluded that Oswald shot Connally out of hatred and resentment arising from amending his discharge from the Marines to "undesirable." Connally did send a two-sentence "handoff" of Oswald's initial discharge complaint, saying that he was no longer connected to the Navy and would pass it on to his successor. Oswald did not apparently keep Connally's letter, but he did keep its fancy "Connally" envelop (James Reston Jr, The Accidental Victim: JFK, Lee Harvey Oswald, and the Real Target in Dallas, 2013) and (Pierre Sundborg, 2016). Did that show fatal hatred, or was that an ego boost to have gotten a personal letter from a famous man? Oswald did "threaten" in his reply, but only to get to the bottom of this problem. The discharge did plague Oswald: it blocked his employment whenever he was forced to admit it. But the discharge debate lasted many letter exchanges after Connally's handoff. Besides, Oswald had got several reasonable jobs and could have built a good resume had he controlled his behavior.

This book argues that Oswald's political egotism was his real driver. As his best friend said, Oswald might kill but only for "a very strongly held ideological motive," a "hunter of fascists." (Mohrenschildt, Lee Harvey Oswald as I Knew Him, 2014)

The fact that Oswald did not make any coherent political statement after his arrest is more evidence that he had killed the wrong man. All his previous life was a search for a system he could stand. With Kennedy at the helm, America looked like it had beaten out Communist states as "the most likely to be fixable," in Oswald's view. Oswald may have concluded that "fixing America" would require "stopping Hitler" in the persons of Walker, Connally, and the ultra-right. Certainly, it was astounding that Oswald did not speak out about Marxism and his beliefs once he had the attention of the entire world. This, after all, was a man who had risked his own life mouthing off in the Marines, in the USSR, in the streets of Dallas and New Orleans. It made sense to risk his life to help JFK improve the best available country – that would make him historically famous, as he craved.

10

# CONSPIRACY THEORIES HAD FERTILE GROUNDS

Oswald, through his grandiose schemes, was connected to much of the world's "dark sides."

Oswald was an unusual young man – perhaps unique. The constant in his youth was his mother, a self-involved person who had little empathy for anyone and little interest in young Oswald. He was affection starved, while his mother blamed everyone but herself for her failings. By chance, Oswald heard about Marxism and Communism at a formative age. He adopted a naïve self-taught Marxism as a shield against his social and academic failures in one school after another. His older brother escaped his mother and poverty by joining the Marines, and Oswald followed but as a unique "Marxist Marine." He read Soviet literature just as Khrushchev was opening cultural exchanges - going to the USSR became his escape from the Marines. Failing to find a Marxist utopia in the USSR, he bailed back to the US, with a young wife and child.

Before Oswald was 24 years old, he had blundered into contacts with leading secretive operations: he was one of few people whose mail was opened by the CIA's HTLINGUAL, the KGB, and the FBI. He knew some Air Force radio and radar secrets. Unknown to him, he had files with the CIA, the FBI, the Soviet KGB (equivalent to the CIA, Homeland Security, and FBI), the US State Department, and Navy Intelligence. He had contacts with the Soviet Emigree Community, the militant side of the John Birch Society with General Walker, the CIA-supported Cuban emigree community of New Orleans, CIA informants like De Mohrenschildt, TV and radio appearances as a Castro supporter, and even an uncle who was connected with the head of the Mafia in New Orleans. He tried to defect and give secrets in the sea of spies lurking in the US and Soviet Embassies in Moscow. He blundered between the Cuban and Soviet embassies in Mexico City – the hemisphere's biggest nest of CIA, KGB, and Cuban intelligence - just when the CIA was making covert use of a future president of Mexico. Oswald communicated with the Communist Party USA, the ACLU and the FPCC, all of which were on FBI watchlists.

That is an incredible list of questionable contacts and coincidences. Oswald bumbled through the twilight world of international espionage like a bitter "Forrest Gump."

No verifiable evidence has surfaced that Oswald was an actual agent. Oswald was considered both too bitterly outspoken and too quietly independent to be an asset to anyone. Yet Oswald, on his own, made big plans and quietly carried them out.

After the assassination, unfounded opinions were naturally commonplace. Multiple parallel investigations in real-time did produce conflicts and mistakes. More sinister, elements of the Federal Government did actively suppress any deep investigation into conspiracies. When Ruby killed Oswald, any truth that might eventually come from Oswald's mouth was lost. Suspicions soared. People everywhere had questions. Conspiracy theory work started immediately, spurred on by Oswald's tossed-off claim that he was "a patsy." Mark Lane published his "Oswald Innocent?" article in the National Guardian less than a month after the assassination (Mark Lane, Oswald Innocent?—A Lawyer's Brief, 1963); Lane argued that leaked misstatements would provide "grounds for reasonable doubt" that would prevent Oswald's conviction, had he lived to stand trial.

By May 1964, the first conspiracy book built on Oswald's "I'm a patsy" comment hit the press. It claimed that two shooters were managed by "the military-industrial complex" led by Texas oilmen but included the mob, the Dallas police and more. Assassin X shot from the overpass, while Assassin Y shot from the TSBD. Neither was Oswald, but Oswald knew enough to need killing. Tippit was supposed to kill Oswald. Ruby knew Oswald and succeeded in closing his mouth. The book was published in France five months before the Warren Report and was soon translated into 20 languages (Buchanan, 1964).

The Warren Commission said little for 10 months. Rumors swirled. People like Lane were quick to question the FBI's role: "[sarcasm!] This remarkable law enforcement and investigatory agency, unable to solve a single one of the more than 40 Birmingham bombings, is now able to function as investigator, prosecutor, judge and jury. No other American agency has presumed to occupy so many positions of trust at one time" and "The Justice Department has already privately expressed 'disappointment' with the FBI report, fearing that it 'has left too many questions unanswered.'" Lane then speculated that the FBI would never change its story, as it would be too embarrassed. He viewed the FBI as "almost completely useless" for future investigations.

Some of the world's strongest intellects questioned the findings. Bertrand Russell, a leader in analytic and logical thought, was inspired by Mark Lane, formed his own ad hoc committee, and published *16 Questions On The Kennedy Assassination*, in paraphrase:

1. Why was the Commission entirely of government leaders?
2. If Oswald acted alone, how is National Security an issue?
3. Why were Commission activities kept entirely secret?
4. Why did the Commission assume Oswald killed JFK instead of asking who?
5. Are the F.B.I., the Secret Service and the Dallas police honest?

6. Oswald headed a list of 23 Dallas subversives, but he wasn't tracked?
7. Why was the motorcade route changed at the last minute to go by the TSBD?
8. How did Oswald shoot JFK from the front?
9. Why has the medical evidence been altered out of recognition?
10. Why did the FBI confiscate key photo evidence?
11. Why does some evidence appear fraudulent?
12. Why did authorities claim Oswald's paraffin test proved he shot JFK?
13. Why did the only eye-witness to Tippit's murder not describe Oswald?
14. [Unsupported] Why was Oswald described as Tippit's killer before Tippit was shot?
15. How did the Commission predict that Marina would reverse her testimony?
16. How did DA Wade make so many wrong observations about incoming evidence?

Russell continued: "We view the problem with the utmost seriousness. U.S. Embassies have long ago reported to Washington [they hear] worldwide disbelief in the official charges against Oswald, but this has scarcely been reflected by the American press. No U.S. television program or mass circulation newspaper has challenged the permanent basis of all the allegations — that Oswald was the assassin and that he acted alone. It is a task which is left to the American people." (Russell, 1964) All good questions, most of which have now been answered.

International interest was intense as well, initially positive but soon trending to "widespread skepticism and outright disbelief." *The Oswald Affair* came out only six months after the Warren Report (Sauvage, 1965). It begins by unfairly castigating the DPD for not following the "elementary police routine" of shouting "Nobody moves!" to preserve the crime scene; he may not have realized that there was an unknown number of shooters with high-powered rifles lurking somewhere – no doubt just waiting to freeze when a brave policeman brandished his trusty pistol and shouted, "Nobody moves!" This book certainly illustrates the problems inherent in listening to excited testimonies – like seven blind men and an elephant. The claim that "any uncertainty, any ambiguity, should be interpreted to the advantage of the accused" is misapplied in the face of the "preponderance of evidence."

Lane then asked: "If Oswald is innocent—and that is a possibility that cannot now be denied—then the real assassins of President Kennedy remain at large." (Mark Lane, Rush to Judgment, 1966)

When the Warren Report finally came out, it concluded that it found no evidence of any conspiracy - even though by then, it could not answer important questions that had multiplied. What was Oswald's motive? Why did he have no escape plan? Why would a Communist kill Kennedy when he was the Communist USA party's endorsed candidate, especially when witnesses said he respected Kennedy? Why did Oswald fail to use his TV presence to spew his manifesto? How could three shots be fired in the FBI's 5 seconds? How could an amateur like Oswald make such difficult shots with a crude rifle? Where was that missing bullet? What about witnesses who heard more than three shots and from other places? Eventually, Oliver Stone's "JFK" examined the Zapruder film and produced the famed mantra: "Back and to the left,"

Oswald went from being presumed guilty to presumed innocent, in many minds (Gallup Polls - Swift, 2013). In the years after the Warren Report release, most Americans became convinced that Kennedy was a victim of a conspiracy. These were not "conspiracy nuts." These were everyday Americans from every walk of life. RFK was never convinced of a lone gunman, declaring that he thought Cubans or Mafiosi had done the deed. Even LBJ grew to repudiate his own commission's conclusions. America was hearing an explosion of disturbing questions but heard no convincing answers. Popular beliefs changed as new experts made new pronouncements, and new witnesses materialized with new memories. The saga of national assassination angst eventually became a story in itself (Reiman, 2019).

Perhaps the biggest factor in the slow response to growing questions was a failure to appreciate their seriousness. The Texas police "knew" they had the right guy and that he had already paid with his life. Justice was done, as far as they were concerned (Weisberg, Whitewash: The Report on the Warren Report, 1965). The police and FBI focused on hard evidence and devalued the conflicting testimonies; experience teaches every investigator that human memory is notoriously inaccurate, especially at times of sudden crisis. Unfortunately, witness unreliability was not understood outside the police (Shaw, 2016).

Further, the FBI understood that Oswald was not a simple nut. He was an erstwhile defector who had spent years in the USSR and who had recently tried to defect again to Cuba. He had unwittingly waded through the domestic and international spying apparatus of the United States, as well as its powerful enemies. That was impressive even if he was regarded as a useless talker by both the Russians and the Americans; neither respected Oswald enough to even track him carefully. Given this underestimation, the FBI feared that a complete 1964 investigation might do more harm than good. After all, the killer was already dead. It could embarrass "innocent bystanders" (i.e., the FBI itself) or might even damage the country, either directly by harming National Security or indirectly by undermining respect and confidence in important services or individuals.

The FBI and others, such as the CIA, wanted to hide their mistakes or internals. The result was a lot of gaps in the story. These gaps, when left unanswered, were filled in by conspiracy theories.

Of all the conspiracy workers, Harold Weisberg was among the most impressive. He spent many years digging through thousands of documents. He used the Freedom of Information Act (passed in 1966) to pry even more documents from the government. His books, starting with "Whitewash: The Report on the Warren Report," are monuments to perseverance in pursuit of truth in Kennedy's death. He documents how the Warren Commission misrepresented and suppressed its own evidence. In later books, he detailed the activities of the FBI and the CIA: he found a vast number of discrepancies, mistakes, obfuscations and lies. His work is much more detailed than the few salient points made below. But Weisberg concluded only that the case should be considered still "open," and that a lot of ass-covering was going on. He does not fully absolve Oswald, nor does he indict others (Weisberg, Whitewash: The Report on the Warren Report, 1965).

Also of note, Sylvia Meagher provided a great service by indexing the entire 26 supporting volumes of hearings and exhibits (Meagher, 1966). She also catalogued a long, thorough set of questions raised by the many mistakes, witness contradictions, and questionable assumptions exposed in the hearings; eventually, she theorized that JFK was killed by anti-Castro activists and organized crime (Meagher, 2013). Many of Weisberg's and Meagher's threads have been spun into various conspiracies.

The Warren Report undermined its own conclusions with its extensive records but a lack of evaluation of veracity. It repeated hundreds of conflicting stories with credible accuracy but little indication of which might be true or why. The Warren Commission allowed only limited access to the Zapruder and other films, even within their own personnel. They decided not to present the actual medical and film evidence to the various doctors to allow them to change or refine their opinions on Kennedy's wounds and that medical evidence (the HSCA later did revise the medical analysis, for example, correcting his head wound trajectory). The Commission inevitably had to stop including what it considered to be "impossibly outlandish" testimonies. Both the reported conflicts and the unreported claims raised questions.

An excellent film, ***The Kennedy Assassination: Inside the Book Depository,*** suggests the doubts that surround any conspiracy to kill Kennedy (Lemmino, 2023). But as that watchable film concludes, we can't prove that there was no conspiracy. Indeed, questions about the Report would likely have receded into history had it not been for actual "conspiring." Once the lone gunman was dead, there was less concern with revealing everything and more concern with not revealing any damaging facts. The Warren Commission allowed important people and agencies to protect themselves with untrue, misleading, and incomplete evidence.

## Jackie Protected Her Family

The first people to protect themselves were the Kennedys. Jackie Kennedy was hugely distraught, with the image of her dead husband burned into her memory. She refused to have her husband probed, sliced, and photographed by random Texans - "the very people who had killed him"; instead, she moved the autopsy to Naval facilities in Maryland – and pressured to make it quick. She insisted that all photos be impounded from Parkland and elsewhere and that the autopsy be performed by friendly doctors whom she could trust not to sell stories or photos to the world. She was backed by her Secret Service protectors, who were willing to shoot their way out of Dallas with JFK's body. She was backed by her brother-in-law Robert, who, as the Attorney General, had some say. And she was backed by the public, who completely understood her mortification. No one wanted their memory of Kennedy to be of a cold, bloody, disfigured lump on an autopsy table.

## Medical Experts Protected Themselves

The decision to have JFK's autopsy done in Bethesda by upset and unpracticed doctors chosen by the Kennedy family had ramifications. The Kennedy family pushed for only a cursory search for bullets instead of a full autopsy. Under pressure, those doctors failed to do some basic gunshot wound procedures: to accurately locate and thoroughly investigate the back wound, to carefully assess the spinal nerve damage to understand the path of the first bullet to hit Kennedy, to model the devastating head wound, to consult with Parkland doctors and generally did not follow established autopsy procedures.

Because the Kennedy family prevented publishing the results, conspiracies boomed around bullet numbers, paths, and origins. For example, the autopsy's initial findings suggested a bullet was still inside Kennedy's body, which made three shots problematic (Weisberg, Whitewash: The Report on the Warren Report, 1965). The HSCA Forensic Pathology Panel excoriated this autopsy as an "exemplar" for bungled work; they corrected bullet entry positions, for example (House Select Committee on Assassinations, 1979).

Some say that the autopsy was not shortened because it did take more than three hours, but much of that time was wasted in fruitless efforts to find the bullet that exited his throat as CE 399. But the autopsy doctors also failed to x-ray JFK's head before unwrapping and perturbing him, thus shifting his fractured skull bones and losing the original entry geometry. Two wounds. Two sets of major errors.

The original autopsy notes and report were burned by their author, Dr. Humes. He claimed the originals were grotesquely stained with JFK's blood but could not explain further. It seems more likely that he was covering his own initial mistake of declaring the back wound as "shallow" – he said initially: "There are no lanes for an outlet of this entry in this man's shoulder." Humes did not realize that his probe was blocked by the layers of tough fascia, the rigor-mortised muscles, and C7-T1 vertebra processes, all of which had shifted given that JFK was not in the same position on the table as he had been in the car. Further, Humes did not know there was a wound near Kennedy's Adam's apple since the Parkland tracheotomy had obscured it. Instead of dissecting the path, he looked for a missing bullet somewhere in JFK's body, using x-rays and exploratory cutting, but found no trace (he did find bruising on top of JFK's right lung). He thought that mystery was solved when, in mid-autopsy, he was told of the "nearly pristine" bullet found on a stretcher at Parkland. Humes concluded that the stretcher bullet was the "missing" shallow back wound bullet and wrote that up in his initial autopsy notes. After the autopsy concluded that Saturday morning, he called Parkland doctors and was told about the "possible entry" neck wound that they had seen. Humes then realized he should have dissected the bullet's path. That would have connected the neck-area wounds with a path direction and angle that would have pointed to the shot's origin. Unable to redo his autopsy, he instead burned his original notes, thus hiding his back wound mistakes – but left the trajectory question muddied.

Because Parkland doctors were given no time for examination, let alone autopsy, it was not surprising that their cursory views of JFK's wounds were vague. The image of Kennedy lying face up with his thick gore-matted hair hanging down gave credence to a massive exit wound towards the back of Kennedy's head - and thus shots taken from the front. While most of the Parkland doctors were careful to avoid certainty in their speculations, some were more confident than accurate, and some were misquoted. One doctor even created a fanciful sketch showing Kennedy missing the back of his head, which ensured that a lot of the public would believe that a shot came from the front. The Parkland doctors had completely missed the wound in Kennedy's back, adding to the confusion about shot directions. The Parkland operating room was crowded, busy and tragic, so observations were hardly done calmly. Mistakes are unsurprising (David S. Lifton, 1980). Many have spun the many medical mistakes into conspiracies, for example, "The Radical Right and the Murder of John F. Kennedy" (Harrison Livingston, 2004).

The Warren Commission itself had little access to the autopsy details, thanks to Earl Warren's squeamishness. The rewritten report, the lack of access, and the variance in answers to autopsy questions led to rampant speculation. For example, when Kennedy's Press Secretary announced his death, he described it as "a bullet right through the head" but pointed to the front of his own head, implying a shot from the front. By 1967, Warren Commission members described the failure to carefully examine the medical and autopsy information as their biggest mistake.

## Oswald Tried to Protect Himself

Oswald made few public statements after his arrest, in the two days before he was himself killed. Mostly, he responded to a few of the many shouted questions, for example:

"[They're] giving me a hearing without legal representation or anything."

"I didn't shoot anybody, sir. I haven't been told what I'm here for."

"I'd like some legal representation. These officers have not allowed me to have any."

"I was questioned by a judge. I protested at that time that I was not allowed legal representation."

"I didn't kill anybody. I am not allowed legal representation."

"They're taking me in because I once lived in the Soviet Union. I am a patsy."

"I didn't shoot anybody. I haven't been told what I am here for."

"I have not been charged with [killing Kennedy]. In fact, nobody has said that to me yet. The first thing I heard about [Kennedy being killed] was when the newspaper reporters in the hall [asked] me that."

"I emphatically deny these charges."

Given Oswald's history as a courageous loner espousing Marxism, it is extremely surprising that Oswald had so little to say when the entire world was listening. He did not claim Kennedy's death or even admit that it had happened. He did not pontificate on any rationale for the assassination. Oswald had a history of brazen talking on any platform he could find. He didn't do that when he had the ear of the entire world.

On the other hand, if he were innocent of the shooting, it would have been "normal Oswald" to go ballistic with claims of the US police state and its brutal crushing of the little man. He didn't do that, either.

Oswald's sudden dazed and then smirking silence is difficult to explain - unless he killed Kennedy accidentally.

The Police and FBI men who were behind closed interrogation room doors, interviewing Oswald, concluded that he was constantly lying about everything. He was contradicting himself. He was denying facts that were easily provable. In short, he was totally uncooperative.

But people outside heard only these few somewhat pitiful denials. And only these pitiful denials were on video for constant replay. There was no video or audio record of Oswald's contorted lies in those interrogations.

## Marina Oswald Protected Herself

Marina Oswald was from the USSR of the 1950s. Born in 1941, only two months after "The Great Patriotic War" began, she was too young to understand the deprivations and terrors of World War II. Her natural father was probably among the 27 million Soviet war dead. She lived with her grandmother for 5 years. Then she moved to Leningrad, rejoining her mother and stepfather. The deaths of a million civilians in the Siege of Leningrad a few hundred miles to the southwest, or tens of millions further south, was a pall over the USSR as it was rebuilding (Priscilla J. McMillan, 2013).

Up until Stalin's death in 1953 (when Marina was 12 years old), she would have heard constant stories of "disappearances," torture, exile to Siberia, and executions. People in Russia were never sure whether the next day that repression might return, so they became careful about talking, especially around strangers or police. In 1959, she moved in with her uncle in Minsk - a colonel in the Soviet Ministry of Internal Affairs. Her uncle was an engineer in forestry and a communist, but he was apparently not connected to Soviet police.

She met Oswald in 1961 at a Minsk party, was married in six weeks, discharged in absentia from Komsomol for marrying an American, and was a mother within a year. Early in 1962, Oswald told Marina that he wanted to renounce his attempt to defect to the USSR. In June 1962, the family emigrated to the United States and settled in Dallas, Texas. The FBI interviewed Oswald and Marina upon their entry to the US. The FBI followed up a couple of times when the Oswalds settled in Texas.

Marina apparently did not know of Oswald's plan for

November 22, but she did know things that would have triggered FBI and police actions that would have prevented the assassination had she come forward earlier. For example, she knew he had a pistol and telescopic-sighted rifle; she knew he had tried to kill General Walker; she knew that he had pushed her all of 1963 to arrange her own repatriation to the USSR; she knew that he was planning to defect to Cuba if he could, even suggesting hijacking a plane. But Marina had always been nervous about authorities: her memory of the KGB in the USSR frightened her into silence with the FBI.

On November 22, Marina was watching the President's visit when the announcer broke in with "shots have been fired!" A half-hour later, Ruth told Marina that the shots had come from the Book Depository; Marina said nothing but immediately feared that Oswald was involved. She checked the Paine garage where Oswald had kept the rifle wrapped in a blanket and was relieved to see the blanket still there. At 3 pm, six policemen pounded on their door. Ruth let them search the house. Marina pointed out the blanket as the place where Oswald kept his rifle. When the policemen picked it up, the blanket was empty. She said she knew then it was Oswald who did the shooting.

Marina knew more about Oswald than anyone else. She knew he was capable of an assassination – he had already shot at Walker. She could have turned him in to the police for that Walker shot. Technically, she was an accessory and could have faced prison or deportation back in April; She also could have been found guilty as an accessory, for either Walker or JFK shootings. The police and FBI did not threaten her, at least during the first days. Nevertheless, Marina must have felt extremely nervous about telling the authorities anything.

Marina was interviewed by the press many times and by the Secret Service and the FBI 46 times (without immunity) between the assassination and her first testimony before the Warren Commission on February 3, 1964. She is known to have made a series of incomplete or incorrect statements. She then wrote her life story, from meeting Oswald to the assassination, and made that available - under oath as true. She started off her Warren Commission interview by saying that she wanted to correct some inexact statements she had made in the past. Through her interpreter, she said, "But now inasmuch as she is sworn in, she is going to tell the truth." And that she understands that she will not be charged with anything (she had been given immunity).

In previous interviews, she had lied about some things connected with the assassination to avoid incriminating herself. Now, she apparently told the truth. Oswald was mentally sound; she recognized Oswald's rifle, which he sometimes cleaned and sometimes took out for practice; she took the famed "backyard photos" of the armed Oswald; she saw his Walker notebook and knew Oswald had missed a shot at Walker; she thought Oswald may have expected to get caught after Walker, but instead fled to New Orleans; she heard him working the rifle bolt sitting in the dark on the porch in New Orleans; Oswald had wanted to hijack a plane to Cuba, instead going to Mexico City to get a visa for Cuba; Oswald's mother had raised him poorly; Oswald was not any kind of agent; Oswald had written Connally about his discharge, which Connally said he passed on to responsible authorities; Oswald did not say anything against JFK, ever.

Marina said that on the 23rd, she met Oswald with his mom at the Dallas jail. "I could see in his eyes he was guilty," and he was afraid. She said she became more convinced as new facts came out. She thought at first that "he wanted --by any means, good or bad-- to get into history." Later, she said, "I think that there was some political foundation to it, a foundation of which I am not aware."

At the end of her February 3, 1964, testimony, Representative (later President) Ford asked: "Mrs. Oswald, after President Kennedy was assassinated, your husband was apprehended and later questioned by several authorities. In the questioning, he denied that he kept a rifle at Mrs. Paine's home. He denied shooting President Kennedy. And he questioned the authenticity of the photographs that you took of him holding the rifle and the holster. Now, despite these denials by your husband, you still believe Lee Oswald killed President Kennedy?"

Marina answered Ford with one word: "Yes."

Marina's previous contradictory statements ended up fueling the conspiracy world. Her maturity and morality soon came under scrutiny when she had a brazen affair in February 1964 with her business manager. The FBI watched her become a chain smoker who drank straight vodka. She was soon being described as lazy, greedy, ungrateful, cold, and anxious to party by those who knew her in early 1964 – but she was very young, a product of Soviet culture, and under unusual pressures.

While she did resume some pre-Oswald behaviors, she did maintain her opinions on the killing for many years. She gradually improved herself, working in a drugstore until her WC interviews concluded, then improving her English at the University of Michigan, and then marrying a Texas engineer in 1965. In 1977, a mature Marina told reporters: "I believe that Lee acted alone in this murder and shot the President, ironically a man whom he respected and admired."

Twenty years later, in 1996 (33 years after the killing), she had completely changed her view. She gave no new evidence but just her new opinion, which was likely influenced by constant interviews by assassination researchers. Marina told the Assassination Review Board: "I definitely think that Lee Oswald did not kill President Kennedy. I think he was given up to pacify people as a patsy. I don't think he was the first one - only the first one we know about. And he wasn't crazy" (Assassination Records Review Board, 1998).

## Ruth and Michael Paine Protected Themselves

Marina called Ruth Paine her best friend. After the assassination, Ruth had concerns that her involvement with Marina Oswald made her an accessory (Priscilla J. McMillan, 2013). After all, Ruth had let Marina live with her. She had driven Marina to and from New Orleans. She had done a lot for her child and then the new baby. She had carried Oswald's rifle to New Orleans and back to Dallas in her car – she said "unknowingly."

Michael Paine, Ruth's semi-estranged husband, had not spent that much time with either of the Oswalds, but he had taken Oswald to an ACLU meeting. Some considered the ACLU to be extreme "left." Michael's father had been a real Communist and had taken youngster Michael to meetings. Michael had spent time talking with Oswald, and he had no witness to verify what had been said.

Probably, the Paines were most worried about the rifle having been stored in their garage. Oswald had brought it into Ruth's home, wrapped in a blanket. Michael testified he had to move it around Ruth's garage to use various tools. Yet both Ruth and Michael insisted that they had no idea what was in the blanket. Michael said he thought it was "old camping equipment." Ruth just said she never inspected it, either in her car or as it lay in her garage. The Warren Commission let them get away with some unlikely claims.

## The FBI Protected Itself

The FBI had several contacts with Oswald and quite a file on him. Marina had also been considered as a possible KGB sleeper agent. FBI agent Hosty had been trying to interview Marina and, through her, Oswald in the weeks before the assassination. His visits had caused Oswald to become furious with Marina, precipitating a fight between Marina and Oswald only a week before the assassination. That fight caused Marina to shut Oswald out for that last week, not only conjugally but for any meaningful conversation. Marina was making fun of Oswald about his FBI paranoia. Had Hosty either persisted in an actual interview with Oswald or had he backed off and not stirred up a fight that isolated Oswald, in either case, Oswald might not have shot (Weisberg, Whitewash: The Report on the Warren Report, 1965).

The FBI used White House concerns about international conspiracy as a lever to get the Warren Commission to accept sworn affidavits instead of uncontrolled interviews. That effectively kept the Commission from investigating the FBI itself.

The FBI should have respected Oswald as a capable man: a man who had been a Marine, a man who had organized a lone defection to the USSR, a man who had conceived of a pamphlet plan to impress Cuba, a man who had the courage, intelligence, and determination to execute these plans. The FBI could have jailed Oswald had they investigated his shot at Walker back in April '63; the FBI could not believe a serious shooter could have missed Walker and so dropped the investigation, guessing that Walker had garnered publicity with a fake attempt. They did not connect Oswald's gun purchases to his potential even after they found the Hidell connection to Oswald in his FPCC pamphlets – that should have put him on a watch list. When Oswald marched angrily into the Dallas FBI office to threaten the FBI people only a few days before the assassination, they ignored his handwritten threatening note. Hosty even knew that his new job was at the TSBD, overlooking the President's route and the single best place to shoot down at the motorcade due to its view down the curved, descending Elm Street.

In defense of the FBI, their main anti-terrorist Hosty was more concerned with ultra-right assassins. Leftist Oswald did not look like a person who would kill Kennedy. Kennedy, while elected as a conservative Democrat, had become a leader for ideas that Oswald also championed - at least a lot more than other American leaders. To non-Texan Hosty, Connally would not look that significant and was never considered an assassin's target.

The FBI jumped to conclusions after the shooting. For example, they guessed about the shot sequence and claimed three shots were fired in less than six seconds. They did not revisit claims such as the reports from surgeon mumbles: the bullet which struck the president in the back was still in the president's body or fell out, thus preventing easy acceptance of the eventual single-bullet solution. They destroyed Oswald's threatening note and memo after the assassination. They tried to hide their intercepted November letter from Oswald to the Soviets. They mis-transcribed Oswald's notebook to remove Hosty's address, license and number. The FBI did not seriously investigate how Oswald got from New Orleans to Loredo, TX, on his way to Mexico City. They may have torn the key "kill Connally" page from Oswald's notebook.

In addition, the FBI was apparently lax in preserving the original evidence and evidence chains of the assassination. The FBI was given most of the physical evidence. For example, the C2766 Carcano rifle had paperwork to trace its progress from Italy through to Oswald's hands – but it had inconsistencies: the importer (Crescent Firearms) told the FBI that C2766 had been sold to Kleins in June 1962, but Kleins' paperwork showed C2766 arriving in Chicago 8 months later – clearly that needed explaining; both Kleins and Crescent say they sent their original documentation to the FBI, but the FBI was only able to produce the Kleins' documents and those only as copies. The FBI should have preserved everything for the most important murder in their history. The "single bullet" CE 399 was given to the FBI at Parkland, but the agents failed to inscribe the bullet or to file their "302" paperwork to create the chain of custody – later conspiracists could wonder if CE 399 was planted to frame Oswald.

### The CIA and DIA Protected Themselves

The CIA had contacts that touched Oswald. The CIA routinely placed agents in and around embassies, along with fancy technologies. When Oswald visited the US and Soviet embassies in Moscow, he bumped into more than one agent. The CIA also cooperated with foreign intelligence groups. For example, the Finns told the CIA about Oswald's visa and travel to the USSR. In our age of computerized records and infinite storage, we may forget that in the early 1960s, a file on someone was a stack of paper and those stacks had to be culled or micro-filmed due to the sheer space they took up. More paper meant more search times. It should not be surprising that the CIA was reluctant to focus efforts on young Oswald.

George De Mohrenschildt did act a little like the newly minted James Bond. He was not a CIA agent, but he did know CIA employees and was considered an "asset." The CIA routinely canvased most foreign-traveling businessmen, so it is likely that George had been involved in some way with the CIA. George knew J. Walton Moore, the Dallas agent of the CIA's

Domestic Contacts Division; George asked him about Oswald before initially helping Oswald in 1962, for example. The CIA may have said that Oswald was "harmless" since George went ahead (Paul Hoch, 1975).

De Mohrenschildt should have reported Oswald's shot at General Walker. De Mohrenschildt apparently guessed that Oswald had taken that missed shot. It was a major terrorist action and one that the CIA would very likely have reported to the FBI. Given De Mohrenschildt's ego, it is most likely that he did not tell his CIA contacts about the Walker shot; his new job in Haiti would have been jeopardized by getting involved with Oswald's incompetent crime, particularly when Oswald could claim that De Mohrenschildt had goaded him into buying guns and "trying to kill the next Hitler."

The CIA did not want to reveal anything they might be doing. The CIA had tried to kill Fidel Castro, sometimes using Mafia contacts, and after 1960, with the approval of JFK and RFK. JFK apparently ordered an end to the assassinations in 1962, but one part of the CIA was still trying to assassinate Castro in late 1963. RFK was not enthusiastic about any investigation into that history.

When Oswald went to Mexico City to visit the Soviet and Cuban Embassies, the CIA was watching. The CIA did not want to reveal their spy tools and contacts, especially once Oswald was dead. The Mexican authorities were also asked to limit their investigations by the CIA and approved by Attorney General RFK; this request was apparently to reduce the chance of exposing CIA operations there or perhaps to prevent any connection imputed between Oswald and either the Cubans or Russians - an idea that might excite Americans to start World War III. The CIA had both machinery and people-watching activities in Mexico City. Silvia Duran, who handled Oswald's visa request, was reported by several people to have "dated" Oswald in the 3 days after he was rejected, though she and her best friend both denied that, saying Oswald was not worthy of dating. Silvia was immediately arrested and "aggressively interrogated" on November 22, apparently at the request of the CIA. She did not waver in her denials but had to be rearrested a couple days later when she tried to flee to Cuba. Chief Justice Earl Warren told his committee not to investigate Mexico City and Silvia Duran. Historically speaking, all personnel at any consulate should be suspected of intelligence connections.

In June 1964, Hoover wrote a letter saying FBI informant Jack Childs had somehow overheard Castro claiming he had extensive information on Oswald's time in Mexico City. According to Castro's overheard talk, Oswald had blamed Kennedy for poor relationships between the US and Cuba – causing problems with his visa; Oswald was so angry that he threatened to kill Kennedy. Hoover's letter was sent to the CIA but not to the Warren Commission. This third-hand story had neither supporting evidence nor did it fit Oswald's situation – the visa was held up by the Russians in order to check on Oswald's past. Nor was it likely that Castro would risk his country and his life with claims about knowing Oswald's deadly intentions months before the killing. Further, Oswald may no such complaint to anyone in the US, for example Marina. However, the CIA and Hoover did not let the Commission know, even if it was a red herring.

In 1976 and 1978, CIA Agent John Whitten said he had been assigned the day after Kennedy's death to investigate Oswald's CIA links. He assembled a staff of 30 and delivered a series of drafts entitled *Preliminary Biographical Study on Lee Harvey Oswald*. The head of the CIA shut down Whitten's investigation after five weeks without further investigation of Cuban or Soviet connections (Jefferson Morley, 2016).

By 2020, Freedom of Information suits were able to extract a little story of CIA involvement. Within 48 hours of Kennedy's death, a CIA-funded anti-Castro student group had published hints that Fidel Castro had worked with Oswald (as a "leader" of the FPCC) to assassinate Kennedy - however, there were no known instructions from the CIA, and the hints appeared to be fabricated to stir up anti-Castro hatred. Some records remain redacted as of 2023 and likely would describe anti-Castro operations, probably in conjunction with the FBI's COINTELPRO program against the FPCC (Fair Play for Cuba Committee). It is unlikely that the CIA did much against Oswald's ineffective one-man FPCC "branch" in New Orleans (Jefferson Morley, 2016).

The CIA itself was concerned about the relationship between the anti-Castro groups and Oswald. Soon after the assassination, the CIA launched a secret investigation where a broad net was cast, looking for any Cuban exiles who might have helped Oswald with money, guidance, or in any way, or who disappeared suspiciously in November '63. The fear seems to have been that Oswald might have been fooled by the anti-Castro extremists. Some have concluded that this investigation implies that the CIA did not believe Oswald was the lone killer. As of 2023, no final CIA report has been found on the results of this CIA inquiry. Many conspiracy ideas include the CIA or rogue elements in plots to assassinate JFK, for example, due to JFK's plans to avoid war in Vietnam (Prouty, 1992).

JFK's own DIA, the Defense Intelligence Agency, also developed and destroyed a file on Oswald. Their research apparently began immediately after the assassination, with illegal snooping on diplomatic channels of both friends and foes. They intended to discover any foreign involvement but found none. They then destroyed their records in order to prevent any public admissions of spying or spy technology.

## The Secret Service Protected Themselves

Some of JFK's Secret Service agents had been out "partying" very late the night before, a firing offense (Susan Cheever, 2013). They had been too certain of themselves when setting up the motorcade route and had ignored the ideal TSBD sniper's location that happened to look down the slope of Elm Street, allowing shots to be made with little left-right motion; their own protocols insisted on that inspection. They had ignored the open windows in buildings like the TSBD. They had not identified Oswald as a threat. They had been overconfident in turning down more police support (Select Committee on Assassinations, 1979).

However, all that said, there was little difference between the Secret Service setup in Dallas compared to other motorcades in other cities. It was judged that having draconian restrictions on people in windows, or bringing in extensive police and military, was out of place in a democracy. They also knew, as Kennedy knew, that it was not hard to assassinate the president with a rifle from a tall building – as Kennedy himself had said that morning. Still, they could have enlisted others to check key buildings – with the TSBD and its Elm Street angle being most likely. The Warren Commission asked if having more sleep would have made them more alert - they had 3.9 seconds to prevent an accurate second shot; however, the Secret Service follow vehicle was travelling only about five feet behind the JFK limo and so would have been under the oak tree that blocked Oswald's first shot in a little more than one second.

The Secret Service also lost sight of their responsibilities after the killing. They should have kept careful notes on the facts after the killing, and not leaked rumors about "shallow bullet holes" and bullet strikes from near JFK's ear up through the top of his head. Some say they should have let a homicide autopsy continue immediately in Dallas, but making Jackie stay a minute longer in Dallas was not something her Secret Service protectors could stomach. The Dallas coroner could have had the body signed over for a remote autopsy and indeed, was ordered to do so by Dallas DA Wade, but apparently, he liked the idea of doing the autopsy himself. He might have been a glory-hunting ass, but he probably would have done a better autopsy.

**Dallas Officials Protected Themselves**

Dallas was blamed by many as a "city of hate" because of its ultra-right extremism. Dallas was a violent city, with more killings than other cities in Texas – and Texas had more murders than any other state. It had earned its grim reputation before the assassination, partly because the famed Texas Rangers had been disbanded over political issues by 1934. For whatever reason, many people outside Dallas blamed the city for JFK's and Oswald's deaths. The Warren Report gave one of its "evidence-free" passes to Texas and Dallas, saying it "found no evidence that the extreme views expressed towards President Kennedy by some Right-Wing groups centered in Dallas had any connection with Oswald's actions." Dallas citizens were briefly apologetic after the tragedy but soon hardened (William Manchester, 1967). The Warren Commission did not investigate whether Dallas' extreme views encouraged Oswald to shoot at Connally.

Mistakes had been made. The Dallas Police Department underestimated the number of people who would come out to see the President. They assumed that there would be no onlookers after the motorcade left Main to turn onto Houston Street, so they did not organize any police presence near the TSBD. They did not watch open windows, with their backs to the passing motorcade (William Manchester, 1967).

Chief Curry, in the car a hundred feet ahead of JFK, leading the motorcade, mistakenly thought shots had come from the "grassy knoll" and sent police there as a first response, letting Oswald get away. He should have immediately established a "stay in place" order for everyone in the plaza area and sealed off the area, especially the TSBD. Patrolman Baker literally let Oswald walk away from the assassination: Baker ran into the TSBD, met Oswald, but let him go just because the building manager said Oswald worked there. Baker should have organized citizens to block every entrance, immediately.

At the time of the Assassination, there was no federal law covering the assassination of the president (other than National Security). The default legal responsibility for the investigation rested on Texas and Dallas. Overall, they did a fair job: they bravely investigated the active shooter site, soon found the murderer at the cost of one of their own, captured him without killing him, and gathered extensive evidence while it was still fresh. They also cooperated extensively with the FBI and Secret Service even when not strictly required by law (Weisberg, Whitewash: The Report on the Warren Report, 1965).

Nevertheless, even small errors were sufficient to seed new conspiracy theories. They did not immediately lock down the TSBD, search and photograph it carefully as a crime scene. When the police first described the rifle they called it a Mauser.

When they described the bullets, they called them steel-jacketed (instead of copper). When they finger-printed the rifle, they did not immediately give the FBI Oswald's right palm print they had lifted from within the disassembled rifle; the FBI found only two blurred prints; later, the Dallas examiner asserted there was still enough palm print for the FBI, thus excusing himself. The Dallas police tried the discredited paraffin testing on Oswald without revealing that it would likely not work given that rifle and its side-mounted scope setup. They confused a map as an escape route rather than a job-hunting map. These were small things, but things that later caused people to doubt that Oswald had that rifle.

Probably the biggest mistakes that the Dallas Police made were (1) not having tape recorders or stenography for Oswald's interrogations, (2) mishandling security around Oswald, (3) reporting to the press that Oswald was guilty and hinting at a Communist Conspiracy, and (4) not pressing their interrogations.

Some critics blame the DPD for not following crime scene protocols in protecting and gathering evidence. However, gathering evidence was not their first priority: their number one priority was finding and neutralizing the assassin(s). It was, therefore, more important to clamber through the TSBD looking for a shooter than it was to meticulously gather evidence. The shooter could have been still at large, including well-hidden within the TSBD. And there could have been conspirators – perhaps even among the Dallas police.


## George de Mohrenschildt Eventually Blamed Himself

Not everyone who knew Oswald could protect themselves from a guilty conscience.

George de Mohrenschildt had become Oswald's "best friend" for a few months through the winter of 1962-63 - maybe Oswald's only friend. It seems likely that George enjoyed goading Oswald into rash political comments or actions. It is likely, for example, that George helped convince Oswald that the Texas ultra-right was a Nazi-like danger to the United States and that Oswald would be a hero if he "stopped General Walker." Oswald seems to have bought his two mail-order guns about the time that George was "encouraging" him. George also seems to have made fun of Oswald, both as a "hunter of fascists" and because Oswald had ineptly missed General Walker; George ridiculed Oswald in front of Marina, so it was sure to have stung (Norman Mailer, 1996). Speculation: there might have been some sexual tension between debonair George and pretty young Marina from his hometown of Minsk.

George left Dallas at that time and was not around in the six months leading up to the Kennedy assassination. Nevertheless, it would be very natural for George to blame himself for goading Oswald.

George went insane in later years, possibly weighed down by the knowledge that he had provoked Oswald to shoot at Walker and then at Connally and, by accident, Kennedy. De Mohrenschildt had, after all, been "Uncle George" to 10-year-old Jackie. George eventually committed suicide. He "was overcome with guilt for his trifling with Oswald." On his death, he called himself "a moral conspirator in the assassination of Kennedy" (James Reston Jr, The Accidental Victim: JFK, Lee Harvey Oswald, and the Real Target in Dallas, 2013).

In a sad coincidence, De Mohrenschildt did make a connection to another famous death. After leaving the Oswalds and Dallas in April 1963, De Mohrenschildt went to perform geology for an oil business and oil refinery for Haiti's President "Papa Doc" Duvalier. Duvalier had a financier partner, who had begun as a poor Egyptian, married into the international arms trade, used the resulting connections to Middle Eastern oil magnates to enter the shipping business, and then attempted oil production in 1964 Haiti. The Haiti deal soon collapsed – it was a swindle. However, that Egyptian when on to buy department stores, eventually owning the Ritz in Paris and Harrods in London. That Egyptian was Mohamed Al-Fayed, the father of Dodi Al-Fayed, who died in the car with Princess Diana in 1997. Diana's death has also produced a considerable assortment of conspiracy theories.

· · ·

## Using the Assassination

Some people have used the assassination to stir up trouble for specific targets. The most common target was Castro's Cuba. The Miami Cuban exiles immediately tried to tie Oswald to Castro, using their CIA connections and Oswald's history. The Nicaraguan government appears to have sent a spy to claim that Oswald had accepted $7000 in the Mexico City Cuban embassy to kill Kennedy. LBJ did not take any of these stories seriously enough to invade Cuba.

Much more common were apparently well-meaning people who thought they saw or heard something suspicious. Many came forward saying that they had seen Oswald here or there. Others said they saw people who might have been the "real shooters." And some people changed their stories over time: witness Helen Markham saw and did not see Oswald shoot Tippit; Howard Brennan gave a description of Oswald in the act of shooting Kennedy but then decided that identifying Oswald might expose him to conspirators who could kill him. As is usual in a sudden event, many people could not agree on what had happened.

Then, there were people who wanted to get money or fame from the assassination. Zapruder set an example by donating his first Life Magazine installment to the Dallas police, asking that it go to the Tippit family. For people like Oswald's mother, making money was about manipulating the event to garner fees from the media. Marina was also not shy as time went on. JFK's murder has produced fifteen minutes of fame for many. It is fair to say that while many try to contribute books or testimony, most do not seem to do it for the small return – very small compared to the efforts. Most have a sincere belief that we need to get to the bottom of a terrible national trauma that still generates stress.

## Little Conspiracies and Big Mistakes

A "conspiracy" is "an agreement between two or more

people to commit an illegal act, along with an intent to achieve the agreement's goal." There were a lot of conspiracies in the investigations that followed the Kennedy assassination. And there were a lot of mistakes.

Overconfident glimpses: in their haste to be the first to big news, many people jumped to conclusions and reported them based on little evidence or only glimpses of evidence: the Parkland doctor who saw a small hole and guessed it was an entrance wound; the Parkland doctors who saw blood-drenched scalp hanging at the back of JK's head and guessed it was a gaping rear exit wound; the policeman who glimpsed a rifle and reported it as a Mauser. That list is much too long to give here. But few were more eager to report their glimpses as fact than was CBS's Dan Rather. He had seen the Zapruder film on November 23$^{rd}$ when Zapruder was auctioning it between CBS and Life. CBS lost access, but Rather hurried to the TV cameras with his guesses reported as facts: JFK was hit first as he put his hand up to his head; JBC was hit second in his chest while turned back towards JFK; Mrs. Connally threw herself over JBC to protect him; JFK was then hit fatally sending his head violently forward; JFK fell towards Jackie's legs; Jackie then crawled out on the trunk, apparently to help the Secret Service agent; the agent then pushed Jackie by her shoulders back into her seat. Rather's quick viewing and overconfident report was wrong in almost every detail. But he was the first to report the Zapruder film – so his guesses became the fodder for many, especially when the film was withheld for years after.

FBI Conspiracies: The FBI destroyed Oswald's threatening note. They may have destroyed a page of Oswald's notebook, one that might have indicated that Oswald intended to assassinate John Connally. Hoover prevented the Warren Commission from questioning FBI agents about Oswald's involvement with the Bureau, instead providing only signed affidavits. The FBI did not diligently pursue evidence that might have pointed to conspiracy. The FBI could have gotten immediate rights to interrogate Oswald by Presidential order, but they did not. They could have immediately insisted that all interrogations be videotaped or at least audiotaped. The FBI could have immediately subpoenaed the people who were known to have inter-acted with Oswald and made the manhunt truly nationwide and aggressive. Instead, under Hoover's direction, they focused on convincing the American people that Oswald acted alone when evidence for that was far from certain. The FBI and Justice Department pressured to avoid investigating Oswald's motives, saying that it might encourage a public assumption of Communist Conspiracies.

CIA Conspiracies: The CIA conspired to suppress investigations of international spy networks but also of possible international involvement in the assassination. They and the FBI raised the "secret" classification on evidence that was embarrassing to them. The CIA triggered a red-herring rumor among Miami anti-Castro zealots, perhaps trying to use the assassination for their own purposes.

The Paine family conspired with each other in swearing that they had no idea Oswald had a gun, either a pistol or a telescopic sighted "assassin's rifle." Wesley Frazier also conveniently mis-remembered Oswald's package size, trying to convince the world that he had not been an accessory helping Oswald bring his rifle.

The Warren Commission failed to create an index for their materials, greatly complicating any later research – at least giving the appearance of obfuscation (Meagher, 1966). The Warren Commission did not interview or ignore some witnesses (Meagher, 2013). The members of the Warren Commission conspired to ignore the autopsy photos and x-rays, obedient to the wishes of Warren and the Kennedys.

The Warren Commission, the FBI and President Johnson appear to have conspired to ignore investigating the possibility that Oswald intended to shoot Governor Connally due to fear of depressing Americans with a "crushing irony." They assumed Oswald's guilt. They also conspired to avoid in-depth investigations of potential foreign country involvements, presumably in fear of starting a major war.

There were many more apparent mistakes than there were provable conspiracies. The FBI agents did not conspire to drop the surveillance interest on Oswald. The FBI did not conspire to drop the General Walker shooting investigation. Jack Ruby did not conspire to kill Oswald. George De Mohrenschildt mistakenly goaded Oswald into assassination attempts. Marina mistakenly married Oswald, followed him to the US, and gave Oswald a cold shoulder the days before the assassination. Even Kennedy mistakenly had the limo go slow with Connally right in front of him in the little jump seat.

Nothing proved to be more mistake-prone than the memories of those present. Said a reporter sitting on the press bus that day, "If I learned anything in Dallas that day, besides what it's like to be numbed by shock and grief, it was that eyewitness testimony is the worst kind." Even that trained reporter, one of 50 on the press bus, felt distracted, confused, and struggled to make sense of his own memories even seconds later. "Seeds of the 'conspiracy' or 'second gunman' theory of the Kennedy murder were sown in that [Parkland] driveway and inside the hospital during the hectic, confused two hours that followed." (Roberts, 1967)

Much conspiracy theory surrounds the thousands of discrepancies amongst imperfect memories, imperfect performances, and imperfect intentions. Many claim that Oswald would not be convicted in a court of law because of these many problems, especially since rules of evidence were sometimes breached. The Kennedy assassination happened in real time in an area permeated with police and agents; a monstrous crime exploding in their very faces, possibly with a still active shooter. It triggered a confused, disorganized immediate response that was very unlike a typical murder scene. With hundreds of witnesses to depose, it is no surprise that hundreds of different views arose. The 27 volumes and nearly 20,000 pages of the full Warren Commission report would have been much longer and arrived much later had every tale been investigated thoroughly. The investigations went much deeper than would a "normal murder." For example, a normal murder investigation would have no problem accepting that Oswald had that rifle, given only the few witnesses and the backyard photos; in modern trials, many murder weapons have no history at all beyond having been stolen at some previous time. Murder trials normally have much fewer witnesses, and even fewer are selected to testify at trial. Some suggest that Oswald could not have been convicted on circumstantial evidence alone, but in fact, most convictions are on circumstantial evidence. Some decry chain-of-evidence breaches, but those do not render evidence inadmissible, only questionable.

The extreme depth of the inquiry, the national security evidence holes, and technicalities might have let Oswald escape a guilty verdict for killing JFK – if he had a very clever legal team who could stand a lot of death threats and if he could stay quiet. Nevertheless, Oswald would still have gone to death row because he would be found guilty of Officer Tippet's murder.

Most assassination conspiracy theories have been attacked, and most have been discredited, if not disproven. A quick debunking was done in (Cohen, 1992). Sites like Quora's "JFK Assassination" and "Debunking JFK Conspiracies" provide modern discussion areas that have taken over from the extensive "alt" email lists and blogs that grew in the 1990s. No conspiracy theory has survived rigorous questioning without resorting to improbable, unproven involvements of many people in government and crime. These conspiracies can't explain how vast conspiracies could incorporate new members given the dangers that some new "conspirator" would expose the attack on such a popular president - or would confess after the fact. These conspiracies are often arcane, complex snippets spun around anomalies like the posting of a money order – but they never explain why these conspirators did not do a much better job, or why they would even choose Dealey Plaza or Oswald. Many other conspiracy theories derive from misunderstandings of evidence (e.g., "back and to the left") or over-reliance on human testimonies (e.g., "saw a shooter on the grassy knoll").

Conspiracies do make easier reading than science. It is easy to say a projectile hit the front of Kennedy's throat if there is no requirement to show an exact trajectory or explain what happened to the projectile, or explain why the windshield was only cracked instead of having a classic bullet-hole or explain autopsy information, though some have tried (Fiester, 2013).

Actual science is hard to perform, hard to understand, and does not seem to get as much attention. For example, consider scientific explanations of "back and to the left": years before Oliver Stone's *JFK* achieved #7 on *Time's* "Top 10 Historically Misleading Films" (Time Magazine, 2011), Itek Corporation had painstakingly examined the motions of JFK and Jackie, frame by frame, and concluded that JFK was driven "back and to the left" by Jackie's worried pressure (Itek, 1975). Yet Stone's wild, un-scienced theory gets massive play and repetition, while Itek's careful analysis has been forgotten. No conspiracy theory fits facts at the level demanded of the Warren Commission's report and many subsequent serious investigations.

There seems little that is provably sinister in any of the bumbling and dissembling of the individuals and organizations involved before and after Oswald's act. That has not impeded the imagination of many who want so much to unravel the assassination. New analyses appear every year, for example, Rob Reiner's four person kill team theory (iHeartPodcasts, 2023).

## Conspiracists Were Right to Look Past Warren

Oswald was neither a lone nut nor JFK's premeditated murderer.

Oswald has been tried, in absentia, in mock courts and by public opinion. Since 1991 and Stone's *JFK* movie, Oswald is usually found to be either an innocent patsy or a co-conspirator. The major reasons for his "acquittal" as a lone gunman have been answered here.

1) Oswald had no reason to kill JFK? Answer: True. He intended to kill John Connally to reveal and block the dangers of the ultra-right. Oswald had already demonstrated his mental equivalence of "American Ultra-Right" with "Hitler-style Nazis." He thought that stopping the ultra-right was a heroic cause worth a life in prison or death.

2) Oswald was a poor shot? Answer: Somewhat. He missed his first shot by waiting too long, leading his target a few inches too much, and hitting a tree branch; he hit Connally with his

second shot; his third shot was blocked by the head of another rider in the car. He had almost 9 seconds in total.

3) Oswald's preparations to shoot and escape were slipshod? Answer: True. He made his plan only two days before the event and expected to get caught – he gave up all his money, for example. He wanted his day in court to harangue the ultra-right.

4) Oswald behaved weirdly after the assassination, not like a classic assassin? Answer: True. Oswald tried to commit suicide by cop after realizing his mistake; during questioning, he gradually resumed his natural smirking and combative style; he had convinced himself that killing Kennedy would not matter.

At least twice, when asked what he thought would happen because of Kennedy's death, Oswald said:

"[Johnson] will probably do about the same thing that President Kennedy would do."

This dismissal of Kennedy's death is enough to prove that Oswald had not aimed at Kennedy. An intentional assassin would not miss a chance to justify rather than diminish his act. Nothing Oswald said suggested that killing Kennedy was something he was proud of or that would bring benefits to anyone ... especially him. His only comment was dismissive - that killing Kennedy was pointless. That sounds like someone who is trying to rationalize his colossal mistake.

The following chapters go into much greater detail about Oswald's shots, and how the Zapruder film identifies them.

# 11

# NERVE RESPONSES AND STARTLES

Oswald's motive can be understood in science. It is not "yet another conspiracy theory".

Oswald's intention to shoot John Connally aligns with what we know of his circumstances, his behaviors, and other evidence. But the only clear physical evidence of Oswald's aim point comes from his first shot. It hit something on the way towards its target. If we can determine when Oswald pulled the trigger, then we can determine what it hit. Our analysis of the event requires some deeper knowledge of how we respond to events – specifically of how our nerves and brains work in the milliseconds of the event – before our brains are fully able to process the event.

Interpreting the Zapruder Film requires a melding of the visual evidence in the film and the physical real-time responses of the people shown in those films. The film records at near the speed of light. Human responses are much slower.

Here is a rough schematic of how physical reactions and memories are created. A full cognitive reaction, such as remembering a bullet impact, takes .3 to .5 seconds or even longer to create in the mind. The very fastest nerve-triggered muscle reactions can begin in .05 seconds when the controlling neuron is directly stimulated, for example, by crushing trauma.

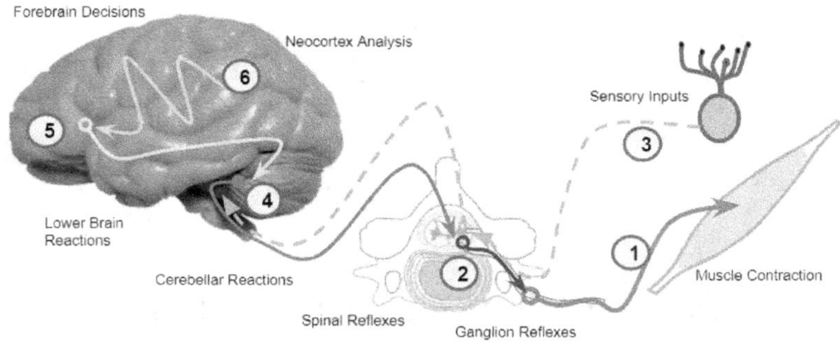


1&2) Trauma reactions are the fastest responses, involving only the Motor neurons directly, beginning in less than 0.05 seconds (1 Z frame). Motor neuron bodies typically reside in ganglia (1) or in the grey matter of the spinal cord (2). A dramatic sudden compression trauma can cause spinal or ganglion motor neuron bodies to fire, independent of normal synapse actions from brain or reflex control. A motor neuron is shown in red; a spinal motor neuron or interneuron is shown in blue:

It is likely that JFK's initial elbows-high, hands-clenched position was due to the bullet traversing next to his C7-T1 vertebral gap, when cavitation compressed the spinal interneuron and motor neuron bodies there, triggering maximal shortening of his arm muscle pairs. Kennedy began his reaction in less than one frame.

3) A classic lower body "reflex" reaction is shown in green, originating with a sensory neuron (3) firing, triggering an immediate motor action by firing the motor neuron body in the spinal cord. Some reflexes, such as the knee-jerk, require only .015 to .3 (3 to 5 frames) seconds in a healthy young person. These reflexes do not involve the brain. Mrs. Kennedy exhibited classic reflex action after her husband's head explosion. Connally's initial right-side "dip" (F 224) and puffed cheeks was likely a solar plexus reaction after the impact of the bullet traversing his chest.

4) Startle reflexes, such as the audio startle reflex, do involve the brain, at least in its lower brain centers. Audio sensory

neurons report a sudden loud noise to "lower brain centers" that operate as hard-wired reflexes – these then activate motor driver neurons in the medulla, which trigger motor neurons in the spinal cord, as in 1 & 2 above. The audio startle is discussed below and causes a blink, then usually jerks in the neck, the arms and so on. The speeds of these non-blink jerks depend on the distance from the lower brain centers, ranging from .1 to .25 seconds (2-4 frames). The audio startle reaction controlled Zapruder's camera "jumps."

5) Trained responses are responses triggered in the limbic- or neo-cortices, suggested in the yellow arrow. Once begun, trained responses are handled by the accelerated smoothing of cerebellar control. Trained responses can be quite rapid, as fast as .2 seconds (4 frames), but are typically a bit longer, up to .3 seconds (6 frames). The Kennedy assassination exhibited trained responses on the part of Oswald, as he rapidly worked his rifle's bolt action, for example. The responses of both Kennedy and Connally to the sound of the first shot represent a kind of training – each responded to the first rifle shot by turning rapidly towards the shooter. This is not true training since they did not explicitly train; rather, they had feared similar nightmare scenarios, and both had training in the sounds of rifles.

6) Thoughtful, intentional actions are driven by analysis and decisions made in the neocortex, suggested by the pink arrow above. These responses typically involve complex analysis after the inputs begin. The time for an intentional response to a totally new situation might range from .4 seconds (7 frames) to many seconds. Mrs. Kennedy's responses up until the fatal shot were mostly intentional.

Each Zapruder frame represents about .055 seconds. We can use our understanding of reaction speeds to explain the effects of Oswald's second shot:

F 222-3: Bullet hit JFK, then JBC, ending in JBC's left thigh after < .01 second.

F 223: JFK begins cavitation-induced trauma reaction, raising his arms with near-clenched hands. Neither JFK nor

JBC are aware of the impact – the sensory nerve data has not been processed yet. All their reactions are by trauma compression or reflex. The bullet's transit has created a cavitation bubble between Connally's ribs and skin. The cavitation pressure on his ribs has caused his $5^{th}$ rib to deform and shatter inwards into his right lung; the shock wave will soon trigger his solar plexus ganglia.

F 224: Connally's cavitation bubble exhausted out through the chest wound, flipping out his lapel. The solar plexus trigger starts a classic "solar plexus"-type diaphragm spasm. His right shoulder went down and his mouth opened. Another classic reflex reaction raised his right wrist with his hat. Neither JFK nor JBC is yet consciously aware of the impact – only about .07 seconds before.

F 228: Both JFK and Connally have now become consciously aware of trouble. This is the earliest moment when Connally begins to set a memory that he'd been "shoved hard in the back." At this point, Connally had turned to face forward. He conflated his "moment of impact" realization with his view at that point.

The startle response is important to show that Oswald targeted Connally. An audio startle is a very predictable event. Understanding that predictability is what makes it 95% certain that Oswald tried to shoot Connally – just given the Zapruder film.

The startle response (or reflex) has been investigated extensively. The definitive work was done in 1939 when high-speed cameras were first applied to understand the reflex. (Landis, 1939) Later work has verified the basic nature of the startle reflex as defined by Landis and Hunt. The startle reflex has been a popular target for research because it is probably the fastest known reflex from the brain and because it is so constant across so many animals, even outside the mammals.

The classic startle reflex does NOT cause gross, asymmetric movements, such as turning the head towards a sound. It causes relatively fine movements that are often undetected by an observer, though some people do "jump" very noticeably. The components of the reflex vary from person to person in degree, but one component is always present in healthy people: the eye blink. A characteristic facial movement and head movements are present in nearly all subjects. Movement of the shoulders, arms, trunk and legs is progressively less common and can be habituated away.

The following elements are present in almost all subjects:

- an eye blink (always; .02 to .054 sec to begin, .015 to close completely, re-opening greatly variable from subject to subject)

- a facial reaction (widening of mouth; in extreme cases, baring of teeth; begins .05 to .14 sec; over in .16 to .45 sec with avg .29 sec)

- a head movement (forward and down, but with chin tilting up to keep eyes level; the neck (Sternocleidomastoid) muscles tenses; in extreme cases, the ears and scalp are moved slightly; it is present in some degree in almost all subjects; begins .055 to .12, averaging .08 seconds

The following elements are visibly present in 20-50% of subjects, depending on their experiences with loud noises:

- a shoulder hunch (begins .1 to .15 seconds)

- an abduction of upper arms, bending of elbows, pronation of lower arms (begins .125 to .195 seconds)

- a flexion of fingers (begins .145 to .195 seconds)

- a contraction of abdomen, forward movement of trunk, bending of knees (begins .145 to .345 seconds)

Some general observations on the startle reaction:

- almost always symmetrical in shoulders, head and eyes

- mild reactions (60%) over in 0.3 seconds; severe may last 1.5 seconds

- present in all ages, from infants to adults

- standing slightly increases speed and amount of startle (P Brown, 1991)

- present in all races, sexes

- independent of training, but training can reduce/increase the extent of reaction

- no voluntary control

- non-directional, no relation to source of sound
- extreme rapidity, initial movement over in less than 0.5 seconds
- the startle mechanism is specific to auditory system (i.e., loud noises)
- some people habituate, but eye blink and some head movement persist
- louder noise creates bigger reactions
- startle intensity increases with excitement in the subject
- no automatic "recovery motion"


Recent research supports Landis' and Hunt's observations, e.g. (Eaton, 1984). Recent research has added that the difference between startle noise and background is important, but that high intensity (e.g. 120 dB) sound will still illicit startle even after 100's of incidents. Oswald's rifle probably produced about 115-120 dB at Zapruder's location, given the angle of the barrel and reflection from the TSBD.


**The Effect of Startle on Zapruder's Camera**

Zapruder's 8 mm Bell & Howell "Zoomatic Director Series Model 414 PD" camera has an integral viewfinder at the top of its box-like design. That viewfinder was not "through the lens" but was coupled to the zoom, so at full zoom, the viewfinder showed about the same image as the lens. At first, Zapruder had his cheek and eye directly against the back of his camera to look through the viewfinder – the natural camera position.

After the first shot, Zapruder's head "ducked," moving down and forward into the camera's back. That head startle caused the camera to rotate about its hold point; the front of the camera tilted up. The film recorded that bump. The head movement begins in about 0.05 seconds for a standing, excited person.

About 0.07 seconds after that head "duck," the startle reflex caused Zapruder's shoulders and arms to "hunch" up. That caused his camera to rotate the opposite way – the lens stopped moving up and moved slightly down; the image shows a sudden downward motion.

A second or two later, Zapruder moved his head back from his camera to see more of what was happening. We know he was no longer looking through the viewfinder because his camera aim wanders so much that by F280, the limousine is almost lost off the bottom of the frames.

For shots 2 and 3, Zapruder's involuntary head duck did not

hit the camera. The camera motion was only due to his shoul-der/arm hunch.  This would tend to drive the camera lens up –
and its image down. This motion begins at about .125 seconds.

12

# STARTLE ANALYSIS FINDINGS

The Zapruder film has become the definitive record of the few seconds that ended Kennedy's presidency. Abraham Zapruder was a Ukrainian-born cofounder of a Dallas dressmaking firm located on the fourth floor of the Dal-Tex Building across Houston from the TSBD. He had gone home that day, at the insistence of his assistant, to get his fancy new Zoomatic movie camera. He had walked down past the TSBD to a precarious position atop a short column about 80 feet from where the motorcade was to pass. He set his camera to "full zoom" and began filming about five seconds after Kennedy's limousine turned onto Elm. Remarkably, Zapruder kept filming despite multiple loud shots until the car disappeared behind trees.

The Zapruder film was developed by Dallas Eastman Kodak, immediately contact copied three times by Jamieson Film Company, then analyzed by the Secret Service, the FBI, and other government agencies. Zapruder sold the film rights to Life Magazine – and Life's editors agreed that the horrible sight of Kennedy's death was not suitable for public viewing. Jackie and the Kennedy family strongly supported the Life self-censorship. Life ended up publishing a few still frames from the film. The actual film, with its key timing information, was initially held from the public, even from investigators up to and including the Warren Commission members. Jackie did not see that film before her Warren Testimony – nor did almost anyone else. Since most Warren witnesses had no chance to compare their memories against the Zapruder film or the other film records of the tragedy, it is unsurprising that the recorded memories are wildly inconsistent with each other and with films.

For years, this most important record of the assassination was held back, seen only by a few experts. During those years, many questions were raised about the murder and were answered by speculations in the absence of the impounded film, engendering the most extensive conspiracy theory cauldron in human history. When a grainy copy of Zapruder film finally emerged and was broadcast on equally grainy TVs, conspiracies evolved to explain any contradictions with the film records, for example, claiming that the Zapruder film was faked or altered. The new theories often had to include more and more collusions amongst a wider and looser crowd of conspirators, though detailed timelines were not provided.

Good copies of the Zapruder film were eventually released. Their new detail, together with high-powered computers, allowed researchers to sharpen and examine each frame of the films in detail, up to the limit of the natural blurring of the 1963-era hand-held fully-zoomed cameras. Fifty years after the assassination, it became possible for any curious investigator to step, frame by frame, to see what everyone was really doing in those seconds.

Assassination researcher John Costella has contributed his frame-by-frame combined edit at http://assassinationresearch. com/v2n2/zfilm/zframe149.html for example (Costella, John, and James Fetzer, eds., 2013). The *Nix* film taken from the other side of the limousine from Zapruder, provide more evidence, as do a number of still photos.

Investigators have shared and published detailed analyses of where and when each picture was taken, especially as related to the Zapruder film. Zapruder frames are numbered; for example, F149 is the 149th frame of Zapruder's motorcade film. Zapruder's camera recorded at 18.3 frames per second, giving the relative time of film events. By looking at the film's background, investigators have tied snapshots and film to Zapruder film frames.

This book examines the Zapruder film to see exactly where he was pointing his camera simply by measuring where immobile objects are in each frame. For detecting startles, only the vertical aim point motion is important since Zapruder's bilateral startle reactions move his camera aim point vertically. The vertical camera motion was measured initially using a ruler and video. More recently, these measurements were replicated with more accuracy, using Google Slide "rulers" on a digitized stop-frame version of the Zapruder film. The results are essentially the same for any analysis since vertical camera motions can be detected with reasonable accuracy, even on blurry editions of the Zapruder film. For example, here is the measurement for F152. The orange guideline at the bottom aligns with the bottom-most extent of the frame to correct for pincushion distortion (green for horizontal) but is not critical for frame-to-frame accuracy. Screen size and units are irrelevant as long as the same setup is used for each frame:

*Vertical: 6.30 screen units; Horizontal: 1.14 units*

. . .

The following shows vertical camera motion measured on the upper left corner of the "Stemmons Freeway" signpost. It shows that Zapruder's aim point changed dramatically from F154 to F155.

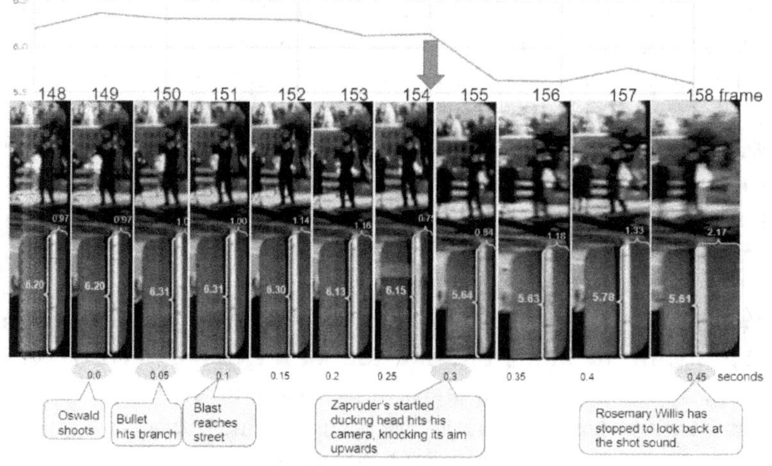


*Abraham Zapruder Film © The Sixth Floor Museum at Dealey Plaza*

Zapruder did not start panning his camera at first; he let the car move into his shot. After being startled, he reacts at F158 by moving his head away from his camera viewfinder. The vertical movements are not huge compared to horizontal panning, which is probably why they have been ignored in the past. But the three jumps are very sharp and very specific to startle reactions.

This startle analysis does not depend on any fancy credentials, or computer analyses, or extravagant intelligence. Anyone with a few days of patience and care can replicate it. The following shows the results of frame-by-frame measurement analysis of the Zapruder camera aim points and, from that, the estimated frames of Oswald's shots.

The measurements use background "fixed points" in the successive images. When switching from one fixed point to another, both the new and old points are used – overlapped – while possible. The following table gives the fixed points that were used for anyone who wishes to verify the analysis. The "overlap" lines describe when a new fixed point is first seen on image; the "switch" lines describe when the new fixed point is adopted as the main measure point. In most cases, the overlapping points yielded similar measures, except in the case where there is extreme blurring.

**Frame Landmark used for Camera Aimpoint spotting**
 145 left junction post shadow & sign top
 204 overlap: right post of sign, at top right
 209 switch: right post of sign, at top right
 224 overlap: third square hole upper right in white wall
 227 switch: third square hole upper right in white wall
 248 overlap: first square hole, next set in white wall
 250. switch: first square hole, next set in white wall
 265 overlap: ring on pole below light fixture
 268 switch: ring on pole below light fixture
 276 overlap: left pant/shirt junction pinkish shirt man
 279 switch: left pant/shirt junction pinkish shirt man
 287 overlap: left junction of red coat and orange pant
 292 switch: left junction of red coat and orange pant
 297 overlap: right side of plant foot of blue pants walker
 303 switch: right side of plant foot of blue pants walker
 307 overlap: right side of next plant foot, same walker
 309 switch: right side of next plant foot, same walker
 313 overlap: middle of white trash spot
 318 switch: middle of white trash spot

The result is best seen as the change (the "speed") in aim point:

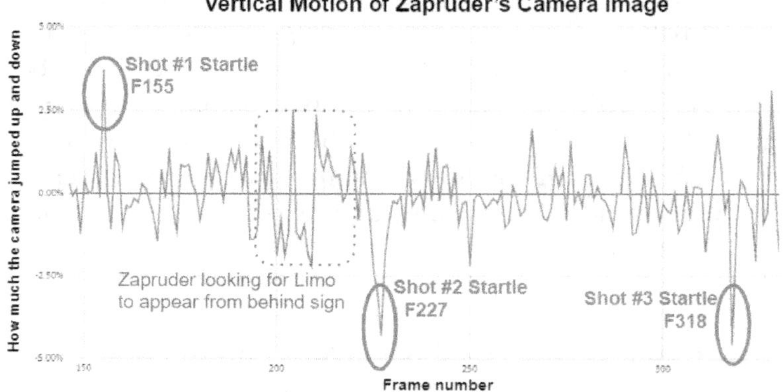



Recently, computer technology has been used to "stabilize" the Zapruder film. This technique also makes use of fixed points but in a much more complete and automated way. It should be possible to extract the stabilizing data used to make vertical frame-by-frame adaptions for an even more accurate view of the camera aim point.

**Reliability of the Zapruder Film**

This analysis of the startle effect entirely depends on the film taken during the actual assassination, primarily the Zapruder film. Some have later claimed that the Zapruder film was a fake, created or altered by the CIA or whoever. Any faked Zapruder film would need to align with the still photographs and the other film taken at the same time. This would need to be accomplished without error and without the use of modern computers and image processing.

The Secret Service first saw the film on November 22, 1963, soon after Dallas Kodak Lab processed it. Three copies were made immediately. There was no time to change the film before copying, even if that technology existed. Zapruder was given the original and one copy. The other two copies were sent to Washington. Zapruder auctioned the film to CBS and Life representatives, with Life winning the bid to own it. The Warren Commission extensively examined the camera and film in early 1964. If any "tampering" had been done, it would have had to be done two hours before the first copies were made. The "tampered film" would have to align with later-emerging snapshots and film. Basically: impossible.

Zapruder sold all rights to Life Magazine for $150,000 ($1,300,000 in 2021 valuation, of which Zapruder gave 17% to the Tippit family) but with the condition that the fatal frame F313 not be shown, that it would not be shown as a film, and that it would be strictly controlled and not given out to others who might exploit its graphic nature (Zapruder A., 2016). F313 was eventually made public in 1975. That same year, Life Magazine sold the rights back to Zapruder's heirs (for $1). In 1999, the Justice Department paid the Zapruder family $16,000,000 for the original print. In addition, the film has been licensed to others, such as Oliver Stone.

Roland Zavada, the Kodak corporate expert on 8-mm film, authenticated the Zapruder film and other photographic evidence for the Assassination Records Review Board in 1998. He said it was impossible to introduce complex coordinated changes onto 8-mm film back in 1963. In his extensive report, he declared that "there is no detectable evidence of manipulation or image alteration on the Zapruder in-camera original, and all supporting evidence precludes any forgery thereto."

Many claims have been made about alleged anomalies that "prove" tampering. Other researchers have shown that each claim has been false as of 2021. A summary of some of the efforts is presented in (Thompson, Bedrock Evidence in the Kennedy Assassination, Accessed on 2/26/2022). Even the shadows in the film have been studied (Farid, 2011).

For example, 46 years after the event, an NPIC worker named Dino Brugioni, who worked on "storyboard" frame stills, recalled that the "mist cloud" that exploded above Kennedy's head in frame 313 was bigger, sharper, and more vivid than the various Zapruder film copies show today. Note that he described the Oswald-shooting direction of that cloud – up and forward from the president. He just felt the cloud seemed altered to be less dramatic. He did not describe any mist cloud ejected towards the rear, nor did he say the limo stopped, nor did he support any other "alteration theory." He did say that two independent teams worked on storyboards; his were not used; the other team, secret from him, had their board preserved in the National Archives. He speculated that the other team might have been using a Zapruder film modified on November 24 by the Rochester Kodak labs under contract with the CIA. Some speculated that the Kodak lab might have modified the Zapruder film, but no evidence has surfaced on who, what, how, and why this was engineered (Horne, 2014). Several authors have attempted to weave together explanations that become broad conspiracies. For example, the Zapruder and other photographic evidence was altered, along with the autopsy data, testimonies, and more: JFK's "death must have involved elements at the highest levels of the U.S. government." (Fetzer, 2007, The International Journal of the Humanities: Annual Review)

The original Zapruder film was damaged. The Kodak developers and Secret Service damaged these frames during their copy and looped viewing efforts. One of the damaged areas is in frames F155-F157: there is a splice mark through the top of F155, the very frame that Zapruder startles. While the original film is damaged at F155-157, it is still visible and undamaged in the first-generation copies: all show there is a dramatic vertical change in aim point at F155, consistent with a startle reaction.

After decades, the various film copies showed varying coloration, suggesting to some that they had been made with "bracketing" exposures. Since the people who had made known copies insisted that they had used the same exposure, some speculated that multiple secret copies had been made. Kodachrome II film chemicals have been extremely stable for decades; however, they degrade in minutes under bright light, such as when illuminated by projector lamps. Slow motion or stop frame projection was particularly hard on the film chemistry – as would be expected when various agents over the pre-digital decades studied the films for clues into the assassination. More likely, then, the fragility of 1963's Kodachrome II chemicals degrade with repeated projection and when exposed to UV and heat. It is not surprising that vivid colors have faded to different degrees over the decades, with the original most protected and least exposed and, therefore, least faded.

The Zapruder film frames are now available in many places, in various enhanced forms. There are black and white slides of each frame, created by Life Magazine, preserved as CE 855 in Warren Commission Volume XVIII; unfortunately, that sequence begins at F171, skipping the keyframes of F133-F169, and is not sharp. The entire film is available from the Sixth Floor Museum and from the National Archives. For the "startle analysis" presented in this book, any full copy that shows the right and bottom frame edges is useable and would reproduce the same results; even distortion is acceptable, as long as they are constant over all frames since only relative frame motion is measured. This analysis was originally done on a bootlegged copy of the film and subsequently was verified on the frame-by-frame internet version at http://assassinationresearch.com/v2n2/zfilm and the Sixth Floor Museum film. The bootleg analysis and the later original film gave the same results (within measurement errors).

There are many discrepancies between witness reports (even those taken in the hours immediately after the shooting) and the films. For example, witnesses did not agree on the number and direction of shots: experienced investigators expected these variations and science explained why (McFadden, 2021).In more extreme disagreements, some witnesses claim that the limo came to a brief complete stop at about the time that the fatal shot arrived. While the Zapruder and Nix films agree that the limo slowed to about 8 mph at that point, that is far from stopping. (The car speed is plotted in **Appendix E: Details of the First Shot**). The heavy limo would have taken at least a second to stop and another second to resume speed – with no automated braking or traction support with old bias-ply tires and drum brakes. Even a one-second stop would mean over 40

Zapruder and Nix frames would need extensive modifications, including adjusting the walking figures in the background and the wind-flapped clothes. That is impossible in 1963 technology. A better explanation of witness recall problems is found in "memory distortion during traumatic events." E.g.: (Dawson & Sleek, 2018)

Note: This book's analysis depends on the motion of Zapruder's 8 mm Bell & Howell "Zoomatic Director Series Model 414 PD" camera. That model has a power zoom with a Varamat 9-27mm f1.8 lens controlled by two buttons on its top. Zapruder set it on full zoom for his entire film. That is verified by the constant height of objects in his images – had he zoomed out, objects would shrink from frame to frame.

Some critics claim that any timing using the Zapruder frame counts is invalid because the Zoomatic Camera was spring-powered. In fact, the Zoomatic camera evolved over time; the Model 414 PD employed a much stronger spring so that it could easily power the camera without changing speed, using technology similar to spring-wound clocks. A much bigger factor in timing is the change in the geometry of the car on its curving, downhill, and speed-changing passage by Zapruder. However, even that is essentially irrelevant to the "startle analysis" since it does not cause rapid changes in vertical aim points.

One other note: measurements account for the curvature of the camera frame. It turns out to be a simple table based on horizontal and vertical measures. For example, a measurement that is taken only .5 units from the right file edge will need its vertical measure increased by .2 units to compensate for the extreme frame curve in the corner – but only for measures done in those edge regions. In the crucial area of F148 through F160 there is almost no movement of the key landmark used for measurements – the freeway sign, so the adjustment for curvature is not material.

. . .

**Blurred Frames and Startles**

The Zapruder film was analyzed by Dr. Luis Alvarez. Dr. Alvarez had excellent credentials: he was awarded the Nobel Prize for Physics in 1968. His conjecture was that the bullet shock wave blast might buffet Zapruder's camera, as well as cause neuromuscular startles.

Dr. Alvarez had his team rate the frames they had access to (F170 through F334) by how blurred each was. *CBS News Inquiry: The Warren Report*, in 1967, reported they found blurs "of neuromuscular startles" at F227, F318, and at F186. They did not calculate the transit time of the bullet but instead applied a fixed 4 to 5 frame adjustment, arriving at F181-2, F222-3, and F313, presumably for bullet arrival frames. They verified that people holding Zapruder-like cameras produced similar blur startles. They required that the holders stay with their eye on the viewfinder, unlike Zapruder, who became curious about the president and took his eye away from the camera.

Alvarez claimed to deduce something about bullet shock waves from his blurs. That is difficult to accept. Alvarez said he was inspired by the WW2 "firing error indicator" used to detect anti-aircraft misses near a towed target, but the little Carcano bullet has a relatively small shock wave, vastly smaller than the anti-aircraft shell shock waves measured in WW2, passing only a few feet from a towed target with highly sensitive microphones. The Carcano bullet would not generate enough power to rotate a camera 80 feet from the nearest track.

Estimated horizontal (red) and vertical (blue) blurring:

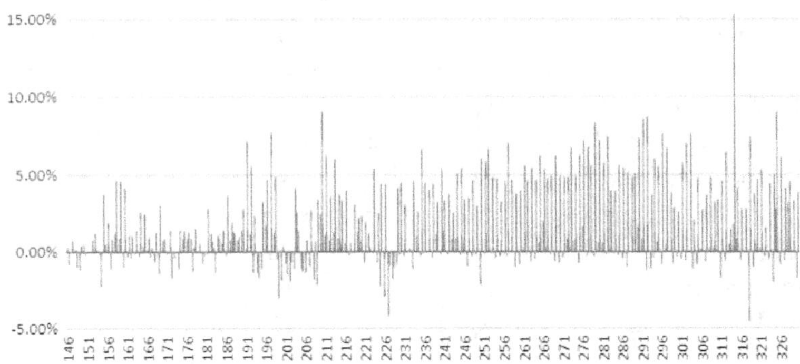

Blurring has an inherent problem: Zapruder was panning from left to right to follow the limousine. The speed of that panning (in red) dwarfed the small vertical jumps (in blue) due to the startle effect. The red values are horizontal motion speeds – the blue are vertical. Alvarez's blurring was almost entirely due to panning motions. Alvarez did notice the blurring that he attributed to neuromuscular startles. It was these motions that led him to suggest shots at F186, F222-3, and F313. Since a shot at near F186 would have to go through the oak tree, Alvarez had his team search the oak tree for an embedded bullet, finding none (Alvarez, 1976).

A more scientific analysis of film blurring was done for the HSCA in 1978 (Hartmann, 1978). Their blur analyses revealed shots fired at about (A) 310 and (B) 190. Hartmann's work denied the Warren Commission's finding of a shot about 210. Hartmann and Scott did detect progressively weaker "blur episodes" at frames (C) 220-228, frames (D) 158-160, and frames (E) 290-293, but these blurs were judged "insufficient to warrant any conclusion concerning the number and timing of any additional gunshots." Horizontal panning blurs simply overwhelmed the much smaller "startle" vertical motions. The HSCA concluded that the first bullet was fired just before F160 and the second at F209 (Sturdivan, 2005).

The blurring at (D) F158-60 seems very close to this book's vertical startle at F155. But these are not the same. The true startle is a vertical motion – that happens at F155. The high level of blurring beginning 3 frames later (at F158) is almost entirely horizontal panning motion. It is NOT a startle. That throws off the timing of JFK's, Jackie's, JBC's and Rosemary's responses by 3 frames or about 0.16 seconds, giving too little time to make conscious responses.

Blurring in the films limits the amount of information that can be extracted. For example, the film is far too blurry to reliably identify people. In fact, if there was not a mountain of corroborating evidence, the Zapruder film is not even accurate enough to be 100% certain it was JFK in the car. The startle analysis depends on judging only the change in aim points;

that change is much greater than the blur distances and is, therefore, highly reliable.

## Oswald's Three Shots

This graph shows the vertical changes in aim points. Zapruder's aim point jumps are marked as "Startles": #1 at F155, #2 at F227, and #3 at F318. Unlike blur analysis, there are three clear jumps, two of which align with known shots.

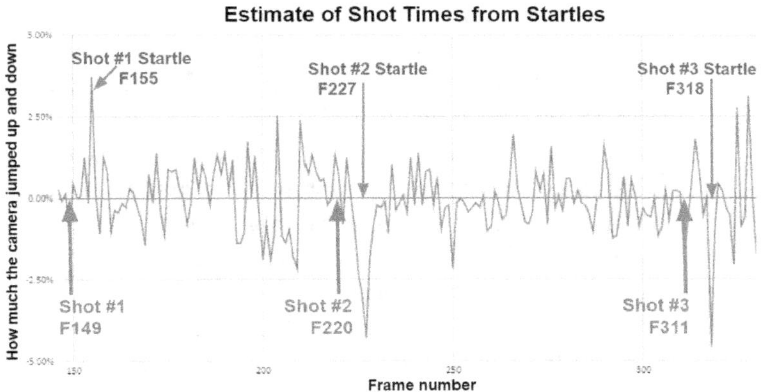


The above graph is also marked with the calculated frames where Oswald pulled the trigger:

- at F149, 6 frames before the F155 "head-bump" startle
- at F220, 7 frames before the F227 "arm-hand" startle
- at F311, 7 frames before the F318 "arm-hand" startle

In each case, the rifle sound took the same time to reach Zapruder; only his head against the viewfinder changed the startles.

.   .   .

This data, knowledge of anatomy and nerve actions reveal answers to some important questions:

1.  How many shots? Three that were loud enough to cause startles. This agrees with most witness memories.
2.  From where? All three shots fit Oswald's TSBD sniper's nest. The first shot sound reached Jackie about .1 second before it reached Zapruder. The second shot caused an arms-up trauma reaction in Kennedy at F222-3, which fits the bullet speed from Oswald's rifle compared to the speed of sound. The third shot arrived a little before F313, again fitting the bullet and sound speed from Oswald's rifle.
3.  How long did Oswald have to shoot three times? He took 3.88 seconds to rechamber and aim his second shot and another 4.97 seconds to make his third shot. He took a total of 8.85 seconds to shoot three times and rechamber twice.
4.  Did anyone else shoot at the car? Any unsuppressed shots would have had to have sound reach Zapruder at the same time as Oswald's. That is not impossible – more analysis will be shown.

The three following chapters detail each shot literally in gory detail. They can be skipped by any reader who is already convinced that Oswald shot, alone, three times: shot one missed; shot two hit JFK with his C7-T1 and then hit Connally, causing all his wounds; shot three killed JFK.

13

# DETAILS OF THE FIRST SHOT

Using the speed of the startle reflex together with the known speed of sound in Dallas that day and the distance between Zapruder and the sniper's nest, we predicted when Oswald shot:

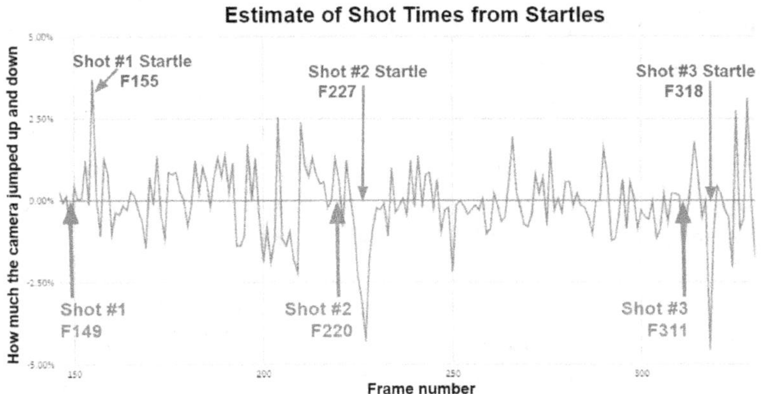



For the first shot, Zapruder likely had his eye on the camera and hit it with his head "duck" – that is why in this shot only, the camera tilts sharply up, initially. The head duck startle reflex begins in .055 seconds and takes 0.06 to 0.12 seconds. The

F155 upward graph spike would be larger except that after about one frame, the arm and shoulder part of Zapruder's startle reaction moves the aim point dramatically back down, resulting in just the short, sharp spike at F155. The first bullet was fired between 0.24 + 0.06 and 0.24 + 0.12 seconds before F155. Each frame takes 0.055 seconds, so that is about 5.5 to 6.5 frames. Oswald fired his first at between F148.5 and F149.5. F149 is substantially earlier than the Warren Commission's conclusions, and at 124 feet from gun to target, it was substantially closer. It is also about the last point before Oswald lost sight of the car under the oak tree.

## What Oswald Saw When He First Shot

We can estimate what Oswald saw at F149 and estimate our error in that estimate. Inches will be important, as we'll see. One source of error is the exact time of the shot: we know only within half a frame of F149. The other major source of error is in the exact position of the car and occupants on Elm Street at about F149. We'll show that we can estimate within about +/- one foot with reasonable confidence.

We do not know exactly Zapruder's startle response, although the auditory startle reflex is quite uniform. We also do not know exactly how far Zapruder's head was from the camera, so the bump of the camera might add up to another 0.02 seconds, but we do know that the head bump preceded the arm motion – so it was less than 0.05 seconds. We also do not know exactly where in the frame that Zapruder started his head duck, but because the image travel is substantial in F155, we know the startle began about the middle of F154 and was overcome by the arm startle shortly after F155 was taken. Zapruder startled around F154.5, +/- 0.3 frames. Oswald fired 6 frames before that: between F148 and F149. In feet, that error is about +/- 3 inches, given the car is going about 11 MPH.

. . .

This is F149 in Zapruder's film. We can use the lane marker end to locate the car on the street.

*Abraham Zapruder Film © The Sixth Floor Museum at Dealey Plaza*

The highway lane marker stripe is just behind the car's left front wheel (in the red circle). Because of the telephoto effects and blurry film, it is hard to measure how far the car has travelled past this lane marker. By backing up the Zapruder film, we can see that the front of the car passes the near end of that lane marker between F143 and F144. Since the car was moving at about 11 MPH (see below for a calculation of the car's speed), we know that each frame represents about 0.88 feet of motion. The easternmost estimate of the car's position would be a shot at F148 with the car moving at 11 mph from F143: [4 frames from F143] * [0.88 feet/frame] = 3.5 feet past the lane marker end. The westernmost estimate: [5 frames from F144] * [0.88 feet/frame] = 4.4 feet. The car's position is only known within about half a frame, about 4' +/- 0.5' past that lane marker when Oswald took his first shot. The accumulated error is 4' +/- 0.8'.

The FBI took photos of a reconstruction of the assassination on December 6th, 2 weeks after the assassination. They were published as CE875: a series of photos of Elm Street taken from Oswald's window. The closest picture to F148-9 shows the FBI car at F140. The car was close to that second lane marker, but unfortunately, it is about where the car was at frame F140. At frame F149, the car would have moved about 8 feet down Elm Street.

The red line shows the reenactment car's position in about F149. But this FBI reenactment car in CE875 was NOT the President's specially modified Lincoln Continental (code-named X-100, or SS-100-X); this FBI car was a production model Continental from 1961-1963, unmodified. Among the X-100 modifications that we should consider:

- X-100 had been literally cut in half, reinforced, extended 3½ feet in length.
- Hydraulic rear seat that could be raised 10½" to elevate the president.
- Auxiliary jump seats - Governor and Mrs. Connally sat in these.
- Partition separates driver from passengers.

This FBI normal 1961 Continental was 212" long, while X-100 was 254", or almost 20% longer. This extended length is in the cab and trunk area - the front of X-100 looks stock. X-100 looks like its cab was lengthened by about 25" to 117", mainly for the partition and jump seats. X-100's trunk area was extended for Secret Service mounts, as well as to support its detachable top and contain its heavy-duty air conditioner.

In the X-100, above, the cab front started at about the same place in the car. After that, there is a slightly increased driver area and a partition. The photo at right is from a lower angle, with a telephoto, but it shows how close the two men were and how Connally was lower and inboard.

In the following "stick figure" X-100, Connally, cramped in the jump seat, would be about in the red circle below at F149; JFK would be behind him, slightly outboard, and in the two-foot extended area of the X-100 cab, about in the blue circle below.

The white reenactment car (shown here at F130 to be out of the way) is a standard Continental. We can use its 17.7-foot length as a "ruler" (the dashed grey arrow) to estimate how far the front of the limo moved from F144 (the green dashed line at the end of that second lane marker) to F149 (the turquoise dashed line). That is 5 frames, or about 4.2 feet, or about 24% (the red arrows) of that white car's length. The green stick figure car, with Kennedy (blue) and Connally (red), shows the car's position at F149 when Oswald took his first shot. Oswald's view was very likely through his telescopic sight, so he would see only a tiny part of this view.

To hit a moving target, the shooter must "lead" that target. The bullet left Oswald's Carcano at about 2100-2200 feet per second; according to Edgewood Arsenal testing, Oswald's ammunition was good quality, with a consistent muzzle velocity of about 2160 fps (Olivier and Dziemian, 1965). The target was about 124 feet away, so the bullet would take about 0.055 seconds – just about one Zapruder frame, to reach the car. In this case, the car's speed of about 11 mph would carry it about 0.88 feet during the bullet's flight. Therefore, from an impact and bullet trajectory point of view, we must look at the car's position at F150 rather than F149:

At F150, in the above, X-100 has moved about 10" (.88') farther down Elm Street. The fuzzy green bar shows the error in the estimate of when the front of the limo passed the end of that lane marker (used above to locate the car at each frame). The fuzzy blue bar shows the accumulated error from the green bar plus the error in estimating the car's speed at that point. It also includes the error in estimating exactly when Oswald shot, given the camera's vertical spike. The fuzzy blue oval represents the area where Kennedy probably sat, given the error ranges, and the fuzzy red oval represents Connally's position. We don't know exactly what part of a target body Oswald intended to hit, and we don't know exactly the posture of the people in the car. Because of this additional uncertainty, the error regions increased to about +/- one foot.

There is little error in the side-to-side position estimates, as we can tell where the car was in the film. The FBI reenactment car did not follow exactly the same path as X-100: X-100 was moving to its left in its lane; by F217, the left front tire of X-100 was on the left lane marker. The stick figure reflects the X-100 course.

Oswald was not a great shot and had practiced only rarely with his rifle. Oswald's refurbished Italian Carcano M91/38 and its budget ammunition were hardly sniper-quality, but at only 40 yards, the rifle was adequate. Its recoil was similar to Oswald's Marine M1, as the more powerful M1 drained some gas to drive its automated feed. While there was a recoil kick for Oswald's rifle that would lift the barrel – the resultant shot would be more directly into the car, not down into the tree branches.

We know that Oswald was not a "real" sharpshooter – though with Marine training, he was better than most people. We have no evidence that Oswald ever practiced hitting a moving target, especially one that was sweeping by in front of him at 11 mph, which is over 16 feet per second. The only record of Oswald shooting at a moving target was with a shotgun in Russia – shots that Oswald missed.

We know there was a shot at about F149. We know it did not hit the car or its occupants when it arrived at F150. The only realistic explanation: **Oswald shot at Connally and hit the lone oak tree branch** a few inches ahead of his desired trajectory.

**Kennedy and Connally Turn to the Shot**

Both Kennedy and Connally turned towards Oswald just after F150.

Oswald wanted to remain hidden - and therefore back in his window - until he shot. If he kept the barrel of his gun entirely within the building for this shot, then the car's rapid motion and steep angle below him would force him to be at least crouching, if not standing.

An important effect of having his gun inside the window is that the building suppresses the noise of that shot for people who are blocked by its frame. Zapruder was downrange at a 30° angle, while Oswald was shooting at about a 48° angle - so at least Zapruder, with no foliage or building between him and the muzzle blast, heard all three shots clearly. But for many other people below, especially under the trees or near the TSBD, the first shot was likely muffled. The speed of sound in Dealey Plaza was about 1125 feet/second. The shot sound took about .12 seconds to reach the crowd on the south side of Elm – arriving at about F151.

Agent Kellerman, who was sitting just ahead of Governor Connally in the Presidential Limousine, described the first shot as sounding very different, "more like a firecracker." Agent Kellerman's sound path at F151 was blocked by oak leaves. Since that first bullet hit in the oak tree, it made little supersonic noise. Other witnesses recalled the first shot as a firecracker or "backfire" sound.

There is no discernible reaction from the agents in the follow car, less than 25 feet behind Kennedy. If Oswald fired from a near-standing position in the first shot, he could have kept his gun barrel out of sight from the agents' car – as would be expected since he did not want to give away his position and get immediate return fire. The muzzle blast was, therefore, blocked by the window frame, causing the agents to fail to identify a rifle shot.

The people in the rear of X-100 would have heard the shot more clearly, unblocked by window frame. JFK had no oak leaves between him and the muzzle blast and would have heard the full blast best of anyone. Connally (JBC) would have also heard it, muffled only slightly by a single oak branch. Both men were well acquainted with rifle sounds. Both men were nervous about driving in an open car - Kennedy was particularly concerned. Jackie and Rosemary Willis, a little girl running about 15 feet south of the limo, also heard it.

In the Zapruder film, we see:

F135: JFK is looking a little to his right (~25°), his arm is up at about 30°. Rosemary Willis, in a red skirt and white hoodie sweatshirt, is beginning her run to pace JFK and Jackie, looking towards Zapruder.

F138: JFK turns his head to his left (it is now about straight ahead); his arm is waving, changing from 30° to 20° or so. Rosemary's father took a picture here – Jackie is smiling. Rosemary's face is showing, so she is facing towards Zapruder and likely looking sidelong at Kennedy.

F147: JFK is now looking to his left, head maybe 45° left.  His arm has dropped to about 5°, and he has stopped waving. Perhaps he is speaking with someone in the car? Rosemary has turned towards Kennedy, with her face half covered by her white hood.

F149: Oswald shoots.

F150:  The bullet hits the top side of the oak branch. JFK is still looking to his left, head maybe 50° left, arm down at 5°, not waving. Rosemary, showing half-face, has run behind another onlooker.

**F151(0.0)**: Startle Analysis: the muzzle blast reached the car here.

[number in () is seconds after the muzzle blast reaches the car]

F160(0.5): JFK is turning his head rapidly to his right; his head is already at about 0° with the car; his arm is still at about 5° (down). JBC appears to have been looking to his left (about 30° left at this point). Rosemary begins looking behind Kennedy, judging from her hood. In the Croft picture, both Connally and Jackie have suddenly stopped smiling and each looks worried. Jackie had been looking slightly left; in about F157, she turned to look behind and to her left, **scowling** towards the motorcycle guard - or possibly towards the muzzle blast reflected from the decorative wall (the crowd suddenly thinned at F150, leaving the reflection path open).

F164(0.7): JFK continues his rapid turn towards the TSBD, head now about 45° right; arm still 5°down. JFK's head has turned 90° in about 0.2 seconds towards Oswald. JBC is starting to turn towards the TSBD on his right; his head is now about 20° left. Rosemary is looking towards the TSBD as JFK's car is past her.

F166(0.82): JFK is now facing about 60° right, his arm still down (JFK completed his head turn in 6 frames or about 0.3 seconds). JBC is now turning his head rapidly right, rotating his head 60° in 2 frames (0.1 seconds). At this point, Jackie also begins a turn, in 1.9 seconds, to her right.

F170(1.04):   JFK is still looking right 50°, his arm down. JBC's head is now 70° to his right.

F173(1.2):   JFK's arm begins raising. JFK is probably executing his pre-planned response to a shot that missed - or a back-fire/firecracker: "If I'm still alive, then try to be cool!"

F178(1.48):  JFK's arm is now up to 30°; he is still looking right at about 50°. JBC is looking almost 90° to his right; the oak trees now completely hide the upper TSBD, so JBC won't see anything. The trees hide the sudden flight of pigeons from the roof above Oswald – a detail that might have alerted JBC or JFK. Rosemary is still looking back towards the upper TSBD.

F183(1.75):  JFK is looking back about 70° right; his arm begins waving slightly.

F189(2.08):  JFK is looking about 80° right; his arm is up to 40°. JBC maintains, looking hard to his right. Rosemary has stopped and is looking back towards the TSBD; she glances towards JFK but then, by F200 is again looking at the TSBD.

·  ·  ·

The Zapruder film is not clear enough to see any definitive startle effects (blinks or head ducking) for these people in the cars or along the road. But JFK, JBC and Rosemary Willis did rapidly look towards the TSBD, at about the time we would expect for an "intentional" response to Oswald's muzzle blast.

By the time the car emerges from behind the sign at F219, the Secret Service man (Kellerman) in the right front seat has also turned his head about 60° to the right. Because of the car's window frame and the film quality, it is not clear where Kellerman was looking at F151.

The head turns of Rosemary, Connally and Kennedy are not startle or reflex actions (Nijhuis and Janssen, 2007). They are intentional, thought-driven, if urgent motions. It takes JFK only 0.5 seconds to decide and turn. Rosemary's turn is hidden, but she's looking back about as fast as Kennedy. Both JFK and the girl end up looking at the TSBD within 0.7 seconds after F151. Connally is only a little slower, at 1 second. This evidence strongly supports a shot sound at about F151 and does NOT support a shot later than about F152 since Kennedy and Rosemary could not complete an intentional turn in response to a shot sound after F152.

## Spent Shells

Three witnesses were directly below Oswald on the fifth floor of the TSBD, watching the motorcade go past. The noise from Oswald's three shots was deafening for them and enough to shake debris down from their ceiling. They reported hearing the action of the bolt and the sounds of the three ejected casings hitting the floor above them. The shells were allegedly found about as in this picture of the sniper's nest:

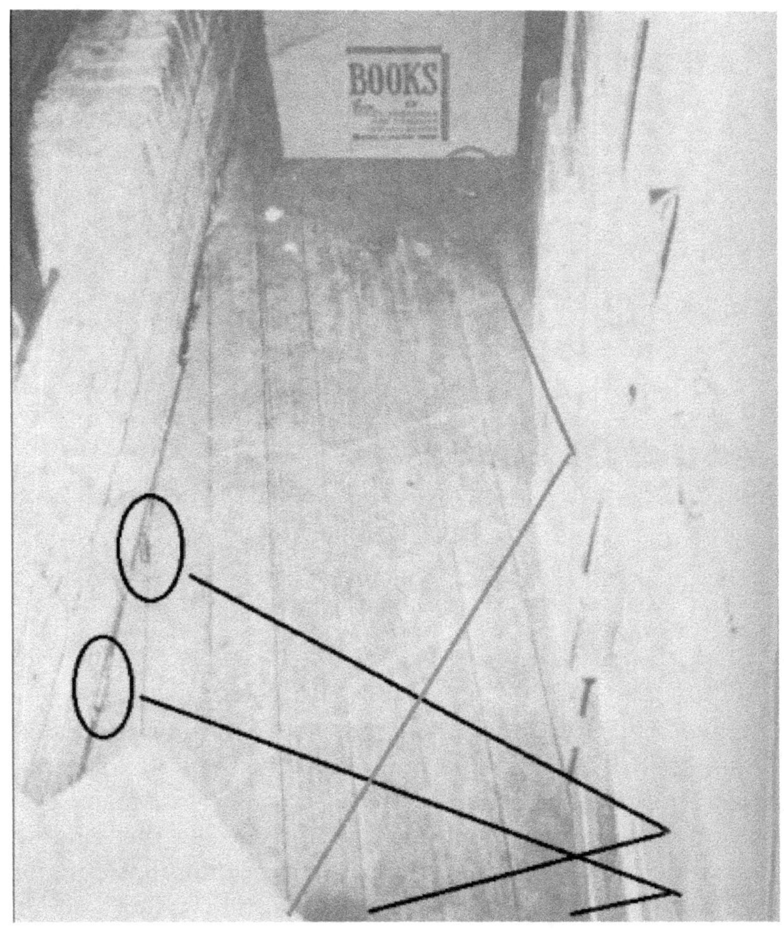
BOOKS

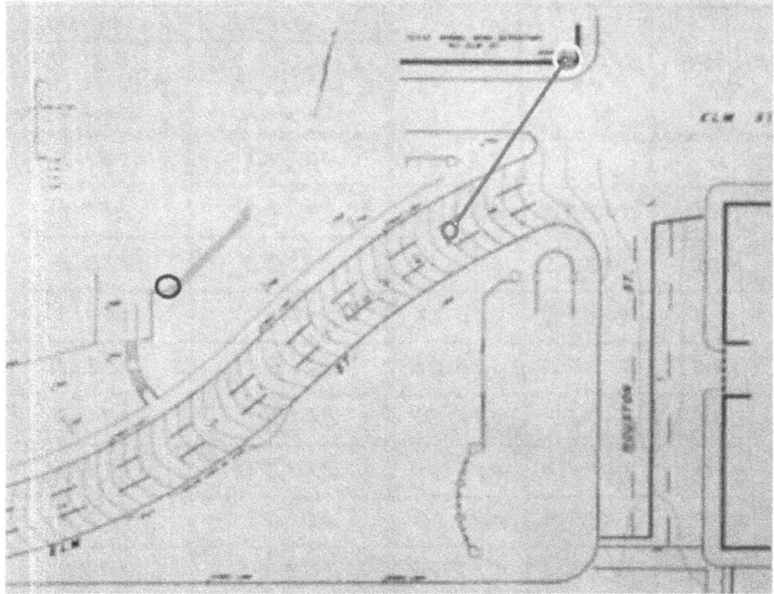

Carcano shells are ejected perpendicularly to the rifle barrel. The first shell is likely the one circled in red. At F149, the trajectory of the first shot is red on the Dealey Plaza map. The rifle would have been pointing at almost 60° out the window and would be fired from a standing or crouching position; its shell would be ejected at about 30° back at an upward arc, as shown by the red lines. It would likely bounce off the boxes and could be expected to end up in the far position, where a lone casing is circled in red (Holland, 2015).

The other two shots were both taken when the car was farther down Elm Street. Oswald likely sat down and used his box stand to take those shots at about a 45° angle from the window frame. The ejected casing would then hit lower and at a more direct angle on the boxes to the right. They would be expected to bounce more directly to end up as the two shells circled in black.

. . .

These spent shells offer some weak collaboration to a shot taken earlier than the Warren Commission's estimates. There is some testimony that the shells were disturbed by the police before being photographed and only replaced "approximately." The Warren Commission reported tests in CE 546-7, showing that the barrel angle of the first shot would tend to eject the first cartridge down the row.

**Was Oswald a Good Enough Shooter?**

Oswald qualified as a "sharpshooter" (scoring 212 and needing 210) in December 1956 after his basic training entering the US Marines. Later, in March 1959, he was barely acceptable in his rifle shooting accuracy (scoring 191 and needing 190 to pass); at that time, Marine rifle shooting required firing an M1 from standing, sitting, kneeling, and prone positions at 200, 300 and 500-yard distances for a maximum score of 250 points, so Oswald had been a moderately good shot - at stationary targets. When briefly available to the public in 1993, KGB reports from 1960 said Oswald was "not a good shot" with either a pistol or shotgun at moving targets. Oswald missed General Walker with a rifle in April 1963 at close range.

| 200 YARDS SLOW | DATE Dec 19 | NO | ELEV | WIND | CALL | VALUE |
|---|---|---|---|---|---|---|
| | ELEV. USED 6 - 0 | 1 | | | ◯ | |
| | | 2 | | | ◉ | |
| | CORRECT ELEV. 6 | 3 | | | ◉ | |
| | | 4 | | | ◉ | |
| | ZERO WIND 0 | 5 | | | ◉ | |
| | | 6 | | | ◉ | 3 |
| | WIND VEL. 0 | 7 | | | ◉ | 4 |
| | | 8 | | | ◯ | 3 |
| | WIND DIRECTION 0 | 9 | | | ◉ | 4 |
| | | 10 | | | ◯ | 4 |
| | | SCORE | | | | 38 |
| | REMARKS | | | | | |

CE 650 is a page from Oswald's Marine shooting record. His score of 38 was acceptable, but the spread of bullets ranged up to eight inches from his aim point. That was for a fixed target, seated, 200 yards away, with no wind, horizontal, after several days of intense practice. His bullet spread at the shorter distances (42, 63, and 88 yards) would be proportionate, ranging from 2 to 4 inches from his aim point at a minimum. On November 22, that spread would have been increased by wind, car motion, fear, and hurry.

Modern snipers receive a lot of training, use excellent equipment, benefit from decades of research and development, and usually have a spotting partner. Hitting a moving target is not something that even great snipers like to try because the odds of a hit go dramatically down. There are whole classes on hitting moving targets. Oswald did none of this.

Oswald could not have known how fast the limo would be going. He could not know if the limo would return to its more normal 25 mph to 35 mph as the crowds slimmed to nothing. He could not have known if it would speed up or slow down in response to his shots. He could not even know where on the street the limo would be going, as it might have swung under the trees to the rightmost lane for example. There is no evidence that Oswald had walked Elm Street to understand its curve and its decline. There is no evidence that he calculated any bullet drop effect for shooting to a much lower target. In fact, there is no evidence that he made any investigation of any aspects of his shots. He seems to have just guessed, on the fly.

There is no evidence that he looked at the weather to know that by 12:30, there would be a 12 to 17-mph swirling uneven cross-wind from the west-north-west, with a 10 to 15-mph component perpendicular to his trajectories. For the final shot, his bullet could have been wind-pushed up to three inches to the left, contributing to hitting JFK.

His "sniper's nest" had boxes for a seat and a precariously tilted box for his muzzle rest. His first shot almost certainly had to be taken from a standing or crouching position and did not make use of any support.

Oswald was not a good enough shot, nor had he prepared enough that we can tell who he intended to shoot on his later, more distant, shots. Just because he eventually hit JFK, we cannot tell that he was aiming for JFK. His past records suggest that if he were aiming at Kennedy at F149, he would have missed by a few inches; with no intervening oak branch, his first shot would have hit Kennedy or the car near him. It did not. It hit an oak branch 2.5 feet from Kennedy's trajectory – but only a few inches from Connally's trajectory.

. . .

That is the most important physical evidence of Oswald's intent to shoot Connally. We all assumed that Oswald shot at Kennedy because that's where his bullets hit – but it is likely we moved the target to the bullet holes in our assumptions.

**How Fast Was the Car Going?**

These calculations depend somewhat on the speed of the car. Some investigators have quoted various speeds, an average of 11.1 MPH. But the car speed changed: the average is not useful.

We can calculate a fairly accurate speed graph by using the Zapruder film, but only as the car gets far enough down Elm Street that the angle is measurable.

A simple approach is to choose two points on the car, calculate how far they are apart, and then see how many frames the camera shoots between the first point passing a landmark and the second point passing that same landmark. The entire limo makes good first-last points; it was 254" long. When the entire car is not visible, the edge of the car trunk deck and the upper corner of the windshield frame are two points about 8.5 horizontal feet apart.

Another approach is to measure the car's position for landmarks along the route and then use trigonometry to calculate true distance from apparent camera distance. That's much more complicated, but fortunately, the two methods give similar results.

The driver, Mr. Greer, did a fair job of maintaining about 11.5 MPH up until F275. From his motions in the car, he heard the wounding of Connally and looked back, slowing the car as he twisted around near F300 - the act of twisting to his right towards the back caused his right (accelerator) foot to draw back, causing this slowing. He then took a longer look back just as the fatal shot arrived at F313. After he turned back around to the front, he started accelerating strongly at about F345, dumping Jackie onto the trunk. He slows slightly a second later at F365 to let the Secret Service man and Jackie get safely settled before accelerating to the hospital.

The Nix film (a Keystone Auto-Zoom Model K-810 with 18 frames/second) and Zapruder film car speed estimates are correlated below. The car is also changing its angle with respect to the cameras, so there is a correction by 1/sin(a), where 'a' is the angle of car movement compared to the angle of the camera (the real speed is the hypotenuse, with the side opposite being the measured film "travel." The speed estimates when X-100 is closest to Zapruder (where the sin(a) is about 1 when 'a' is near 90 degrees) by measuring how long it took for a known segment of the limo (for example, the distance from the top of the handhold to the passenger divider) to pass a fixed background point. The estimates are probably accurate to about +-.5 mph near F310 and less accurate at smaller values of sin(a) - i.e., in the earlier and later frames.

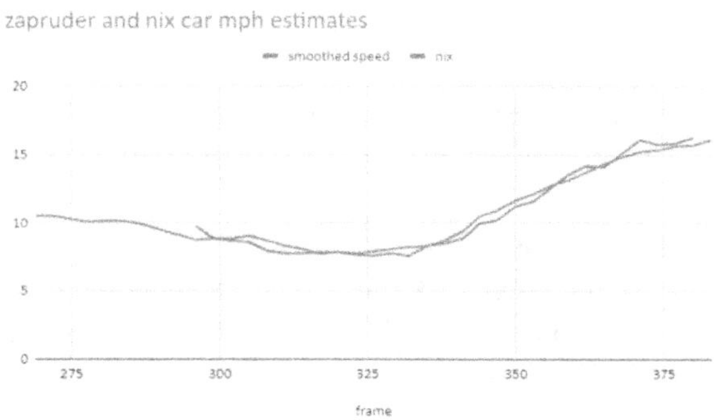


It is inaccurate to measure the speed of the car in the

frames before F270 because the car is far away and is coming too directly towards Zapruder to accurately measure points and positions. The Jack Martin film shows the car passing at about 10.6 mph about 1.5 seconds before the first shot (Martin, 1963); a detailed analysis would likely show that Greer was accelerating towards 11 mph at the key section of the first shot. Greer held the car steady until he noticed the second shot. The early frames (F137 through F147) show a light blue car going into the turn from Houston Street onto Elm Street; that car is going about 9-10 MPH as it turns, as judged by landmarks it passes. It is likely that the JFK limo was going about 10.5 to 11 MPH speed in the F150 area.

The Robert Hughes film does record the limo as it turns from Main Street to Houston Street and then turns onto Elm Street. By measuring the number of frames a specific point on the limo takes to pass a fixed background object, the limo speed can be estimated at about 7.8 mph in turning 90° from Main and about 8 +/- 0.5 mph in turning about 118° onto Elm. Although the turn was eventually greater, by 28°, the turning radius was less because the motorcycles fell back, allowing the limo to cut the corner. The Mark Bell film, taken as the turn completes on Elm, also shows the limo going about 8 mph. It is likely that Greer pushed the speed back towards 11 mph on Elm Street.

### Did Oswald Set Up His Rifle for the Moving Target?

The FBI test-fired Oswald's rifle to determine how rapidly the weapon could be fired and the area within which three shots could be placed. They found that all of the shots were a few inches high and to the right of a 250'-distant target. The FBI agents noted a defect in the cheap 4x18 "BB-gun scope" setup; they could not tell when the scope defect occurred. The scope was side-mounted: it stuck out and could be damaged by dropping the rifle, say, during a hurried escape.

The FBI tester reported that the crosshair ring was out of position and could not have been set "true." The crosshair ring was held by a simple leaf spring, which made adjustments impossible if that ring bumped off its spring. The FBI claimed, "The fact that the crosshairs are set high would actually compensate for any lead and bullet drop which had to be taken. So that, if you aimed with this weapon as it actually was received at the laboratory, it would not be necessary to take any lead whatsoever in order to hit the intended object[sic]. The scope would accomplish the lead for you." However, this high-right setup would only assist on the second and third shots. During the first shot, the car was moving mostly from left to right. It was also moving with much more relative speed: about 9 inches of trajectory compensation would be needed.

Oswald would not have known the geometry of his window shot until a day or two before the shot and would have had to guess the adjustment without test-firing that rifle, without knowing the target's speed or its exact position when he shot. The most likely explanation is that the side-mounted scope was damaged when Oswald dropped the rifle during his flight from the sixth floor.

**Where did the first bullet go?**

Startle analysis concludes that the first bullet hit a specific tree limb in line with Governor Connolly. As suggested by Gerald Posner in *Case Closed*, the bullet lost its copper casing on impact with the tree limb, and the core then ricocheted away down the street. A piece of copper was found on the street - possibly a part of the copper jacket from Oswald's first bullet.

· · ·

At the time of the assassination, a man named James Tague was standing down Main Street only a few feet from the overpass. He was later found to have a small unnoticed wound in his cheek, which he thought happened during the assassination. When he and Dallas Sheriff's detective Buddy Walthers examined the area, they found a place that appeared to be a "very fresh scar" impact on the nearby curb. They surmised that a bullet core had hit the curb, and a shard of concrete had hit Tague. Fortunately, they took pictures.

The red line estimates how the first bullet's lead core (or significant part of the core) deflected off the oak branch (green circle) above Connally. The bullet fragment spun off at subsonic speed and was tumbling – a supersonic fragment would have made considerable noise, but none was reported. It flew 420 feet to the curb in about .6 sec, dropping perhaps 6 feet due to gravity. That core fragment (weighing up to 130 grains) likely hit the top curved section of the curb (the blue circle), still going over 600-800 ft/sec - plenty of chipping power. See WC CE251 for a picture. The Warren Report states that metal from the scar was "spectrographically determined to be essentially lead with a trace of antimony [consistent with Oswald's other bullets]. The mark on the curb could have originated from the lead core of a bullet."

Given all evidence, it is likely that part of the first bullet core hit that curb and sent a small concrete splinter into Tague's cheek. The bullet fragment(s) might have taken a lower trajectory, as there was also a mark on the street, in line with the above tree and the curb near Tague. If so, the bullet would not have to deflect as much and would have started from the branch a degree or two below horizontal.

A witness, Virgie Mae Rackley, testified to the FBI that she saw "something bounce from the roadway between her and the Presidential automobile." (FBI Questions Rachley, 1963) It is possible that it was the stripped copper cladding of that first bullet, as suggested in "A Technical Investigation Pertaining to the First Shot Fired in the JFK Assassination" (DeRonja and Holland, 2016). DeRonja and Holland investigated whether the first bullet hit the overhanging traffic signal or its arm; their theory was critiqued by several: no trace of impact on the traffic light mast arm, a ballistically impossible ricochet angle, and too complex a subsequent trajectory (Vaughn and Myers, 2016).

## Is a 26° Bullet Tree Limb Deflection Possible?

In theory, the branch impact separated the copper jacket from the soft lead bullet core. The core deflection of the first shot would have to have been near 26°: the trajectory from the rifle was about 29° from horizontal, the oak branch was about 16 feet above the road, the curb was 420 feet away from the branch, and the curb was not quite in line with the shot. At 3° declination, it would have lost over 12 feet plus tumbling drag and gravity, enough to use up the 16-foot initial height plus about four feet of terrain ground slope to get down to curb impact level. If it were slower, it would need a slightly higher angle of deflection to reach the curb.

Hunters and others have done research on bullets traveling through twigs and branches. Deflection is normal, but for modern bullets it is much less than 26°, usually measured at less than 5° degrees.

The Haig team did a reconstruction of a Carcano bullet hitting a live oak branch. Unfortunately, they set up their target branches so that the bullet struck the side of a small branch at over 60° (Haag L. A., 2013). At that angle, the bullet deflected very little because it was in contact with the oak for a very short distance. Oswald's bullet was deflected much more than this.

The startle analysis indicates a specific branch was hit:

. . .

This branch is growing away from Oswald. It is growing in a slightly downward direction. Photos from the sideshow that lower tip branches of all these oak trees angle down (droop) at about 10°. A rifle bullet would do serious damage to an oak branch if it hit at Haig's 60°, but if it struck at a small angle, less than 20°, its spin could peel off its jacket and ricochet the lead core far downrange with a 26° deflection.

On the left, we see the oak tree bushing out over the street in a telephoto shot. On the right, we see the shooting angle and the suspected angle of the ricochet towards Tague.

## The Skipping Stone Theory of Bullet Deflection

A bullet can ricochet from a 10° down-sloping branch, coming in at 19° (with respect to the branch) and exiting at 13° with respect to the branch (-3° with respect to the horizon):

The bullet hit at a shallow angle, less than 19°, spinning about once each 8.5" of travel.

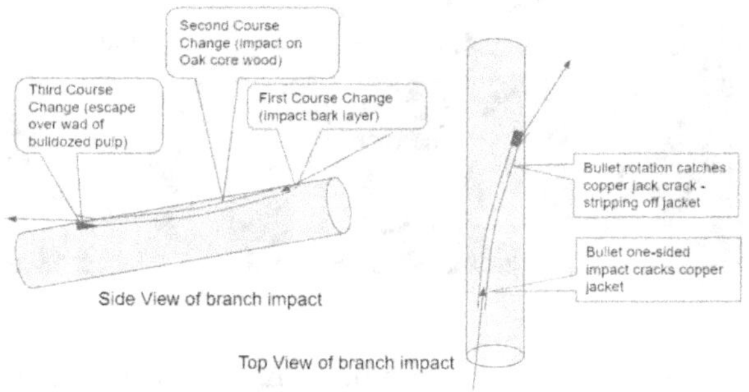


It will dig through the softer bark to about a quarter-inch depth and then hit the hard oak core, which deflects gradually until it bounces back up away from the branch. The stress of the initial impact fractured the copper cladding. The bullet's spin stripped the copper jacket once the crack caught in the wood. A bow wave of shredded wood built up ahead of the bullet core and completed its exit deflection at about horizontal and a few degrees to its right.

This bounce effect has been studied and verified as possible, though not yet with Oswald's exact setup. Tests showed that for a hardwood, the angle of impact (in this case about 19°) could generate an EVEN LARGER angle of ricochet departure (in experiments of oak-hardness wood, the departure angle is about 25°). Netherlands testing was done with 7.65 mm Browning FMJ pistol ammunition, which is lighter (71 versus 160 grain) and slower (918 vs. 2100 ft/sec) than Oswald's bullet; further, the test was done on furniture wood rather than a raw oak branch. These differences could tend to reduce the ricochet angle for Oswald – a departure angle of 7° is certainly possible, if not expected. A 7° departure angle would have Oswald's first shot "core" departing at about 3° below horizontal, or about what we would expect to carry across to the curb on Main St.

The test bullets lost about 70% of their speed – in Oswald's case the bullet core would likely exit at about 600-800 ft/sec and would tumble. See (L. Koene, 2013).

It is possible that one of the casing fragments (CE 569) is from the stripped casing of the first shot. The other had human organic material on it, according to advanced DNA testing done in 2000.

The author tested a Carcano using bullets of the same general batch as Oswald's. We did not try to hit a small oak branch as our setup was not steady enough to reproduce exact targeting; instead, we used an oak log. We did reproduce a large-angle ricochet but did not see a stripped casing in our four test shots. A better setup is needed to hit a fresh-barked small oak branch.

**Conclusion: Oswald Panicked and Hit the Branch**

Oswald was likely very nervous about shooting. It would mean the end of his life as he knew it since he had no escape plan - he had left his assets with his wife. He was looking through a narrow-field cheap, 4x18, dim telescopic sight:

*Abraham Zapruder Film © The Sixth Floor Museum at Dealey Plaza*

With the car accelerating slightly to over 11 mph, it swept under him at about 16 to 17.6 feet per second. His scope had a very narrow field of view of less than 10 feet; the X-100 limo was 6.5 feet wide. When the oak tree flashed into his view, Oswald would have less than 0.3 sec to decide and shoot. A third of a second is just about the reaction time we would expect if he was ready but hesitating to pull the trigger. By the time he saw the branches and shot, that branch would be about dead-center in his scope. The combination of car speed and Oswald's reaction time made it much more likely that Oswald's shot bounced off that lone sloping oak branch.

What at first might seem a "one-in-a-million" shot was actually likely.

**14**

# DETAILS OF THE SECOND SHOT

Oswald fired his second shot about 7 frames before Zapruder's camera jumps: F220 – about 3.87 seconds after his first shot (See **Chapter 12: Startle Analysis Findings**). Zapruder had moved his eye away from the camera to see what was going on; the camera moved by slower 0.12 seconds "arm/hand startle" rather than the faster 0.05 seconds "head duck."

Oswald's shot at F220 travelled 188 feet in about 0.09 seconds (1.7 frames). It struck President Kennedy at about F222.

The above detail from the Warren Commission's CE875 album shows the short FBI car at about F225. At F222, the car was about 3 feet nearer, at 11 mph. The red circle shows where Connally sat, a few inches to the right and down in his jump seat. The blue circle shows where JFK would be sitting, slightly higher, slightly to the right, and a little more than two feet behind Connally in the X-100 limo. Had Kennedy not been there, Oswald would have hit Connally. Kennedy's head mostly blocked JBC, although through Oswald's telescopic sight, Connally might have seemed more exposed. Still, only a driven egomaniac would try to shoot Connally at this point. Oswald was a driven egomaniac.

The Warren Commission concluded that a single bullet probably traversed the soft tissue of JFK's lower neck, yawed slightly and entered Connally's back a bit sideways, traversed his chest wall along his fifth rib, broke 4 inches of that rib with contact and cavitation, exited raggedly from his chest below his right nipple, then broke his wrist bones at about 500-800 feet/second, and finally buried itself a little way into Connally's thigh at about 200 feet/second. The bullet hit no bone directly until the wrist, by which time it was slowed to below its fragmentation energy. Many aspects of this bullet's behavior have been examined: its abrasion collar, stable flight, shored exit, yawing, bone breaking without deformation and low-speed thigh puncture are assessed scientifically (Sturdivan, 2005).

In the Zapruder film, two men are seen clapping at F223. At F227, the nearer man ends his clapping and is looking down past the car towards the TSBD, although the President is approaching his nearest point. That is an intentional movement. The sound from F219-220 reached that man in about four frames at F223-4. His clap stops four frames (about .22 seconds) later. He is clearly looking back at the TSBD by that frame.

## Parkland Doctors Guess an Entry Wound

Several Doctors at Parkland Hospital saw what they believed was an "entry wound" in the front of Kennedy's throat.

The Parkland doctors did not have a chance to get the full story and make a careful analysis. They hurried to undress the dying President, cutting off his shirt and tie as he lay on his back.  His shirt, before and after:

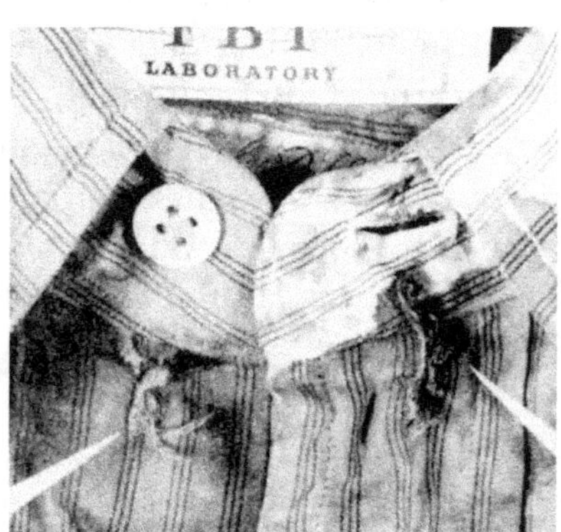

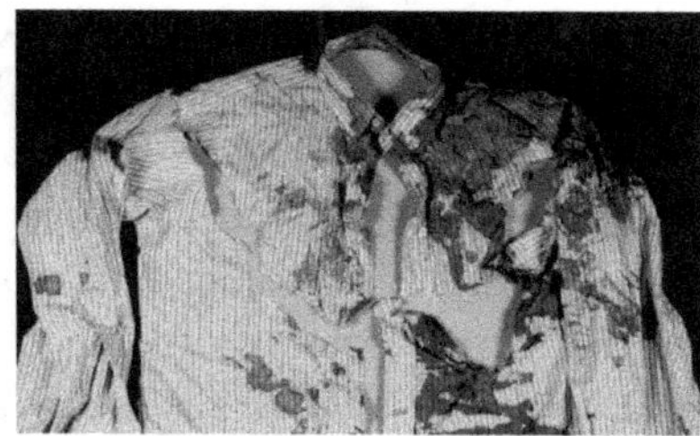

At left, the President, before his death, is wearing that pin-striped shirt and narrow tie. The bullet came out his throat a half inch under and just to the right of his top button. Still travelling at high speed, probably 1800 feet/second, the bullet pushed out a cone of fascia, skin, and four layers of quality shirt, all against the resisting tie. The cone pushed the tie knot slightly to the left. The bullet burst through the stretched fascia and skin, ripping small holes in this quality material and nicked his tie knot, all in less than one-thousandth of a second. This shirt was tight and strong, and the bullet was still oriented straight enough that the cloth held the underlying skin and kept it from blowing out in a typical exit wound.

Four Parkland doctors reported a small round, slightly ragged wound just right of JFK's tie/trachea, below his Adam's apple/larynx. They did not have time to carefully clean the oozing blood from that wound to determine if it had the telltale inward bruise ring of a true entrance wound or the ragged outward fraying of an exit wound. They noted his larynx was slightly displaced to his left, which usually suggests a collapsed lung: they inserted chest tubes but did not find any deflated lung. Dr. Perry then did a tracheostomy right through the neck wound and saw a small, ragged laceration of the trachea on the anterior lateral right side of the trachea. He justified destroying the neck wound, saying the oral intubation wasn't effective, so he needed to get into the trachea ASAP. Later, he was second-guessed, as he could have gone in just below the wound. Only doctors Carrico, Jenkins, and Jones saw the neck wound before Perry's incision, and none of them made any examination of it. In the immediate press interviews, they said that based on its small size, "it appeared to be an entrance wound." Perry described the wound directly as "an entrance wound" but then clarified, saying they were "not able to determine if the neck wound was an entrance or exit wound. ...no work was done to find the trajectory." Some press people published it as "an entrance wound," but the Parkland doctors complained they were misquoted or that they were not careful in their speaking. None of the Parkland doctors had experience with military full-metal-jacket wounds. Perry heard of Oswald's ammunition and later explained that "a full jacketed bullet without deformation passing through the skin would leave a similar wound for an exit and entrance wound."

Tests were made of the entrance and exit through flesh that did not hit bone. The entrance and exit holes were relatively similar –but the exit area was not shored by shirt and tie and the multiple tough fascia layers of the human lower neck. The exits, given shored conditions, would have been even closer to entrance wounds in appearance (Sturdivan, 2005).

Kennedy came into the hospital with a thready, weakening pulse that stopped while they were doing CPR. Had they looked at his back, they would have seen the small entrance wound next to his spine between his last cervical vertebra (C7) and his first thoracic vertebra (T1). They could have looked at his suit coat and shirt to see how the fibers bent, verifying the bullet's direction. The holes in JFK's suit and shirt backs do match Oswald's 6.5 mm bullet but are 3 or 4 inches lower than the autopsy wound: JFK's shirt and suit coat were bunched up due to his constant waving while seated, as proven by other photos and the George Jeffries film.

Many questions would likely have been answered had Jackie and LBJ let JFK's autopsy proceed in Parkland. The President would have been flexible, not in rigor mortis. The throat incision would still have been small since both back and throat wounds would have been known immediately, and clothes would have been available. The autopsy would have had knowledge of JFK's and JBC's seat positions. The nature of Connally's wounds, done by a single bullet, slowed to a yaw and originating from about JFK's throat location, and the single bullet itself would have led to a single bullet fact rather than a "theory."

Unfortunately, the Parkland doctors did not exchange observations with the autopsy team in Bethesda. The autopsy team never knew that there had been a wound where the tracheostomy incision had been, nor did they know the circumstances of the shooting, nor were the President's clothes available. The Parkland doctors never saw the back entrance wound, had no time to probe, and were sidelined for the autopsy by Mrs. Kennedy's wishes. Each group tried to make sense of the wounds from their limited knowledge.

**Autopsy of the Neck Area Wound**

The autopsy team's Dr. Hume did not do a good job with the neck wound. By the time of the autopsy, rigor mortis had frozen JFK's muscles into a coffin-laying posture. His fascia, muscles, and spine were substantially shifted, so the bullet path holes were no longer aligned. Dr. Hume tried to probe the path but was blocked after only an inch or so; Humes speculated out loud that the bullet might have only gone in a little and had fallen out in Parkland during heart massage attempts – two FBI agents reported this speculation as fact, confusing things forever after. Humes asked for full-body X-rays to look for a bullet that might have remained in the President's body. Humes then removed most of JFK's internal organs and sliced them up to look for the bullet path down through the lungs, or even lower – but found nothing below the top ribs; he found only bruising of the top of Kennedy's right lung and strap muscles – consistent with a low-cavitation (slender) bullet passing just above. Humes gave up trying to probe the path - he was afraid his probe would just create a new path.

About this time, word came that a bullet had been found on a stretcher at Parkland. Humes repeated his guess that the stretcher bullet had fallen out of JFK's back wound. The

Kennedys (through Doctor Burkley) were pressing Humes to avoid cutting up JFK any more than was necessary, so with the stretcher bullet explanation, Humes decided to avoid opening JFK's neck to trace the actual neck bullet path.

When Humes wrote out his draft autopsy report, he apparently included his shallow back wound theory. His autopsy drawing was inaccurate; he later excused himself because he thought photos would be available. His measurements proved useless later: he measured from the shoulder blade and skull prominences that depend grossly on posture. In the morning, he called Parkland to discuss his findings, and especially the anomalous shallow back wound, with Clark and Perry. That's when Humes found out about the hidden neck wound. Humes rewrote his final autopsy report to include his new bullet track and then burned his old report - he later said "because it had JFK's blood on it," but eventually, he just said he "forgot" why he burned it. His bad measurements and the two FBI notes reporting his "shallow bullet theory" remained to confuse the issue; the autopsy viewers were sworn to secrecy for 15 years (National Secrets Act) and could not challenge this misinformation even if they knew of it.


The Warren Commission eventually agreed that the path of the bullet matched the angle of the bullet if fired by Oswald, given JFK's position in the car, but a better autopsy would have eliminated many wrong ideas then and now.

While Humes did make important errors during the autopsy, he did end up making an important contribution. When Warren Commission member Arlen Specter interrogated him about the neck wound, Humes realized that the bullet had transited Kennedy's neck without hitting anything solid; that meant it would not be deformed and would still be going fatally fast. Where did it go? He and Specter then concluded that the neck bullet hit Connally, though Humes could not believe it had stayed so pristine. Commission leader Earl Warren protected the Kennedys by refusing to let anyone see the admittedly horrifying JFK autopsy images for fear of leaks to the public. Humes had to testify without access to his own autopsy images; worse, he brought rough sketches based on his own imperfect memories, which further confused the wound understanding. While Humes testified that having the real images would not change his testimony, he and Warren did not realize that the rest of the World would want to make their own judgements.

## Kennedy Starts to React in F222

President Kennedy reacts to the F221-2 bullet by immediately grasping towards his throat.

Doctor John Lattimer et al. proposed that his position is a kind of "Thorburn position": arms raised to ear level, elbows bent towards the throat, fist clenched (John Lattimer M. D., 1977). The Thorburn position was describing a person who had suffered spine damage four days earlier, not someone who just had a traumatic injury. Much argument has resulted on whether this neural effect could apply to JFK.

In fact, Kennedy's response is quite different. The Thorburn effect was due to permanent injury to a few spinal nerves. Kennedy's arm motions were due to temporary high pressure that squeezed all the nerve bodies, causing their axon roots to act as though the pressure-induced ion imbalance was the nerve body "firing."

When this bullet passed through Kennedy's neck, it slowed from 2000 feet/second to about 1800 feet/second. About 20% of its kinetic energy transferred into Kennedy's neck tissue - basically to accelerate tissue out of its way. That tissue kept moving away from the bullet's path even after the bullet had passed, thus making a widening, temporary chasm called cavitation, much as a rock dropped into a pond makes a temporary hole in the water. That cavitation compressed the tissue around it with violence.

The HSCA analyzed Kennedy's back wound. They concluded that JFK was leaning forward at about 14°; the bullet arrived at about 21° downward, but the street slope of 3° and JFK's "forward lean" (explained below) reduced that to an almost flat path through his neck, relative to his vertebrae. JFK's upper torso was turned about 5° to his right; the bullet was moving about 9° right to left relative to the car; thus, the bullet traversed his neck at about 13-14° towards his left, emerging through his tight collar, to hit John Connally.

Many critics have rightly questioned this "forward head lean." The HSCA estimate, shown in the black and white below, has JFK looking down – as though tying his shoe, some quipped. But we know JFK's head was likely erect at F 222, as shown in many motorcade photos. But seated in the car, JFK was showing "forward head posture," as many of us do when we are relaxed, tired, or perhaps beginning to lean towards Jackie when she complained about a motorcycle backfire (Jackie had turned from her leftward scowl to her right and was leaning towards JFK in a speaking attitude by F 222). JFK's neck was sloped forward, but he bent his head to appear erect, for example, in the (Croft) picture at about F160, shown below:

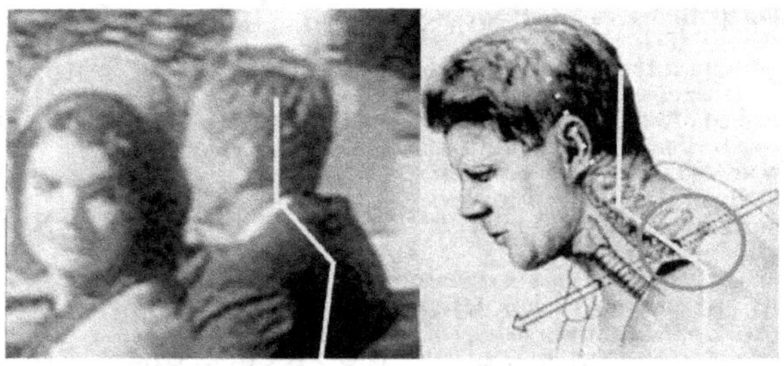

That spinal bend positioned JFK's neck area so that Oswald's bullet appeared to take an almost flat path (the HSCA thought "upward") when JFK was laid out on the autopsy table.

Some critics have asserted that a bullet could not get through the spinal processes without hitting bone and concluded that the bullet had to enter much farther from the spine. Not so.

That forward head posture caused an upper spinal bend that opened a gap between the transverse processes of JFK's C7 and T1 vertebrae so that Oswald's bullet drilled between the C7 and T1 processes very close to his spinal column. Its cavitation was minimized by bone and muscle. It bruised the top of his right lung (without hitting it) and passed over his right first rib. It missed his right carotid and jugular, nicked his esophagus, and tore through the extreme right side of his trachea (the trachea probably deflected it 2-3° to the right). The bullet crossed above his collarbone/breastbone. Its undamaged round nose pushed out a cone of JFK's fascia, skin and two layers of double-cloth dress shirt. That growing cone shoved his tie a little left. The bullet burst through the cone, fraying the right side of the tie knot and yawing on towards Connally.

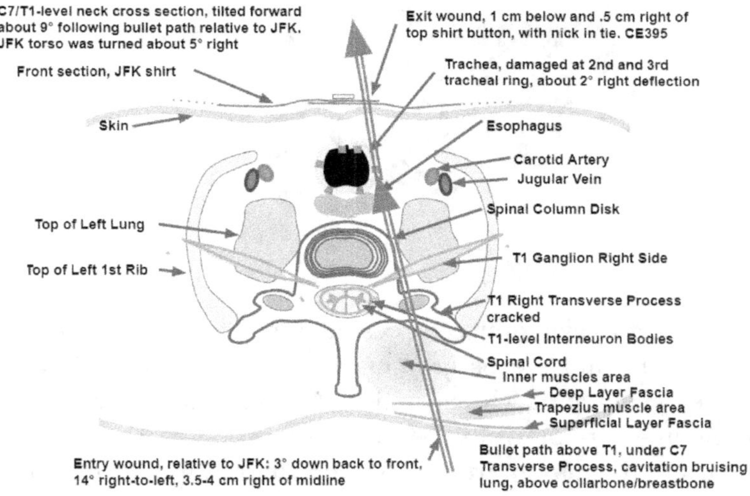


The above schematic illustrates how the bullet passed between the right transverse processes of Kennedy's C7 and T1 vertebrae. Realignment from posture change, the three tough fascia layers, and the post-wound rigor mortis and swelling made probing this wound very difficult for the unpracticed autopsy doctors. Civilian pathologists, accustomed to the accuracy demanded in trial evidence, would have dissected, but these three men chose to avoid taking time and further damaging JFK's body. For that reason, there remains debate about this bullet's path. The autopsy doctors had no Zapruder film to understand how the President was seated, leaning slightly forward, with his right arm raised, causing his shoulder to be higher than during the autopsy. Further, a small X-ray anomaly on C6 was taken as a bullet fragment by some. The presence of a fracture in the T1 transverse process suggests that the bullet passed near enough to have its cavitation pressure do that damage (Wilson, 1992).

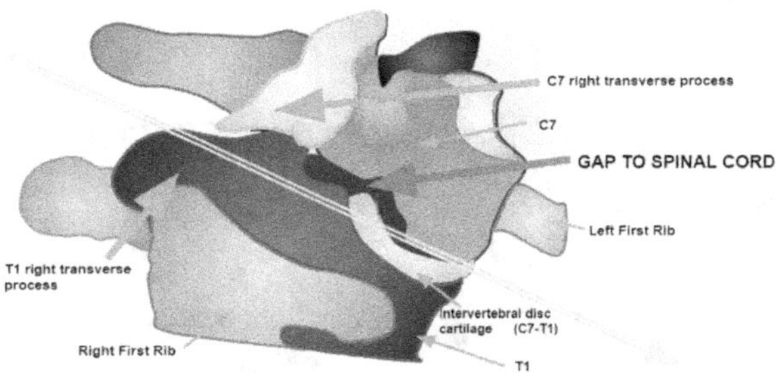


The bullet's cavitation compressed the nerve bodies in the spinal cord and plexus grey matter in the C7-T1 gap - very suddenly and hard. The cavitation was magnified by the shape of the intervertebral gap. Severe compression of nerve bodies can cause them to squirt out their ion content, mimicking what happens when they "fire" – in this case, a very strong "fire" that did not recover quickly via ion transport. The result, in Kennedy's case, was that the nerve bodies in the T1 brachial plexus all behaved as though they had fired - very hard and without immediate recovery. Poor autopsy records muddled the question. An embalmer, sworn to secrecy for decades, eventually did confirm the "near C7" location of the back entry wound (Fallstrom, 2013).

The nerve bodies in the T1 brachial plexus are the interneurons and reflex neurons whose axons control the shoulders, arms, hands, and some muscles in the chest and back. The bullet cavitation compression caused **every** nerve body in the T1 brachial plexus to fire immediately. As a result, **every** T1-controlled muscle in JFK's back, chest, shoulders, arms and hands went into "maximum contraction" and stayed there while the squeezed nerve bodies tried to recover their ionic content.

This compression firing is **not** a reflex: it is an artificial action that begins as soon as the nerve axons conduct from T1 to muscle. There was no "reflex delay"; no sensory nerve sent some reflex-worthy message up to the spine. Therefore, the response time between bullet axillary nerve passage and muscle movement is the path time for axon to muscle contraction - less than 0.05 seconds. That is why JFK is already reacting in arms and hands by Zapruder frame F224.

## Kennedy's Elbows-raised Position

Kennedy's odd position after F222 resulted when all the T1 ganglia muscle nerves in the shoulder and arm fire to their maximum at the same time. The muscles of the shoulders, arms and hands are paired - one for each direction of motion around each joint.

For example, the deltoid muscle moves the arm up towards the sky under control of the axillary nerve; it's paired with the Latissimus dorsi (lat) muscle under control of the thoracodorsal nerve. When both axillary and thoracodorsal nerves fire to their "max," their muscles will fight to raise (deltoid) or lower (lat) the arm around the shoulder joint. Depending on their natural strength and depending on their current length (muscles weaken as they shorten), the stronger muscle "wins." With arms down, the long deltoid is typically stronger, so the arm moves up. As the arm moves up, the deltoid muscle shortens, making its pull weaker. Meanwhile, the paired lat muscle lengthens - which makes its pull stronger. Eventually, the weakening deltoid's power just balances the lat's increasing power, and the two muscles pull at balance. The target shoulder joint, pulled at maximum force by both muscles, becomes "locked" in place at that balance point. The balance point of a typical male's shoulder is reached when his elbow is raised to almost ear level. Because deltoid and lat muscles are relatively similar in strength, Kennedy's left arm took all of .6 seconds to reach ear-high equilibrium as these strong muscles fought each other.

The same equilibrium was reached with his other arm and hand muscles: his elbow was pulled in by the bicep until the lengthening triceps balances - for a typical man, that will be about a 30° angle towards the shoulder. His rotator cuff muscles balanced when his arm was a little forward from pointing straight out. His wrists balanced at about neutral. His fingers closed, almost to fists, because finger-closing muscles are much stronger than opening muscles.

By F225, less than 0.15 seconds, Kennedy's hand clench and elbow-bend positions were already established. His left arm rose slowly but was fully up by F235. Throughout, his arm muscles were at maximum pull, as rock-hard as they could get. Neither Kennedy nor anyone else could have moved his arms and hands without breaking something.

Because the bullet traversed his neck on his right side, the nerve bodies in his right T1 motor ganglion were more rapidly and severely compressed. That caused his right arm and hand to move more quickly and more powerfully into the clench-equilibrium position. His right arm was also already raised, so it had less distance to cover. His right hand reached its high at about F243 at about his eye level, then gradually sinking to about 45° by F312, as Jackie pulled him over towards her.

Famed "1984" author George Orwell recorded a similar wound he received in the Spanish Civil War. The standard Spanish military 7mm Mauser round was similar in shape, speed, and weight to the Carcano 6.5mm round. Orwell's wound was also clean through the middle of his neck, missing bones and key blood vessels. Orwell reported a painless, violent "electric shock" and a false flash of light; his right arm was completely paralyzed as his legs crumpled and his head banged on earth. Orwell felt no pain for many minutes until he was loaded on a stretcher; then, his right arm came somewhat back to life. He had pain, dysfunction and numbness in his right hand and arm for years. His wound was so unusual that doctors trooped by to admire a man who survived a through-and-through neck wound.

**Kennedy's Rigid Back**

The compression and firing of the T1 brachial plexus would also have some effects on his back posture. There is some variation in how back muscles are controlled, and so it would be difficult to predict the effects of sudden muscle contractions in Kennedy's back. However, it is possible that suddenly rigid muscles did contribute to a rigid posture.

There are some afferent (sensory) nerve bodies in the T1 brachial plexus. Upon compression and firing, these might have caused some immediate and strong sensations, such as sudden phantom pain that would appear to be coming from arms or hands. Sudden pain might cause further tensing of muscles, those not controlled by the T1 nerves. As Lattimer points out, the sudden compression might have damaged Kennedy's spinal cord and, therefore, interrupted communications to and from his brain from below his T1. It is also true that afferent stimuli are filtered for attention; often, strong pain sensations are ignored at first, as with George Orwell.

Some have suggested that Kennedy's "back brace" kept him upright. He was wearing a light canvas lower abdominal belt (without actual stays), held in place by an elastic wrap (McHugh, 1967). It is unlikely that this light support would have inhibited any determined effort on Kennedy's part.

In any case, the Zapruder film shows that Kennedy sat rigid for a couple of seconds. Then his arms started to relax a little, and he started to bend forward a little. He was pulled to his left by his concerned wife, but his posture changed only a little until the impact of the third shot.


## Connally and the Single Bullet

Connally did not recall hearing the shot that hit him. That bullet had travelled twice as fast as the sound of the rifle. The shot sound reached Connally a tenth of a second after his body was being severely injured. It is not surprising that he would not attend to the sound.

After drilling relatively cleanly through Kennedy's neck, the second shot yawed slightly and hit somewhat sideways in Connally's back. It punched a neat .8 x 1.5 cm near-elliptic hole through Connally's coat, shirt, and skin just behind his right armpit. Slowed to about 1500 feet per second, it careened tangentially, grazing the outside rib cage on about the same 20° downward path as Connally's 5th rib at that point. Its tangential contact and cavitation burst 4 inches of his 5th rib, sending shards that punctured his right lung. It exited through muscle and skin, creating a 5 cm round "sucking" exit wound just under his right nipple. Slowed still further to perhaps 6-800 fps, it went sideways through Connally's wrist, fracturing his radius (a bullet can break bone as low as 213 fps). At about 2-400 fps, it ended up embedded slightly in his thigh (a bullet can penetrate the skin at 163 fps) (Belkin, 1979). A copper-jacketed bullet like the Carcano can resist deformation at 1000 fps in a "head-on" bone impact but is less resistant to a sideways blow; the sideways impact with wrist bone did flatten it a little. The bullet (CE399) was found on Connally's stretcher with only a flattening, as though it had been hit hard broadside with a hammer. CE399 was only a bit bent and flattened. A little lead core squeezed out its back, leaving a few grains in Connally's wrist and probably his thigh.

Connally's torso was turned about 30° to his right. Connally was tall, at about 6' 2", and would have had trouble sitting in the small folding jump seats. He seems to be sitting sideways at about 20° when seen from above, but there is no proof. His sideways seating would explain why his left leg was in the path of CE399.

At F222, he was turning back to face the front (after having turned towards the TSBD after the shot sound at F151). His torso was leaning slightly to his right. The bullet, after leaving Kennedy's neck at about a 21° angle down, traversed Connally's torso at about a 20° downward path. The 3° down-slope of Elm Street was cancelled by Connally's very slight rightward tilt (towards the oncoming bullet). Connally's right arm was raised; the rightward twist of his shoulders drew his right shoulder blade out of the path of the bullet.

Connally's testimony in the Warren Report is compatible with this "single bullet theory" when neurons are considered. He reported being hit in the back by the second shot. A tenth of a second after F222, his dramatic F224 right-shoulder dip is a result of the bullet's impact on his chest and the solar plexus diaphragm reflex contraction. The slowing bullet reached his thigh in less than .01 seconds. On its way, it triggered the reflexive flip-up of Connally's right wrist and hat. JBC continued his leftward turn– his brain had not had time to understand the impact. It took about .25 to .35 seconds for Connally to realize, consciously, that he had been hit. He was looking straight ahead when he understood the impact. In later testimony, he never realized this delay between strike and realization: he honestly insisted he'd been hit about F230 when he first faced forward. Once aware that he'd been hit, Connally again turned right, doubling over, and looked back towards Kennedy. About F285, he "fell" backwards into his wife's lap. He believed that his wife pulled him over. His wife did not remember whether she pulled him or not. The Z film does not show pulling, suggesting that Connally ducked backwards himself.

The surgeons who operated on Connally said they thought all the wounds in Connally had been from the progress of one bullet, slowing as it damaged him. They also thought that Connally was probably hit by a yawed bullet because of the elliptical entry wound, though they suggested that a tangential strike could produce an elliptic entry. A yawed bullet is much more likely because it would be consistent with the path through Connally; a tangential strike would continue left (lung) or right (arm):

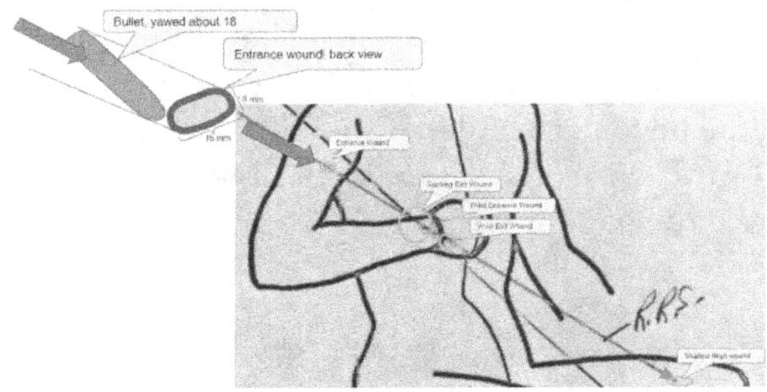

While the surgeons agreed that a single bullet had done the damage, they did not think that CE399 could have been that bullet. That bullet was barely damaged. The surgeons did have experience with gunshots, but less experience with Carcano stable bullets that had slowed through one person and then hit enough soft tissue in Connally to slow it to below its crumple speed. The bullet is "digitally available" as CE 399 at the National Institute of Standards and Technology. It is marked with incomplete chain-of-custody initials.

The fact that CE399 was slowed and yawed argues strongly for the single bullet theory. President Kennedy was the only "slowing agent" close to the bullet's path. Traversing Kennedy's neck provided exactly the slowing demonstrated.

Many have modeled the single bullet trajectory. One group came very close to getting exactly the CE 399 result with a physical test (Anatomical Surrogates Technology, 2009). Their bullet was slightly left of where CE 399 hit Connally and, therefore, did not follow the same exact path: it hit two ribs solidly instead of hitting the 5th rib tangentially. It was close enough to the real event to leave a slightly more damaged bullet that had too little speed left to enter their thigh model.

. . .

The idea that CE399 was conspirator-planted begs the question: why deposit a slightly flattened bullet as a fake? What possible explanation would there be for a slightly damaged bullet, other than having been slowed through the soft tissue of at least two bodies? It is hard to produce a CE 399, other than as the single bullet trajectory!

Other investigators have done a complete job of explaining CE399, the orientation of the two men in the car, the angle of the car, and so forth. For example, see "Case Closed" by Gerald Posner and the work by Failure Analysis Associates, which Posner cites. Forensic scientists Michael Haag and Luke Haag modelled the bullet for the PBS documentary *Cold Case JFK* in 2013, showing it going through 3 feet of pine without deformation as well as demonstrating the single bullet theory.

A small amount of lead was missing from the back of CE399 – and a similar amount in small grains was found in Connally's right wrist. It is virtually impossible to make partially flattened CE399, extrude a small amount of its lead core, then stick those grains or equivalent bits in Connally's wrist.

In F224, Connolly's right lapel flips up. Posner says that this establishes the exact moment when the bullet passes out of Connally's chest. The transit time through Kennedy's neck and Connally's torso would be less than 0.01 second, much less than the .055 of a single frame; further, the lapel is not in the bullet's direct path. Latimer modelled the lapel flip and concluded it took about one-tenth of a second – about two frames (John Latimer, 1996). It is more likely that the slowing bullet's cavitation pressurized a cavitation "bubble" between Connally's ribs and his skin; the deflation of that pressurized bubble forced the lapel out rather than the bullet itself. The bullet thus traversed Connally at F222, and the cavitation ejecta followed .05-.1 seconds later to move the lapel just after F223; that lapel was therefore "out" at F224.

The bullet's impact caused a "solar plexus" reaction in Connally at F224. The solar plexus (celiac plexus) is a complex of radiating autonomic nerves and ganglia wrapping the front of the aorta, just below the diaphragm. The bullet's pressure wave triggered a solar plexus diaphragm spasm, like a punch in his stomach. The sudden tightening of his right-side diaphragm caused him to hunch over slightly, particularly on the side of the impact: his right shoulder went down. His mouth opened to exit air impelled by the sudden solar plexus reflex diaphragm contraction. The timing of this response is consistent with an F222 arrival time.

## Kennedy or Connally as Target

The freeway sign blocked the critical instant when the bullet hit Kennedy and Connally – only Connally is visible. We do not know exactly how Kennedy was sitting, nor do we know exactly how Connally was crammed into the jump seat.

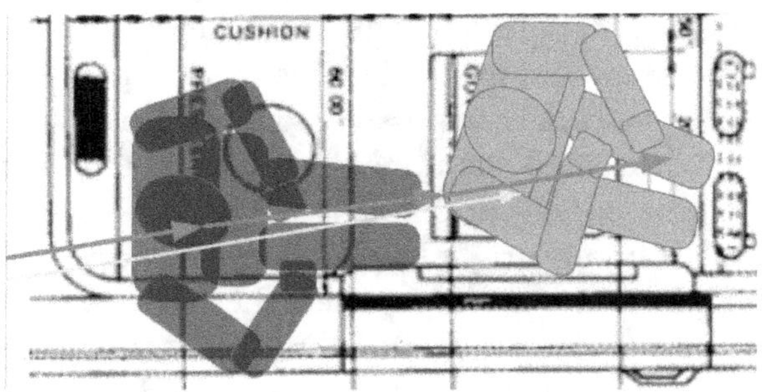

. . .

Since Oswald was unschooled in hitting moving targets, he may have thought his bullet would travel so much faster than the car that he would not need to lead his target by much. The yellow arrows above show what Oswald might have aimed at, assuming he ignored the car's slow travel. He was 11° to the right of and 22° above the car at that point. The orange arrow shows where such a bullet would hit were it fired along the yellow line, based on the car's actual 11.5-12 mph (it moved 17-19.5"). The red arrows show where the bullet actually went.

Oswald was blocked by the tree until about F210, so he had only a half second to acquire, aim and fire (at about F220). That is a very short time for someone unpracticed in moving targets. Connally was only partially exposed. We really cannot say much about Oswald's intended target. If he shot at Connally, he was certainly unconcerned with the life of the brown-headed man sitting behind Connally; if so, he must not have realized that it was Kennedy.


**Witnesses React**

At F255, AP photographer Altgens took his famed "picture #6," looking towards the TSBD at the limo with a stricken JFK. His photograph shows 21 faces enough so we can see which way they are looking, including 10 of the faces in the middle of the Croft photo. In Altgens' photo, taken about 5.7 seconds after the first shot (at F150) and 1.8 seconds after the second shot (at F222), we can see how people actually reacted to the shots:

9 Faces remain fixed on JFK.

9 Faces have looked to their left, generally towards the TSBD and Oswald's nest.

3 Faces are looking behind the limo, perhaps at the Secret Service car.

0 Faces are looking to their right, towards either the knoll or the overpass.

In the background of the Croft photo, we can see the end of the stone wall, and thus, we can locate where these people were standing. The people on the right (east) end of Croft's picture were roughly 120' from the Sniper's nest on the sixth floor. The people at the west end of Altgens' #6 picture are about 120' from the nearest point of the grassy knoll fence. Overall, these people cover a middle area between the knoll and the nest.

The Altgens photo provides unequivocal evidence that people who noticed the first two shots thought they came from somewhere behind the limo – regardless of what they later remembered or thought they remembered after discussions with others.

**15**

# DETAILS OF THE THIRD SHOT

Almost everyone agrees that a shot hit Kennedy's head fatally at between F312 and F313. We have shown that Zapruder startled at F318. See **Chapter 12: Startle Analysis Findings.**

Our startle analysis shows that the jump in Zapruder's camera is consistent with a third shot at F311 from Oswald's Nest, 268 feet away in the TSBD – about 4.97 seconds after his second shot and 8.84 seconds after his first shot.

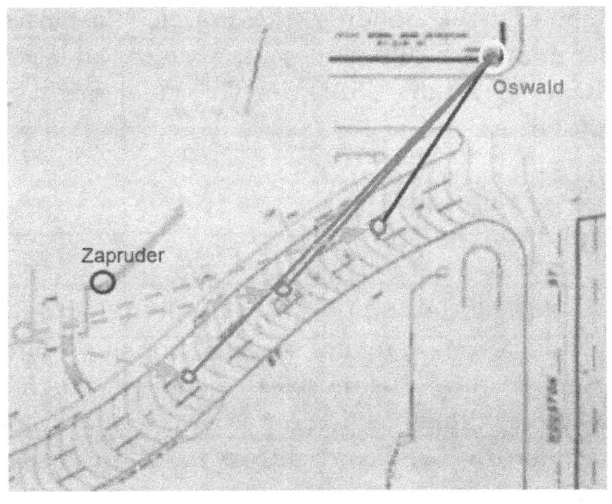

It would not be consistent with a shot coming from the "grassy knoll," for example. Suppose a shooter shot from behind the fence on the grassy knoll, say from the green circle in the above. Zapruder was standing only 50 feet away. Sound energy dissipates with the square of the distance: Oswald's rifle blast went from about 150 dB (or more) down to about 121 dB over the 264 unobstructed feet to Zapruder. A similar blast from the grassy knoll would be at 133 dB when it reached Zapruder. The Nix film shows the grassy knoll but does not show any shooter there (Itek, 1967). Any muzzle blast of a "knoll" shot arriving at F 313 would reach Zapruder in less than one frame. His startle reflex would be about 3.5 frames sooner - so his camera would jump 3.5 frames sooner. Zapruder's camera jumps do not line up at all with any loud noise coming from the grassy knoll.

Given the bullet speed and the speed of sound, we can calculate that the shots are entirely consistent with Oswald's TSBD window. Since there were two shots with known impact points and times and their distance from Zapruder, we can narrow the shooter's likely position to less than one hundred feet of that Sniper's Nest. Although that includes the highest floor of the Dal-Tex building, the muzzle blast from there would have a very different echo pattern and would be screened enough by the TSBD that Zapruder might not hear enough to startle.

## In the Car Before the Third Shot

The third shot effects are critically dependent on the motions of JFK, Jackie, and JBC. As a result of the second shot, Kennedy was forced into an upright, arms-up, elbows-out, initially rigid posture. His muscles, operating at high tension, locked his arms in that position for at least several seconds. He did manage to turn his face slightly towards Jackie right after he was hit.

Mrs. Kennedy (Jackie) may have been unaware of the

meaning of the first muzzle blast at F151, but she stopped smiling and turned to look to her left; then she turned to her right. At the impact of the second bullet in F221-2, her head points at the crowd through the gap behind Connally, her head turned about 70° to her right – she is probably looking at JFK. By F223, Kennedy's left elbow lifts quickly, in a strange way. Jackie can still see JFK's face.

Starting a half-second after JFK was hit in the neck/back and 4.6 seconds after Oswald's first trigger pull:

F233 (4.6 seconds after F149): Jackie turned more towards JFK, who began turning his head slightly in her direction. Her right hand rose towards JFK's raised left elbow at 0.7 seconds after the impact, consistent with an intentional response.

F244 (5.2 seconds after F149): Jackie's right hand grabbed JFK's left arm, which was by then up to Jackie's mouth level. Jackie's hand, in a white glove, shows just on the end of JFK's left elbow. Two frames later, Kennedy starts leaning towards Jackie: Jackie was pulling on his arm with her right hand.

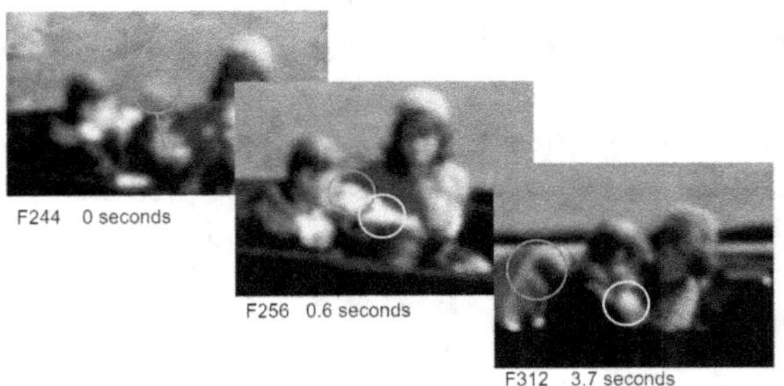


*Abraham Zapruder Film © The Sixth Floor Museum at Dealey Plaza*

F256 (5.8 seconds after F149): Jackie's left hand also grabs JFK's left forearm; Jackie now has both her hands on JFK's rigid left arm.

. . .

F260 (6.1 seconds after F149): Jackie starts a small motion towards JFK: she is pulling harder on his arm and, therefore, pulling herself towards JFK. Her force is moving JFK's elbow down and back, twisting him towards her. She is pulling hard enough down that she rises slightly up out of her seat (we measure her body position compared to the car frame). During this motion, it appears that Jackie shifts her attention to Governor Connally briefly; judging from his mouth, he may have said something, maybe "no, no, no!"

The car slows down a bit from this point, probably due to the driver raising his foot off the gas as he twists right to take a quick glance towards the rear of the car. A half second later, the car is down almost to 9 mph; it will reach its slowest about a second after this, at about 8 mph in F320.

F270 (6.6 seconds after F149): Jackie has hesitated in pulling on JFK, as she shifts to look at Connally for a second. JFK has stopped any further lean towards Jackie.

F290 (7.7 seconds after F149): Jackie turns her gaze back to JFK and starts to lean towards JFK's face. JFK also starts to lean more towards Jackie, so she probably is again pulling on his elbow with her two hands. She has not moved either hand – they are both on JFK's left elbow. We can see that Jackie has pushed hard enough to raise her right elbow up off the seat back.

## Oswald's Third Shot

Oswald probably spent a half-second to a second to look at his second shot results. He would see that Connally was definitely hit as he bends down his right shoulder to an unnatural position and bends forward towards the right side of the car (he is sitting at about 20° to his right because of his long legs in the little seat).

Oswald probably lost sight of his target while he rechambered and re-aimed his rifle. After less than three seconds (about F270), he would again have his target in his crosshairs. If his target was JFK, he would have seen JFK's head presented high and virtually still – Oswald would likely have shot right then. But if his target was Connally, Oswald would have seen a more complex target motion.

At F270, Connally had turned in his seat to look back at JFK – and coincidentally towards Oswald. About one-half second later, Connally appears to start ducking backwards towards his wife. The Zapruder camera has drifted enough that we have only a partial view into the car, but by F292 we can see that the sun is striking Connally's nose; by F300, his upper lip is getting sunshine. His head was clearly tilted so that the back of his head was approaching his wife. His wife has leaned towards Connally and probably touches him about F307. Connally levered himself backward from an F282 0° upright to an F307 30° lean backwards towards his wife; he covered that 30° arc in about 25 frames, or about 1.37 seconds. The top of his head traveled about 18" at a speed of about 1 mph.

Connally's bottom remained in the same spot in his jump seat. In F307, it seems that Connally's body and face are aligned, meaning that his entire torso is now angled backward from the jump seat towards his wife. His head, by F307, is at the same level as his leaning wife's. Connally appears to pause his backward motion, probably because he hit his wife's hands; he then starts turning his head towards the car front. At F313, he is still held up by his wife.

Oswald watched this motion through his telescopic sight for about 2 seconds. At F270, Connally's head is clear and looking back in Oswald's direction. But then, within a second, Connally turns and rotates backwards and might soon be hidden by the back passenger (JFK). If Oswald were shooting at Connally, he had to take a shot at a moving head in a moving car.

By the time Oswald decided to shoot, at about F304, Connally's head would be about half visible above and to the right of Kennedy. He had paused his backward move, stuck on his wife's hands or shoulder. Kennedy had leaned to his left and forward, putting his head at about the middle of the rear bench seat. Oswald pulled the trigger at F309; the fatal bullet arrived between F312 and F313, just clipping the top right of JFK's skull. Just 2 inches to the right or an inch higher, and it would have grazed JFK and killed JBC.

Only an expert shooter, or a man driven by ego and a fear of failing another assassination (General Walker's), would take such a difficult shot – if he knew JFK was just to the left of his target. As with the second shot, there is no reason to assert that Oswald was aiming at Kennedy rather than Connally, given that the two men were only inches apart in trajectory. Because Zapruder was filming down into the car, it foreshortens the distances. Consider the Moreman photo for a different perspective .2 seconds later (between F315 and F316).

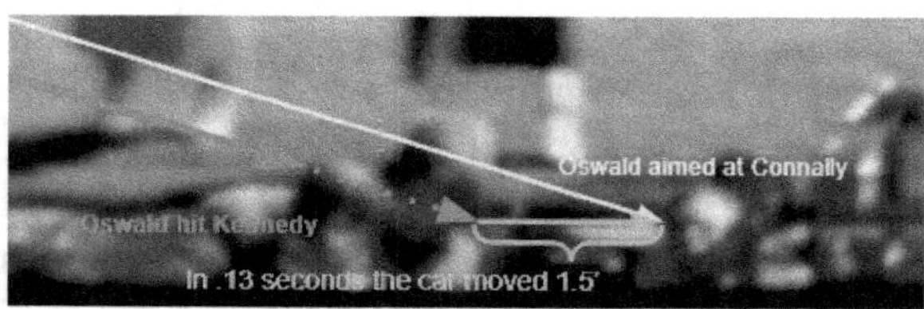


*Abraham Zapruder Film © The Sixth Floor Museum at*
*Dealey Plaza*

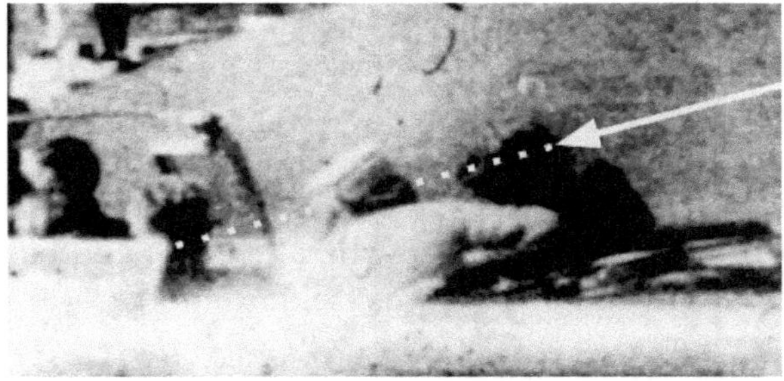

We have no evidence that Oswald had practiced shooting at moving targets. He did not know his muzzle velocity, nor the speed of the limo, nor the drop in the street, nor the wind, nor the distance to Connally. He certainly could not have figured out a proper lead for his shot.

It is possible that Oswald just assumed that his bullets travelled so fast that he could ignore the "slow" motion of the car. If Oswald shot without considering the car's ~8 mph motion at F310, then the car would travel about 1.5 feet during the bullet's ~0.13-second flight feet. That put the very top of Kennedy's head into the path of the third bullet – as shown above.

**After F313**

JFK was dead immediately.

F313 (9 seconds after F149): JFK's exploding head is driven slightly (about 2 inches) forward towards Jackie's face. Jackie still had both her hands on JFK's left arm, but she had moved her own head and torso around in front of JFK's face.

F323 (9.5 seconds after F149): A half-second later, Jackie begins to recoil back as JFK falls "back and to the left." Her right hand, maybe both, let go of JFK's arm. For a heartbreaking moment, Jackie looked down into her husband's destroyed skull. Her surprise turned to visceral shock. She spent close to a second looking down at Kennedy's shattered head and its surreal flesh-colored piece of skull that is thrust at her face in F327. By about

F325, Connally has gotten his shoulder around in front of his wife, and he starts rotating down to her lap.

F329 (9.8 seconds after F149): Jackie has put her right hand on the back of her husband's neck while her left hand has moved to his chest. JFK slumped towards Jackie's lap.

F332 (10 seconds after F149): Jackie has begun to stand up, instinctively distancing herself from her husband's bloodied or instinctively looking for help. The Secret Service agent, Clint Hill, who was specifically responsible for her, had been the only agent to leave the follow car and was now grabbing onto the trunk-mounted handrail. Jackie had likely seen him by F347, as she has turned her head about a third of the way in his direction.

F338 (10.3 seconds after F149): Agent Greer, the limousine's driver, had slowed the car to about 8 mph as he was looking at the wounded men behind him, first in his rearview, and then by turning around. At F338, he stepped hard on the gas and the powerful car accelerated. By F340, Connally's head was in his wife's lap and she was lying over his torso.

F345 (10.7 seconds after F149): The sudden car acceleration rocked Jackie back onto her right elbow, which was on the seat back. At F350, she has dropped JFK and is trying to catch herself with her left hand on the seat back.

F358 (11.4 seconds after F149): Her right hand gripped the seat top, but her torso was already being carried towards the trunk by the continuing acceleration. Her gloved right hand had no leverage to stop her from sliding out onto the polished, down-sloping trunk.

. . .

F364 (11.7 seconds after F149): Jackie tried to catch herself by straight-arming her right hand on the trunk. Her gloved hand slides about a foot on the polished trunk as Greer continues accelerating. Agent Hill can't jump onto the accelerating car and will soon be left dragging behind it if Greer continues.

F370 (12.1 seconds after F149): Agent Greer has seen Jackie's (or Hill's) predicament in his rearview mirror and lifts his foot off the gas. The car had jumped from 8 mph to 15 mph in about 1.8 seconds; it continued to accelerate for another half second, up to 16 mph. Fortunately, Jackie's thighs hit the seat back and stopped her slide. Agent Hill took advantage of the drop in acceleration to get his foot on the rear platform. In the Zapruder film, the zoom foreshortened the image so it looks like Jackie is approaching Agent Hill, but in reality, she has slid towards the middle of the trunk – as is visible in other photos.

F380 (12.6 seconds after F149): Jackie has lowered her body and moved her right arm to help brace herself. Jackie begins to push herself back into the car. Agent Hill has gotten both feet onto the car. By F384, Jackie was able to move her right hand back up the trunk.

F390 (13.2 seconds after F149): Agent Hill touched Jackie's right elbow with his fingertips, but she is already on her way back into her seat. Jackie is looking down to where JFK has slumped partway into her seat. She had to squeeze around his head to sit down, which she does by F419 (14.7 seconds after F149) or before. Agent Hill had let go of her elbow sometime before that. Jackie will now cradle JFK's head for the agonizing drive to the hospital.

. . .

Agent Hill's recollection of helping Jackie back into her seat is wishful thinking (Hill, 2013). By F408, Agent Hill was climbing onto the trunk to shield its passengers. There is no evidence of skull or brain matter on that trunk (the reflections claimed by some in the Nix film are not present in the much closer and clearer Zapruder film) and no evidence that Jackie grabbed anything in the less than two seconds she slid about on that trunk.

**Tracing Two Head Movements**

When the fatal shot hits at F313, 4.97 seconds after the second shot, Jackie is bending low towards JFK's face. She is still gripping JFK's elbow with both hands and is probably still leaning her body weight on that elbow. She is very likely still pulling Kennedy back and to his left so that she can get her face near his. JFK's arms have come down a little from his F235 position, but they are likely still near rigid since Jackie's hands have not changed their position much. JFK has tilted about 22° towards Jackie; JFK is leaning forward about 10° and has twisted about 20° to his left – all mostly because of Jackie's pulling.

In the next frames, Kennedy does fall back and to his left. His head and torso rotated about 10 inches back and 10 inches left in .5 seconds – about 14 inches total. (A free-fall object would move over 40 inches in .5 seconds.) This relatively slow fall to his left has been misinterpreted in many conspiracy theories.

Kennedy's head motion has been analyzed carefully for the period of the third shot. It is straightforward to use the Zapruder film, frame by frame, to measure where Kennedy's head is relative to the back seat. His head distance is shown in blue below; a higher value means his head is farther from the seat (more forward). Jackie's head is shown in red, in the vertical direction relative to the far side of the car; likewise, a higher number means her head is farther from the seat (more forward). The Y axis is about equal to inches.

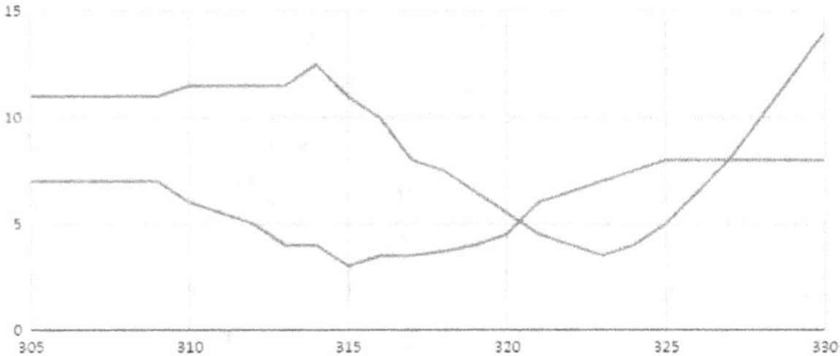

In the frames just before F308, Jackie had been distracted by Connally shouting - we see that her head was steady. Then, at F309, we see her head ducking, and at the same time, JFK moves slightly forward – likely because the car suddenly slowed and all the passengers moved forward. Jackie was pulling herself around to look in Kennedy's face, using her two arms on JFK's elbow for leverage. When she pulled to move to the right, she was exerting a force that would move Kennedy to the left as soon as his lower body tensed muscles relaxed, as they would at F314. This was first noticed in 1967 (Itek Corporation, 1967) but has been inexplicably ignored.

At F313, JFK's head snaps forward by 2.2 inches (Myers, 2007); this is the result of the bullet's impact, transferring almost its entire energy as it traversed the president's head. See (Costella, 2021) for a concise demonstration. The NIH paper "Gunshot-wound dynamics model for John F. Kennedy assassination" (Nalli, 2018) observed that the snap forward was first noted in the 1960s. Only the President's head moves in this way. Experts have measured the film more accurately and concluded that his head moved forward 2.1–2.3 inches (Thompson, Six Seconds in Dallas, 1967). Various formal investigations eventually concluded that Oswald shot a bullet that struck high on the back of Kennedy's cranium. Its impact left a "beveled" oval hole of about 6.5mm by 15mm. The bullet was shattered by the strength of the convex skull bone. Bullet and skull fragments fanned out, liquifying brain with a cavitation pressure "cone." The cavitation pressure then pushed out the upper right mid-skull from the inside, creating an extensive hole and cracks (Nalli, 2018).

There is still considerable disagreement about where Oswald's third bullet struck. The autopsy reported it as "slightly above the EOP' (External Occipital Protuberance). The Bethesda team expected that photographs would provide the exact locations and so gave only rough estimates. Unfortunately, the Kennedy family and their supporters refused to allow the use of the actual photos and x-rays, and even when made available, the photos and x-rays were not up to modern standards and remain hard to read. Kennedy's head was thoroughly shattered on its right side and had been bumped enough that its shattered bones were loosened. The Bethesda doctors did not shave his head, nor did they take extreme care when cutting open his skull and removing his brain. As a result, the entry hole was never accurately located. Later ballistics tests were done with direct rather than tangential strikes. The forensic reviews that followed the Warren Commission all agreed that the entry wound was on sloping skull, about 3.5-4 inches higher than the EOP, in the president's cowlick, and the wound was amongst fractured, shifted bone pieces. The autopsy doctors should have done a better job of piecing it together. Not everyone agrees (Sturdivan, 2005).

## A Grim Impact

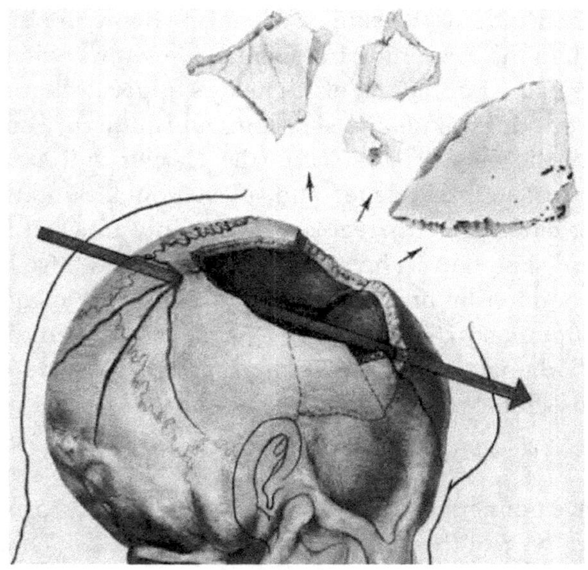

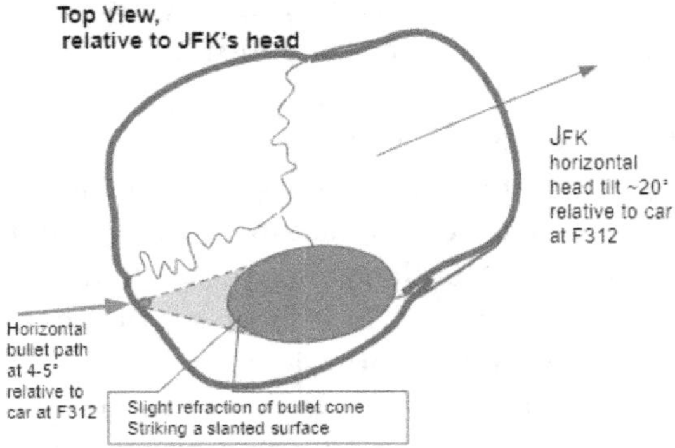


Kennedy's head was tilted left and down relative to the car. Relative to the oncoming bullet, his head was tilted down almost the same as the bullet's angle, and to the left by about 20° (Select Committee on Assassinations, 1979). The bullet fragment cone did not push out Kennedy's skull - cavitation energy did that. The bullet's energy went about 12% in skull penetration, 64% in cavitation, and the remaining 25% was expended in hitting the inside of the skull. Cavitation energy, about 3 times greater than the remaining fragment exit energy, created a very strong pressure bubble under Kennedy's upper right mid-skull, pushing out dura, skull and skin until all ruptured. Some skull pieces tore loose from the scalp (the Harper and Delta fragments); most stayed attached and splayed out around the hole. The mist cloud exited irregularly where not blocked by skull pieces and skull flaps. The result was a big hole above his right ear, surrounded by broken scalp, skull, and gore (Nalli, 2018). The documentary *JFK: Inside the Target Car* recreated the shots, the skull damage, and the splatter patterns, all supporting Oswald as shooter (Discovery Channel, 2008).

Some have pointed out that Kennedy's head would have to have absorbed "90% of the kinetic energy" of the bullet (Thompson, Last Second in Dallas, 2021). The claim that Kennedy's head moved forward by 2.2 inches is misleading: JFK's head was struck off-center and rotated so that the back of his head appeared to move 2.2 inches; by rotating, his head presented slightly more in its narrower (side-to-side) dimension causing the boundary of background-head to appear to move a little less than the head actually moved.

Once again, an immediate autopsy in Dallas would likely have been more effective. His fractured head would not have to endure long travel to Maryland and stresses that relocated skull pieces. The autopsy would have been carried out by people who were experienced in forensic autopsies for court-appropriate evidence, who would have been careful to identify the scalp and skull entry wounds before the head was further damaged. The pressure to observe the Kennedy family's wishes would have been diminished.

## Why Did a Single Metal-Jacketed Bullet Do So Much Damage?

The lead doctor at Parkland gave a nearly correct analysis an hour after Kennedy's death. Dr. Clark said, "I felt it was a tangential wound ... striking obliquely, not squarely or head on... If it strikes the skull at an angle, it must then penetrate much more bone than normal, therefore, is likely to shed more energy, striking the brain a more powerful blow. Secondly, striking the bone in this manner may cause pieces of the bone to be blown into the brain and thus act as secondary missiles. Finally, the bullet itself may be deformed and deflected so that it would go through or penetrate parts of the brain, not in the usual direct line it was proceeding."

The most important error in understanding JFK's head wound was in locating the bullet entry. The Parkland doctors did no investigation. The autopsy doctors apparently did not first locate the scalp entry hole, which would have been relatively unequivocal (and is what is estimated in this book and at the last minute by WC's Ford and by later forensics). The autopsy doctors apparently first examined the skull, taking JFK's brain out to look at his skull from the inside to find the entry wound. They did not understand that JFK's skull had shattered and that the entry hole area was broken into pieces that had shifted during JFK's transit to their autopsy table. The autopsy team located the entry near the external occipital protuberance, but their position was based on skull pieces that had shifted within Kennedy's skull. This misunderstanding caused much later questions and conspiracy thinking: an entry at the external occipital protuberance could not reasonably cause the damage given a shot from Oswald (Aguilar, 2014).

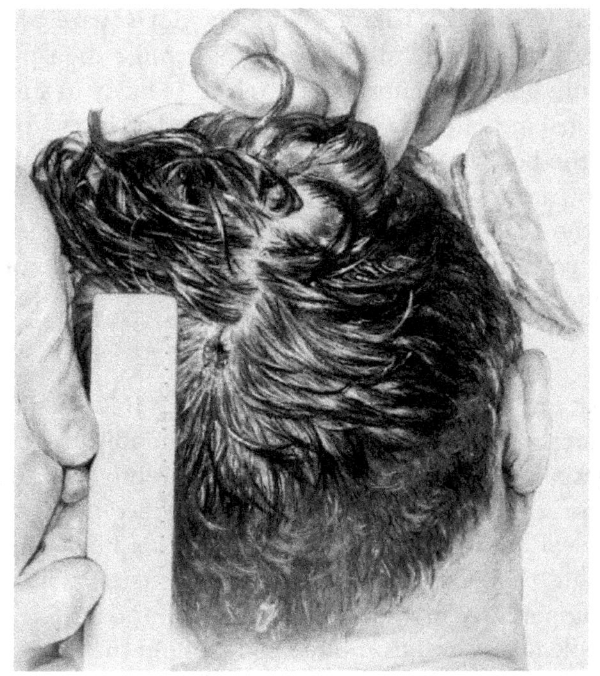

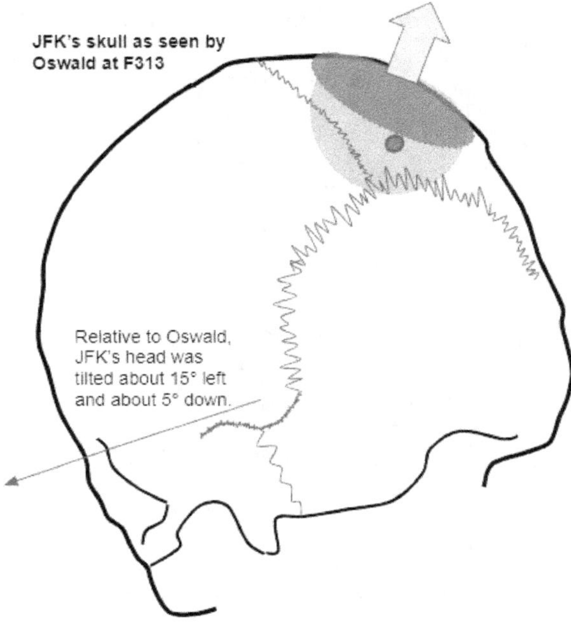


The headshot analyses were further misled by a failure to look at Kennedy's head position at F313. Alverez, Nalli and his critics did not emphasize the actual geometry of the fatal strike. Kennedy was leaning to his left. His head was tilted further left and down. The bullet arrived right of midline and traversed slightly "upward" and to the right relative to Kennedy's head. If we look at Kennedy's head from the direction of bullet travel, the bullet has struck quite off-center both laterally, horizontally and vertically. It was, as Dr. Clark suggested, a tangential strike. It was an inch from glancing off. It was within another half inch of missing entirely.

The one man who got the best understanding of JFK's head wound was the mortician who reassembled it for embalming. He said he was "under orders from the White House Secret Service and the FBI not to discuss any factors relating to points of entry of bullets, nor their effects." He did say informally that "the President had been shot at the very top of the cranium and approximately the 7th vertebrae." He died in 1976 and never testified under oath.

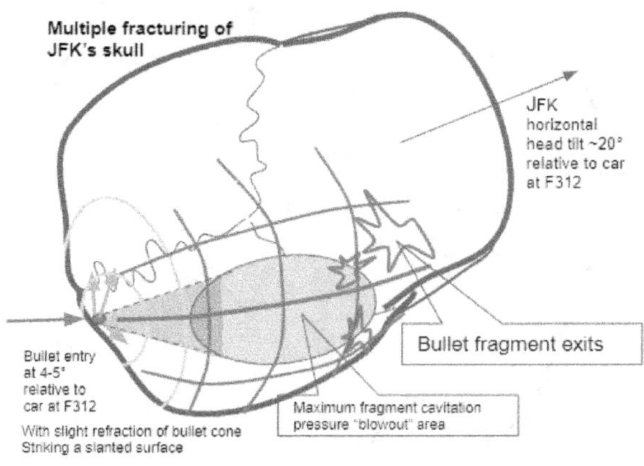


*(This is theoretic, to show fracture types.)*

The bullet did not traverse the skull in the middle and did not distribute its cavitation equally; rather, its energy focused just under the right top skull. That created a wound that was more towards the back of the skull than the front. Kennedy's head had extensive fracturing from four causes:

1) From the Zapruder film, the bullet struck Kennedy's angled skull at between 45 degrees and 65 degrees - JFK's head was tilted forward about 27° and to his left at about 18° (Myers, 2007). The bullet hit on the sloping surface of his skull, punching a 15mm by 6mm elliptical hole. The high stability and jacket of the bullet did reduce the initial transfer of energy to the skull at the entrance so that the skull was punctured relatively cleanly at the first entry, with radial cracks extending slightly from the arrival end of the ellipse. (shown in **green**)

. . .

2) The force of the impact caused an indention in the skull at the impact sight, like a bowling ball dropped on a trampoline. The stretch in and then rebound out caused characteristic circular fracture arcs centered around the impact site. Because of the relatively small energy transfer on impact, this trampoline fracturing was minimal and lost in more extensive tile fractures that followed. (in **tan**)

3) The high angle of impact fractured the bullet. The effect of hitting a solid skull at a sharp angle caused a high bending stress on the bullet, causing it to fragment as it bent.

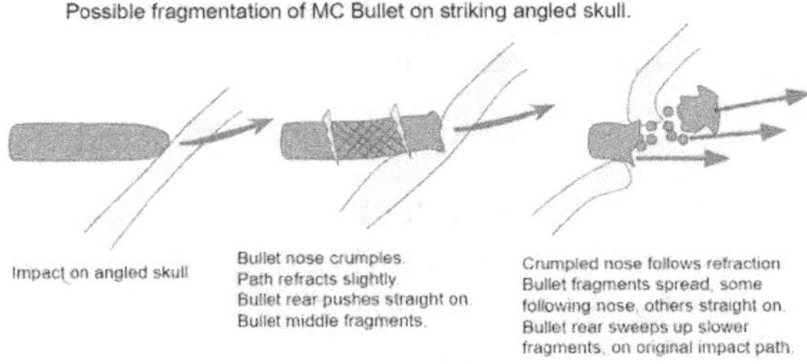


The bullet became a cone of bullet and bone fragments. That cone of fragments transferred about 65% of the bullet's total energy into a compression cavitation. That cavitation hit the top inside right of JFK's skull almost immediately since it was only 1–3 cm away from the cone center path. That pressure burst out the top right of JFK's skull, causing "tile fractures" around the maximum cavitation point above JFK's right ear. It was this cavitation wave, traveling at right angles to the bullet/fragmentation path, that caused the massive upward/forward blowout seen in the Z film. (in **blue**) The tile fracturing was widespread because Kennedy's scalp and dura resisted the expansion, spreading the explosive force all the way back to the entry area.

. . .

4) Most of the tiny remaining bullet fragments in the cone embedded inside the skull as it was being blown apart; the few bigger pieces punched out through fissures or made small holes above JFK's right eye. Examiners found outward beveling, showing three separate exit points. Three pieces ended up in the car – two hit and cracked the windshield. (in **purple**)

It was this complex multi-cause cracking that shattered JFK's head. His scalp was mostly still in one piece, hiding the extensive interior damage. His scalp had only a 5mm entrance hole near his cowlick (the true entry wound position); a large hole above his right ear to the center line, where the cavitation pressure had pushed some skull "tiles" out; a few small holes where bullet fragments had exited in JFK's scalp above his right eye.

Why did the impact of the bullet traversing Kennedy's neck do little apparent damage, while this head impact caused extreme destruction of Kennedy's head? The key: the high-angled impact on hard skull. That impact caused shattering stress on the long, thin bullet, which converted the jacketed bullet into an expanding mass of bullet and bone fragments, to act very much like a fragmenting bullet. That fragment "cloud" transferred a high percentage of the bullet's kinetic energy into cavitation. Another key to the skull destruction was the fragment cloud's path, which was so near to the upper right skull. A final key was the resistance of the scalp and dura, spreading the cracking force throughout the upper right skull. Its cavitation pushed out the skull from the inside, fracturing it and tearing the scalp in a stellate pattern. The result was that the cavitation fracture pattern included most of Kennedy's upper right skull in tile fractures, a few lost skull pieces and dislocated bone. It was not surprising that an entry and exit wound could not be easily identified, as both were lost in cavitation fractures and still covered by mostly intact scalp.

.   .   .

A modern analysis of various bullet trajectory damage was done by scientists in Germany. Their extensive study agrees with the rougher analysis in this book. They modeled scalp, skull, spinal fluid, and brain, even the folding of the bullet casing. They tested not only the wound as presented here but also the effects of the autopsy doctors' "near EOP" claim in 1964 and many proposed conspiracy claims. They showed that impacts at the low EOP, or from grassy knoll shots, or south knoll shots, or the "Storm Drain" all failed to produce damage as seen in JFK: these tests "rigorously exclude hypotheses in regard to shot origins other than the TSBD." Only a bullet from Oswald's area would produce the observed "specific skull bone crack formation" and bullet fragmentation (Then, Nelson, Vogl, & Roth, 2022).

A lot of the upper right side of JFK's head was fractured skull held in a rough place by the scalp, except where the cavitation blowout hole had taken out a lot of upper right bone. A large piece of skull, attached to the scalp, hung down, showing as an orangish area over Kennedy's right ear. It would have been impossible to pick up JFK's head without some skull pieces moving about. When Kennedy was laid out on his back, the wound shreds drained to the back of his hair; at Parkland, the wound was not examined, leading some to see the gore-soaked back of his head as an exit wound.

The autopsy doctors also had trouble with JFK's head wound. The Parkland staff had apparently recognized that the extensive skull damage had made Kennedy's skull very fragile: they wrapped his head separately to stabilize it. When the autopsy doctors began their work, they (unfortunately) unwrapped the skull before they did skull X-rays: some fragments shifted. When the autopsy moved on to his head, they did not first find the exact scalp entrance wound, for example, by shaving the entrance area. They apparently did some sawing to remove his brain, causing further shifting. Then, when they searched for an entrance wound, they peeled the scalp back from his skull, again causing shifting. At one point, they complained that at least one piece of Kennedy's skull fell out onto the table. All this shifting of shattered skull made the entry point very hard to pinpoint. The doctors concluded a low, occipital strike on looking at fragments, but they did not reassemble the skull. The scalp preserved the real hole, but not all people reported the scalp location, not realizing that scalp stretch was less of a problem than bone fragmentation.

The Warren Commission did request ballistics testing but did not test tangential strikes on a head with scalp and dura. Their results were eventually reported by (Olivier and Dziemian, 1965). Later, forensic experts, for example, the HSCA investigation, realized that the fragments, when reassembled, put the bullet entry about 10 cm higher. They did not do new testing with the higher entry point. The tests also did not use the Zapruder film to precisely position the tilt of Kennedy's skull for a tangential impact. Even so, they verified that the jacketed bullet could fragment on entry and cause massive damage.

A few witnesses remembered hearing two final shots, very close together. Sadly, there were two sources of a loud bang: one was the sound of Oswald's muzzle blast, but about .1 second earlier was another "bang" – the horrible sound of a skull exploding and of bullet fragments hitting the windshield and its frame. While Kellerman and others were very familiar with gunshot noise, it is unlikely that any had experience with the explosion of a skull at close range. Thus, Kellerman's "flurry" of two shots was likely the skull and fragment impacts followed closely by the arrival of the gun sound.

## Why Did Parkland Doctors Describe a Posterior Head Wound

Parkland doctors were responsible for trying to save JFK, not for tracing bullet paths. They did not investigate JFK's wounds, but they did see damage.

All saw JFK on his back, with massive gore in his thick hair and, particularly, draining towards the back of his head. They saw massive head damage, with shredded brain tissue and extensive vascular damage that allowed immediate leakage of any new fluids they pumped in. There was also skull, brain and scalp that had been displaced and hung outside his head towards the back. Some could look down into JFK's partially-emptied skull. Without an actual examination, the Parkland doctors reported a somewhat consistent view of a massive head wound towards the back of JFK's head:

Dr. Carrico: "a [fist-sized] defect in the posterior skull, the occipital region." Only Carrico did any examination of JFK's back, by running his hands up from brace at belly-button level to neck; he said he did not feel any important wounds there.

Dr. Perry: "a large avulsive [stuff coming out] wound of the right parietal occipital area."

Dr. McClelland: "right posterior portion of the skull had been extremely blasted ... the parietal bone was protruded up through the scalp and seemed to be fractured almost along its right posterior half, as well as some of the occipital bone being fractured in its lateral half." In his post-op report, McClelland called it "a wound to the left temple" but did not describe an entrance wound there nor why he thought that, nor why he said "left temple" when no one reported damage to the left temple.

Dr. Clark: "large, gaping wound in the right posterior part."

Dr. Jenkins: "a great laceration of the right side of his head (temporal and occipital)."

. . .

None of the Parkland doctors said anything definite about how many bullets might have hit JFK's head. They described the damage as very extensive. The senior doctor, Dr. Clark, said he had inspected the fatal head wound: "it could be an exit wound, but I felt it was a tangential wound ... striking obliquely, not squarely or head on." Dr. Clark "could not say how many bullets hit or where they came from." Dr. Clark described the "likely tangential" head wound in the 2:30 pm press conference and consistently thereafter. His speculation of a tangential head wound turned out to be exactly as eventually asserted by the HSCA years later, but it did not get the media play of doctors who suggested a front entry.

Another puzzle: one frontal X-ray shows a bright white 6.5 mm circle that looks like a bullet cross-section, but no such anomaly shows in other X-rays. This white circle looks like a guessed entry-point marker added during x-ray copying, at about where JFK's scalp had its entry hole. Critics jumped on this 6.5 mm spot as a clumsy attempt to fake evidence. No one ever admitted adding that mark, but that may be because those X-rays were not made public for decades (Aguilar, 2014).

The Parkland doctors all agreed with the updated autopsy findings in the Warren Report: two bullets, from behind and slightly above. They all said that they never said (or intended to say) anything that was not consistent with the eventual autopsy findings, though they admitted they might have been misleading in their words to the press. Note that seven of the Parkland medical doctors and med students later changed their story, saying they believed JFK had been shot from the front because it looked like the throat wound was an entrance and the head wound was an exit; these people feared "unusual witness deaths" and declined for thirty years to help find "the truth."

. . .

Meanwhile, the Kennedy family demanded that they be given all the autopsy info, preventing independent verification of the medical data. It was grudgingly released to later investigators. Some may think that now they've released it all, and maybe they have. After all, there is the "Assassination Records Act," but that act applies only to information that was in government hands. It specifically exempts the Kennedy family.

Even in 2023, there may be missing information withheld by defensive people making personal decisions, be they Kennedys or Doctors or many others.

**Why Back and to the Left**

After the initial impact at F312-13 and a 2" forward head lurch, JFK's head and torso moved rather smoothly back and to his left from F314 to F321, moving about 10 inches back in one-third of a second. Authors have variously described Kennedy as being "slammed," "catapulted," "snapped," "thrown," or even "rocketed" back and to the left "violently," "massively," "dramatically." In reality, the highest speed Kennedy's head achieved in the back-left direction was about 1.45 mph, and it was relatively steady until impeded by Jackie and the seat. The 2.2" motion forward, at F 313, showed that Oswald's bullet had accelerated JFK's head at about 2.3 mph, considerably quicker than the back-and-left fall. Later (F327), Jackie pulled JFK's broken head to her at about 6 mph. It would be more accurate to say that Kennedy toppled sideways at less than 1.5 mph to his back and left. Note that the telephoto compression makes speed estimates inaccurate, but Kennedy's torso length allows corrections.

Gravity helped topple JFK. Kennedy started in a left-overbalanced position, leaning forward and left, with his head twisted left and down. He had perhaps been holding himself so as not to collapse on Jackie. When his brain was destroyed, motor nerves stopped working. Once he stopped resisting, gravity alone would gradually accelerate him at up to 1.4 mph down, translating to back-and-left as he rotated on his thigh-spine angle. But he initially accelerated faster than by gravity alone.

Some have suggested a "jet effect" may have contributed to this motion: ejected matter and the recoil of stretched scalp did exert some force created by the cavitation pressure at right angles to the bullet fragment path. Note that the original Alvarez Jet Effect proposed that material ejected out the exit hole would impart backward motion; the jet effect in this book concerns a bullet/bone fragment cone traversing just under the top right skull so that its cavitation forced out that top skull, blowing ejecta up perpendicular to the bullet's path – as shown in the Zapruder film. The explosion of material from the top of Kennedy's head would have an equal and opposite effect on that head, driving it a bit down and left. Since his head remained in alignment on his torso (instead of flopping to the left on his neck), this jet effect does not explain any major back and left movement of his entire torso. The NIH paper agrees that a jet effect of any direction did not account for the preponderance of back-left motion.

The NIH analysis suggests a neuromuscular reaction. Severe brain injury with a rapid increase in pressure can cause "Decerebrate or Decorticate Posturing": involuntary rigidity, flexion or extension of the arms and legs; Opisthotonus can result, characterized by extreme arching of the back. The right side of the brain does control movement in the left side of the body, so a leftward-biased motion is conceivable. The Zapruder film does show an arching of Kennedy's back in F 314 through F 316, consistent with Decerebrate Posturing. However, while JFK's back arches, and his torso "gets taller," it does not show an asymmetric stiffening that would directly account for a left-and-back motion.

Others have speculated that this motion was due to a second projectile's impact (Thompson, Six Seconds in Dallas,

1967) (Thompson, 2021) but have not explained how the projectile would transmit so much energy as to move the entire body "back and to the left," or how the projectile would not exit the left side of the president, or how the projectile would transmit its force uniformly on the entire torso instead of just moving the head alone to the left. Kennedy's head stays in the same position relative to his torso and does not bend at the neck, as would be expected from a sharp blow to the head from the right.

What else might have sent JFK back and to the left?

Jackie pushed him that way. This was concluded back in 1967 and never refuted, but it seems to be forgotten (Itek Corporation, 1967).

When JFK was hit and reacted at F223, Jackie had been surprised and uncomprehending. She was confused by his strange posture and expression as he turned towards her with his elbows unnaturally high. She immediately grabbed his left elbow and started pulling it down; he tilted towards her in response. Two seconds later, she paused, frightened that Connally suddenly shouted, "No, no, no!" She then tried to twist herself in front of JFK's face: her right hand was pulling down on JFK's left elbow; her left hand was pushing on JFK's left forearm. Kennedy had moved only slightly beyond his first tilt. When Kennedy went limp at his brain death at F313, Jackie's considerable continuing pressure moved Kennedy back and to the left. At F316, 0.15 seconds after impact, Jackie's head ducked down, and she thrust out due to physical (rather than auditory) startle, adding to the force pushing JFK back and to the left. At that point, JFK was far enough over-balanced that gravity continued his back and to the left even as Jackie withdrew her hands.

Kennedy's head stayed in about the same position with respect to his spine; no body-moving force (for example, a projectile or jet effect) could act only on the side of his head without tilting his head out of spinal alignment. That is a strong indication that the toppling forces are acting on his whole torso rather than just his head: Jackie is pushing on his arm and gravity takes over. In addition, JFK's Opisthotonus arching torso thrust against Jackie's hands, which were on his elbow and forearm. That asymmetric force appears to contribute to Jackie's pushing JFK back and to the left.

At F320, Jackie began sitting up, raising her head. This is likely because when Kennedy's head exploded, she responded in surprise. Normal reaction time begins between 150 and 300 milliseconds; Jackie reacted by F320 (about 330 milliseconds). A tenth of a second later, we see her suddenly letting go of her husband's arm, releasing their pressure on Kennedy by F324. Kennedy continues toppling due to gravity, landing in Jackie's lap. We can see Kennedy's right arm relax from its F222 cavitation-induced tensing, starting 0.2 seconds after that fatal shot.

This entire sequence, from bullet impact to Jackie's hands leaving Kennedy's arm, takes from F313 to F324, or about 0.6 seconds.

This is not the only time when Jackie moved her dying husband. At F327, Kennedy has slumped towards her. She reaches with her right hand and grips him by the back of his neck, and pulls him towards her. In the three frames from F327 to F330, Kennedy moves at twice the speed of his famed "back and to the left" as Jackie pulls his head towards her breast. In less than half a second, she realizes that his head is completely destroyed and that he is dead. F337 captures this moment of inconceivable woe: Jackie's face is as eloquent as the famed "Scream" painting – only real.

**Blood Mist**

The exploding blood and brain mist was caught in the 10-15 mph WNW wind when it sprayed above the car. Some spatter made it to the front of the car's windshield, but most ended up in the car; Agent Kellerman, in the right front seat, said "body matter" was all over his coat. Some of this mist was blown back onto the oncoming motorcycles behind the car (as can be seen in the stabilized Oliver Nix film). Some skull pieces fly up and forward, unaffected by the wind, as reported by others such as (Nalli, 2018). A motorcycle cop, himself traveling at more than 8 mph just behind the limo, was dusted by brain matter mist; he concluded that the mist had shot towards him, not realizing that he had driven into it as it blew with the wind; that policeman's early story convinced some Dallas police that a shot had come from the front. Other pieces might have been slung in arbitrary directions by their initial scalp attachment, even towards the rear of the car. The Zapruder film does not show any chunks on the trunk. Most of the mist showered the inside of the limo and its occupants – including the driver and agent in the front seat.

Parts of the fatal bullet exited JFK's head and hit the windshield, leaving a star-like, non-penetrating crater (CE 349-351) and a dent in the windshield frame. Two fragments of this fatal bullet were found in the car, CE 567 and CE 569, and are now digitally available at the National Institute of Standards and Technology. These bullet fragments did not have enough remaining kinetic energy to do more than crack the glass.

The bullet fragments were tested by "neutron activation." Oswald's bullets were made from scrap lead containing antimony; neutron activation gave the mix for each big fragment (having ballistic marks from Oswald's gun) and several of the small bits (Rahn, 2004). It did reveal that there were two quite different clusters of very close composition, and each group containing a fragment ballistically matched to Oswald's rifle; that grouping does suggest that:

- A single bullet struck Kennedy and then Connally.

- A second bullet killed Kennedy.
- No other bullet was likely involved.

Neutron activation is now accepted as trial evidence, and is considered reliable, of high accuracy. (Randich, 2006)


**A Second Shooter is Unlikely**

Regardless of bullet fragments, some speculate that a second shooter killed Kennedy at or near F313. While not impossible, it would be difficult to understand and needs a great deal more than hand-wave explanations.

Any second shooter would need to avoid startling Zapruder or must startle him at one of the three known places– since we saw only three startles. A typical rifle creates a 150-160 dB blast, and the best factory suppressors (sometimes misnamed "silencers") will cut that sound energy by 30 dB or even, in exotic equipment, by 40 dB. There have been specialized suppressed rifles producing only 85 dB, a noise which Zapruder would not likely notice. A suppressed muzzle blast could have been masked amongst Oswald's much louder blasts and echoes.

A "silenced" second shooter would need a subsonic bullet to avoid its supersonic "crack" over any nearby heads. Such bullets substitute increased mass for velocity to maintain killing energy. But what happened to any such bullet? Why did the bullet impact spray matter forward in the Zapruder film? The fine mist did end up on the motorcycle cop, but much more of it ended up forward in the car. It is simpler to explain that small amount of mist as hitting the motorcyclist due to the WNW wind and the motion of the motorcycle.

Synchronized shooting has been suggested. But the car's speed was unpredictable, and any bullet impact must be within 0.05 seconds, or it will show easily on the Zapruder film as separate accelerations. How could shooters synchronize accurately? As it turned out, only Zapruder and Nix cameras were capturing the event, but there could have been several others – how would these conspirators deal with more complete

Zapruder-quality recordings? Even a nearby suburb's TV camera might have chosen the uncrowded Dealey Plaza for filming.

Some believe they heard a shot from the overpass or knoll area. Of 190 witnesses, 172 had an opinion on the number of shots, with 79% saying "3 shots." (Thompson, Six Seconds in Dallas, 1967). However, only 64 had an opinion on the shot origin: 25 mentioned the TSBD, and 33 mentioned the knoll or overpass areas in front of the limo. There is an excellent analysis of the reasons that it is hard for people to determine shot origins: besides echoing, the bullet shock wave precedes the muzzle blast wave, depending on the distance from the bullet path and shooter. For Oswald's Carcano bullet, traveling at an average speed of about 2080 for the third shot, people standing along Elm near or beyond the limo at F313 would hear the muzzle blast .1 to .25 seconds after the bullet crack. The muzzle crack has much less energy but is generated all along the path of the bullet, and so it can confuse the origin (McFadden, 2021). Zapruder himself reported that he heard two sounds for each shot, which he attributed to echo. For Zapruder, neither the Dal-Tex nor the County Records buildings were ideal reflectors, so he may have heard the bullet cracks (Sturdivan, 2005).

A believable second shooter scenario must have a complete trajectory map: from shooter to victim, traversing the victim, and from victim exit to final bullet (or fragments) positions. For example, a shot that is claimed to have entered JFK's throat must have come from a specific spot, at a specific Zapruder frame; if it was claimed to go through the windshield, then a demonstration of the cracking is needed; otherwise, its trajectory must be shown to avoid hitting the car or other occupants; it would have to have explainable sound and startling; when it hit JFK it would have to have an explainable disintegration tied to observed data; if any part of the projectile exited JFK it would have to have an explained trajectory. Apart from the projectile, the shooter would also have to have an explained "trajectory" and motivation. Any shot through the windshield would need to explain why deflection would be controlled, why the noise of the impact on the glass would not make the driver and passengers jump, and why the shooter could expect such a tiny cracking that only a few people every claimed that saw an actual hole. If any other person was involved, there would need to be a detailed understanding of their movements and motivation– before and after the event. So far, there has been no believable, detailed explanation.

In any case, the motions caught on Zapruder's film and the other records are fully explained in this book, without any second shooter.

## 16

# JOHNSON'S FIRST DAYS

Oswald was very wrong about the importance of Kennedy's death. Killing Kennedy was a disaster for the US and the World (Salinger and Vanocur, 1964). This book argues that Oswald made one of the worst mistakes in US history.

In the words of the "most trusted man in America" in 1967, Oswald had hurt the world. News anchor Walter Cronkite, in closing *CBS News Inquiry: The Warren Report*, predicted:

*We have found there has been a loss of morale, a loss of confidence among the American people towards their own government and the [people] that serve it, and that is perhaps more wounding than the assassination itself. The damage that Lee Harvey Oswald did the United States of America, the country he first denounced and then appeared to re-embrace, did not end when the shots were fired from the Texas School Book Depository. The most grievous wounds persist, and there is little reason to believe they will soon be healed (CBS News Inquiry, 1967).*

Kennedy's death unified most of the world in an outpouring of grief. No leader had the love of so many people. His funeral, though quickly arranged, was attended by 220 foreign dignitaries from 92 countries, five international agencies, and the papacy. Its worldwide TV coverage transformed the TV industry. Major US TV networks broadcast continuous live coverage, suspending commercials for days, throughout the US and in 28 other countries. The BBC and other networks gave major time, likewise even in the USSR, Cuba and Japan. Nearly everyone watched their TV or gathered around public TVs; most of that audience was shocked, many weeping. Only a few on the American ultra-right expressed any "happiness."

People around the world described JFK as a uniquely capable leader who had saved the world from nuclear war. He was described as: courageous, intelligent, rational, practical, principled, patriotic, energetic, intense, careful, caring, confident, respectful of all, purposeful, humorous, self-deprecating, witty, engaging, mostly honest, and remarkably even-tempered even under severe stress. He was one of the few presidents who could enter a room full of antagonists, listen to viperous personal castigations, yet emerge unintimidated and unencumbered by rancor or vengefulness. In the crucial decisions, he did what he thought was right, independent of maelstroms of self-serving or mis-informed advice. He gave Americans hope, a new respect for politics and national service, and a new pride in being American (Salinger and Vanocur, 1964). A special issue of *Life Magazine* reminded everyone of Kennedy's virtues soon after his death (Henry R. Luce, 1963).

Had Kennedy continued to a second term, he would have set the course of America and the world in an entirely better direction. Perhaps we would still "ask not what your country can do for you, ask what you can do for your country."

Thanks to Oswald, the manipulative Lyndon Johnson became president – something Johnson could never have achieved on his own. Johnson was driven by self-aggrandizement with little genuine interest in the citizens of America. His presidential decisions would be driven by his egotistical need to be "legitimately" elected to greatness that surpassed even FDR's.

In his first hours, Johnson did a good job of calming the nation. He went to great lengths to prevent any nuclear war (some say too great). He allowed key parts of the government to hide their mistakes in the assassination, but also in their daily operations. However, if Ruby had not killed Oswald, Johnson's first months as Presidient might have had a much different course, virtually uncontrolled and unpredictable. By luck or design, LBJ dodged that disaster.

Unfortunately for the country, Lyndon Johnson did not stay lucky. Where his predecessor had abundant self-assurance, Johnson had mostly self-centered ambition. His results:

- LBJ restricted the Warren Commission, generating near-universal mistrust.
- LBJ started a war to ensure his own election and bask in the aura of "war president."
- LBJ's war destroyed his connection with youth, enflaming a youth rebellion.
- LBJ promised a "Great Society," but his war destroyed his ability to deliver it.

Johnson ultimately failed, fumbling all the key aspects of Kennedy's programs.

- He undermined the Kennedy assassination investigations by allowing too many secrets.
- He passed Kennedy's civil rights but failed to implement them to suppress state and local tyrannies.

- He overpromised results from civil rights legislation, ignoring Kennedy's admonition that American's had to address civil rights in their own lives.
- He launched the Vietnam War and further split America by lying about it.
- He ignored JFK's prudent budgeting as he impoverished America with war and poorly managed giveaways.
- He turned Kennedy's "self-improvement" into an underfunded Great Society dream that squandered the best opportunity for effective racial integration.
- He gave too little to boost the needy but could not build national support for even that little giving.
- His increasing paranoia and prevarication stimulated national division and mistrust.
- He cemented America into a systemic racism that Kennedy had sworn to fix.

Ultimately, Johnson's failed war and social policies became the driving forces for deepening the polarization of America.

**Johnson Destroyed Trust in the Federal Government**
Since 1958, the Pew Research Center has polled Americans about their trust in government:

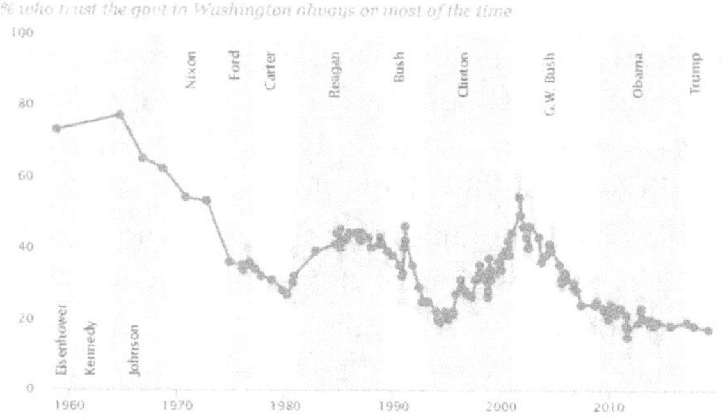


*(Pew Research Center, Washington, D.C., 2021)*

During the Eisenhower and Kennedy presidencies, trust exceeded party lines. Most people believed that each president was trying to do his best for the country, even if they disagreed with the exact policies. People also understood that the government, firmly rooted in the US Constitution, was "bigger" than the changes wrought by party politics. They trusted in the idea of the government.

That does not mean that Americans universally believed what Kennedy said. Americans are sophisticated enough to know that foreign policy, particularly in conflicts, cannot stand the truth. When Kennedy said, "we shall bear any burden" to support the cause of liberty, they understood it in the context of his next sentences: those who "strongly supporting their own freedom." Or for the poor, we would "help them help themselves." No one expected Kennedy to give details of the Missile Crisis or foreign negotiations. Several presidents had affairs or private issues, but none admitted them in office – at the time, few would have expected that candor unless the sex was criminal or compromised national security. However, most Americans did not tolerate self-serving lies that damaged the country.

Trust had reached a high, in the months following Kennedy's assassination, of nearly 80%. The combination of

Johnson and Nixon cut that trust in half. By 2020, only 17% of Americans said they could trust their Federal Government to do what is right "just about always" (3%) or "most of the time" (14%). Johnson was shown to be lying about his war and his ability to follow through on his domestic agenda. Nixon was exposed for his "secret plan to end the war" and then fatally for his "dirty tricks" subversion of democracy during his election campaigns, headlined by Watergate.

Unfortunately, the press and governmental attacks on these presidents laid the foundation for the fracture of the American polity that plagues America in 2024. Vague criticisms were trumpeted by hostile press long before they could be proven, causing presidential supporters to believe they were seeing ferociously partizan attacks by a biased press. Both Johnson and Nixon vilified their attackers and impeded the investigations. All but their gleeful opposition became bored, dismissive, and disbelieving. Conservatives and their "silent majority" saw the proceedings as evidence of a powerful Eastern Elite. Progressives and their "discouraged majority" saw the proceedings as evidence of a powerful oligarchy.

Trust in government rose during the initial Reagan year. Reagan was a known TV personality who was comfortable in front of cameras and presented an upbeat story. Had the public become aware of his traitorous pre-election deal with Iran, he might not even have been elected: Reagan insiders, apparently including John Connally, arranged to have Iran keep the embassy hostages, undermining Carter's deal. Iran freed those hostages minutes after Reagan's oath of office. While widely suspected, Connally's and Reagan's traitorous deal remained secret until 2023.

Reagan grappled with the Iran Contra fiasco, his War on Drugs, and his tax gifts to the rich. Reagan also was the first to trash his own government when he famously quipped:

"The nine most terrifying words in the English language are: I'm from the Government, and I'm here to help."

Trust in government sank again. Voters did not even trust their own party's people.

Americans would have been even more untrusting if they knew that Reagan brought the world closer to nuclear war than the famed Missile Crisis. Reagan pushed over a thousand new nuclear-tipped missiles into Western Europe, declared the Soviet Union an "Evil Empire," and excited the KGB with saber-rattling. Soviet spies mistakenly reported the new Pershing 2 missile could destroy Moscow and most other large Russian cities; these solid-fuel rockets could, they feared, "decapitate" Russian political and military in ten minutes, using maneuverable earth-penetrating ("bunker buster") warheads; hundreds of new cruise missiles would join ICBMs, bombers, and the rest of the arsenal to "end the Evil Empire" in a few hours. The Soviet spies were wrong: the Pershing 2 had too little range, too small a warhead, and no ground penetrator. In ignorance, the Soviets feared a Reagan first strike. The Soviet military went to the equivalent of DEF CON 2, "ready to launch." That was a few nervous fingers away from hundreds of millions of deaths – all unknown to any but a few. British spies reported the danger, and Reagan quickly backed away. The lucky result was the 1988 Intermediate-Range Nuclear Forces Treaty, which removed most IRBMs from Europe (Macintyre, 2018).

Clinton's administration improved trust in government from about 20% to more than 40% - despite his Monica issues. Apart from upward spikes for the first Iraq war and for 9/11, trust steadily eroded through G.W. Bush, Obama and Trump until it reached its 2020 value of about 17%.

Trust in government is different than trust in the president. Since Truman, three presidents have benefited from war enthusiasm: Truman (WW2), George H. W. Bush (1st Iraq war), and George W. Bush (9/11 attack). Only two peace-time presidents had high popularity consistently in their terms: Eisenhower and Kennedy.

.   .   .

## Presidential Approval Ratings

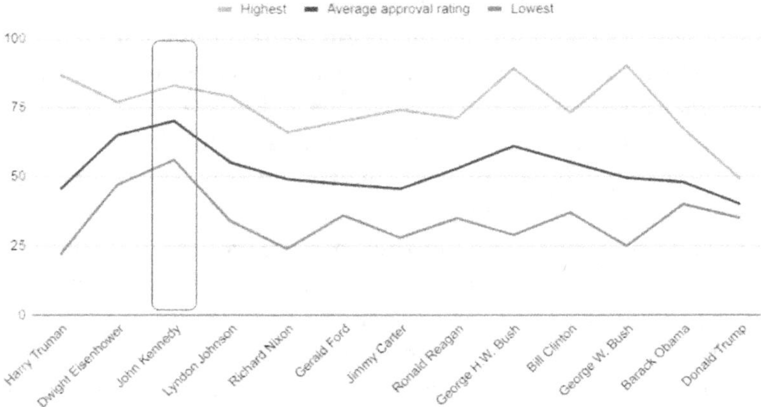


JFK had the highest non-wartime favorable rating of any president, at 83%. Perhaps more importantly, Kennedy was disliked less than any president, without exception: 56% still liked him "at his worst" rating. Kennedy was able to generate enthusiasm both for his government and for himself. These highly favorable numbers support the assertion that Kennedy would have won reelection in 1964 and that Kennedy would have been able to wield a strong, moderate hand in passing his second-term legislation.

Johnson, on the other hand, squandered trust both in the government and in his presidency. His continual lies about starting and "winning" the Vietnam War were enough to tarnish him personally. His passage of his "Great Society" legislation should have been a big plus, but because his war drained all funding, he ended up over-promising and under-delivering for essentially all his major government-funded programs. (Medicare, Medicaid, and Social Security ran under their own taxes and so were stable). Johnson's devolution from civil rights support to "law and order" president managed to anger everyone, while his poorly thought-out policing programs may have increased crime rather than controlled it. His political machinations added a grim Machiavellian cast to his presidency, even after he withdrew from the 1968 race.


## LBJ's America?

Some authors laud LBJ as the president most responsible for creating modern America. In a bad sense, that is true. LBJ did trample America's early 1960s promise into an ongoing festering mire of factionalism and disinformation.

Recent revisionism of LBJ and his legacy stems mostly from reviewing the 632 hours of taped conversations that were made by LBJ during his presidency – "unprecedented nuance and complexity" as he "agonized about Vietnam" and his legislation. Time has made LBJ's Vietnam disaster seem less damaging, particularly in the light of the "War on Terror" begun in the early 2000's. Time has also eroded the understanding of what LBJ did and did not do in his 1960s Civil Rights bill passages, so that now most remember only the bill names.

The contrast between JFK's imagined future and LBJ's actual disasters is detailed in a companion volume by this author.


## Diminished Trust Apart from Johnson

Truman had suffered a massive drop in credibility after presiding over what appeared to many to be a Soviet take-over of Eastern Europe, then a Communist revolution take-over of China, and then a Communist attempted take-over of South Korea. As was discussed earlier, it was not Truman's fault: his armies would not have beaten the Soviets had he illegally reneged on the wartime agreements of the Tehran, Yalta, and Potsdam conferences. It was perhaps a bad call to support the exploitive and ill-regarded Nationalists in China. Truman and Eisenhower could only have "won" in Korea by a unilateral world-appalling nuclear war; as it was, the Chinese carefully did not press their advantage and fought only to reestablish their North Korean ally. The calm and personal integrity of Eisenhower restored confidence.

.  .  .

Some Americans, particularly the "Boomers" born after World War II, had begun to lose trust in many authority figures, not just the Federal Government. Network TV entertainment remained focused on relaxation, but TV news programs reported scandals in business, such as contract-fixing, stock manipulations, organized crime, union crimes and crimes against unions. TV social news reported sports "point shaving," shady gambling, record industry "payola," quiz show fixing, sex scandals, divorce scandals, and more. "Seeing" crime was more unsettling than reading about it.

As TVs spread and TV's powerful scientific mass marketing took hold, viewers were increasingly encouraged to buy for their egos. Efficiency experts needed in World War II influenced corporate America: cheaper, just-good-enough products and "planned obsolescence" undermined some faith in consumer products. Rachel Carson's 1962 "Silent Spring" exposed the unintended or intentional poisoning of water, air, and soil by big corporations.

All that said, it is difficult to say that products were any shoddier after 1963, or marketing was sleazier, or crimes were more egregious. Cars, for example, went from expected (accident-free) lives of 50,000 miles in the 1930s to 100,000 miles in the 1960s; Cars were faster, safer, and generally better liked. Housing felt better in the suburbs, with clear "picture windows," fancy kitchens, central heating, and comfortable plumbing in "manicured personal mini-mansions." Kennedy's tax cuts (passed by LBJ), successful fight against inflation, and pro-innovation attitudes launched ten years of growing economy despite Johnson's mistakes.

.  .  .

The intellectual Counterculture did pick up on the sinister relationship between Eisenhower's "military-industrial complex" and Johnson's war. Even though Kennedy had dramatically increased defense spending to defense industries, he had spent to "make us safer" and had successfully used his increased weaponry for aggressive peace initiatives. The "evils" of the military-industrial complex did not impinge on average people until the Vietnam War protests.

In general, life was getting better in 1963 – if people chose to look at the good side in relative terms. Kennedy seemed to get people to think positively – increasing trust. The dramatic turn in trust correlates with the assassination, Johnson's war, his failure to lead towards positive patriotism, his dishonesty, and his bungled race relations.

**Polarizing America with Media**

LBJ's Vietnam War divided the free press. The 1964 press were cheerleaders for war, praising Johnson's apparent retaliation for the fabricated "Gulf of Tonkin" insult to America. But the press had instant video, embedded reporters, and an investigative attitude. Johnson's war story started to fray. By 1967, and especially by 1968, the US press and mainstream media had become critics of the war. The anti-war kids had been "proven right" and were in ascendance in the media.

The Nixon administration was launched by a conspiracy to block peace in Vietnam. The quasi-legal ongoing attacks against antiwar figures gradually morphed into illegal spying and sabotage of American citizens. The leak of the Pentagon Papers triggered the Nixon "Plumbers" team to find that leak, and later to undermine the leading Democratic candidates while generating faked support for Nixon's policies. Nixon's top-down conspiracy generated a landslide win in the 1972 election. Even JFK's memory was trashed: Nixon's men faked documentation to "prove" that JFK ordered Diem's assassination to damage any future Kennedy family politicking. The Nixon conspiracies did generate major effects, though they were far less dramatic than killing JFK; the Nixon conspiracy was unwound in a long, clumsy investigation despite the FBI leader's apparent collusion. Again, the mainstream media had been instrumental in dismantling a Conservative presidency. Liberals appeared to be gaining strength – but there was a growing scandal fatigue.

A vocal "New Left" was energetic, composed primarily of activists and intellectuals. This New Left had espoused McCarthy in 1968, splintered after RFK was killed, had been completely confused by Nixon's machinations, and enjoyed moral superiority buried with McGovern. The New Left spent their time arguing with each other, with adherents of Euro-Socialism, Communism, anti-Imperialism, anti-Capitalism, or even Maoism. While they did articulate problems, they could not agree on solutions and failed to create loyal, enthused adherents. They did provide convenient fringe strawmen for the TV pundits to spread fear or ridicule to most Americans.

Americans continued to voice high levels of trust in news media, especially in TV news, for accuracy, fairness, and coverage. The rare polls indicated trust levels in the 60% to 80% levels for news and reporters. In 1972, news anchor Walter Cronkite achieved the title "most trusted man in America" and kept that through to his retirement in 1980. People of the 1970s believed their reporters much more than their government.

Conservative big businesspeople, big money, and the emerging neoconservatives feared the investigative reporters. This loose oligarchy aimed to use right-wing extremists to enlist support from middle Americans. To create a defensive narrative, they funded a network of think tanks inspired by the Institute of

Economic Affairs think tank that had countered liberalism in Britain since 1955. The right-wing think tanks espoused aggressive corporatism and Milton Friedman's Nobel Prize-winning theory of "greed is good." They wanted to inoculate the public against the radical New Left. Ayn Rand's Foundation for the New Intellectual (1968), the American Enterprise Institute (1970), the Hoover Institute (1972), the Business Roundtable (1972), the Heritage Foundation (1973), and the Cato Institute (1977) formed a mostly cooperating network of pro-corporate anti-regulation anti-socialism anti-union anti-integration propaganda. They asserted that anti-war and pro-civil rights groups were "Communist-linked."

The New Right seems to have learned a lot from the success of the "British Security Coordination" group in 1940-41. The British set up a truly vast conspiracy involving thousands of US employees and agents who worked to get the US into World War II to help Britain. That group learned to generate fake news into their captive "Overseas News Agency" (similar to UPI); their generated "news" was then broadcast worldwide over the WRUL multi-language shortwave facilities; their fake news was then picked up by regular newspapers and radio stations. The resulting "news" they called "whispers" that had been laundered of all connection with the British originators. These "whispered rumors" might even be ridiculous, but their goal was to "induce a certain frame of mind in the general public, not necessarily to deceive the well-informed." (Usdin, 2018)

A key element of the new background think-tank growth was their discipline. These think-tanks almost always agreed with and supported each other, with consistent positions and consistent phrasing. Unlike the original centrist RAND think-tank (1948), they did not depend on government grants. Unlike the left-wing Institute for Policy Studies (1963), they did not lead open debates or protests or raise the "rabble" directly. While the New Left was ever more visible and often contemptuous of unbelievers, the New Right "thought leaders" stayed in the background, hid their core values, and instead absorbed right-wing activists while developing wedge issues to build loyal single-issue followers among the "forgotten Americans" - the "silent majority" – powerless people who feared "the destruction of America" by left-wing radicals.

The George Wallace brand of "segregationist conservative" had to be defused. The segregationist vitriol was co-opted and spread over feminism, gay rights, and big government socialism. The oligarchic interests of lower taxation, lower regulation, and independence of financial structures such as the Federal Reserve, Stock markets, loans, and international banking could be hidden behind a general diatribe against government overreach. Most importantly, the oligarchic imperative of increasing national, state, and personal debts could be blamed on that amorphous government.

A consistent alternative-fact-base evolved - whatever would focus "silent majority" listeners away from critiques of oligarchic behaviors and towards oligarchic-conservative - goals. Independent old-school conservatives were gradually edged away from the public. Over time, radio became a mouthpiece for a cohesive right-wing world narrative, merging the evangelicals with the anti-communists. Their radio shows used "simplify and repeat" of consistent messages to win devoted believers. This was much different than the hodgepodge of harangues constantly roiling the fractious New Left or the wider Democratic Party.

Under JFK, talk radio had been restrained by the Fairness Doctrine and tax-exempt status investigations to the point that partisan talk radio declined dramatically. Ironically, his death provided tinder to reignite talk radio in the 1970s. One of the first topics that excited the new talk radio shows was the Kennedy Assassination conspiracy theories – topics that had no Fairness Doctrine issues. The conspiracies themselves often involved government agencies - that resonated with talk radio listeners and TV viewers. Soon, the public agreed that "it was a conspiracy, man!" Talk radio was back, though still somewhat restrained by the cumbersome Fairness Doctrine. That restraint was too slow and legalistic to apply to political rather than personal attacks. Carter's "moral presidency" was crushed by increasingly one-sided radio. Reagan's election was a major triumph, another turning point in US political, financial, and social history.

Before 1977, TV networks provided news as a public service, not looking for profits. In 1977, a news show, *60 Minutes,* demonstrated that money could be made from a news magazine format. At the same time, the number of available channels was growing as cable-based media exploded. A "profit" motive was one way of encouraging news formats to capture market share amongst many more competitors. CNN and CBN were born. The new *Right Wing* soon organized the new media to create a faithful following, but the Fairness Doctrine was still an irritating rein.

In a monumental hypocrisy, a deal between Reagan's representatives and Iran's leaders made a few months before the 1980 election sealed Carter's loss in the 1980 election. Iran kept the American hostages until after Reagan's inauguration; Tehran freed them that same day. Worse, the Reagan administration began secretly selling arms to Iran a few months after the election - even though the US was "enforcing" an arms embargo against Iran. Ultimately, various investigations uncovered part of the scheme. In 1987, Reagan admitted that there was a deal to trade arms for the hostages but insisted that he hadn't known much about it. All in all, the Iran-Contra deception was an early example of "alternative facts" establishing a more right-wing acceptable narrative; it demonstrated that carefully managed herd mentality could overcome facts or ethics.

Reagan's removal of Fairness Doctrine constraints allowed the US radio and soon TV networks to generate streams of conflicting "alternative facts"; listeners gradually became committed to a "fact" base that derided competing narratives as "fake news" and non-believers as idiots, sheep, criminals, or traitors. The US populace has been fragmented into factions that can't even agree on enough facts to support intelligent arguments.

The "General Social Survey" polling, begun in 1972 and carried on by the National Opinion Research Center for the National Science Foundation, was able to track the effects of this new manipulation of media. Their data was analyzed by Hunter Pearl (UPenn) and showed a dramatic decline in trust in the media:

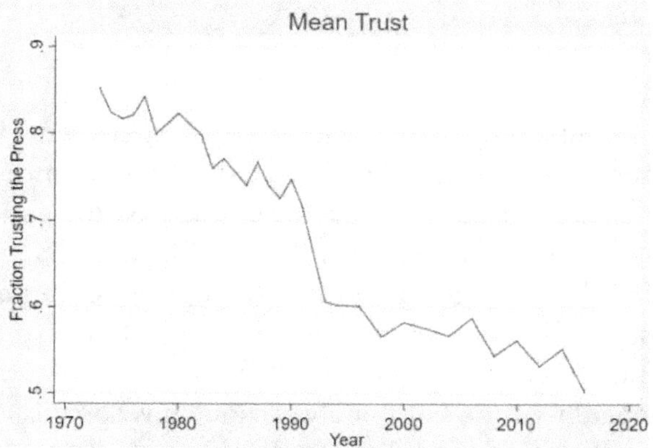


Hunter found this decline was general but was slightly more pronounced for educated people and for Republicans. Regardless, the result of the creation of "strategic media narratives" has been the destruction of trust amongst most Americans.

By 2000, nobody knew who to believe. Most people joined an "echo chamber" with their friends. The left wing did not create consistent think-tank-generated storylines, but they gradually fumbled into their own alternative fact bases. Across the political spectrum, many concluded that the other side must be evil for believing what "just could not be true." Or if a lie was exposed, they might ignore the exposure with "what about … long list of distracting issues," or with "they're all crooks." They were soon back to believing what their crowd believed, with contradictions forgotten.

In 2000, the personal attack rule and the "political editorial" rule were repealed, allowing stations to launch personal and political attacks without even telling the target that they were under attack. Each faction now interprets the other factions' actions in the worst light, but the ultra-right has come to dominate "talk" radio with constant invective. By 2016, a man was elected by simply echoing the established talking points of right-wing talk. He guaranteed himself 41% of the voters and enough electoral college votes to win. His platform was the talk-radio platform: to attack the Federal Government from within, "drain the swamp," shrink the bloated government by appointing untrained and hostile people to slash its parts, say whatever was needed to drive the "lib-tards" crazy. No other developed country has this level of division and anti-government hostility.

As of 2020, the media has joined the government in pervasive mistrust. Only 13% of Americans had a "great deal" of trust in media, and only 41% had at least a "fair" trust in their media. In 1976, before the think-tank coordinated assaults on media trust, 72% trusted their media (Dalio, 2021).

. . .

Lyndon Johnson must be held responsible for starting the slide to the caustic politics of 2020. LBJ broke from the Kennedy directions of hope, enthusiasm, and self-improvement. Nixon added fuel to that fire. American voters, already mentally segregated by Johnson's Vietnam War, fractured into two believer communities with conflicting "fact" bases.

Without the depressing context of Johnson's crime, anger, and war, it is highly unlikely that Nixon would have won, or even run, in 1968. A more likely result would be a continuation of the Kennedy "New Frontier" under another fiscally conservative Democrat. The Kennedy conservative approach would have become entrenched: analyze, experiment, measure, adjust, and then commit long-term. Instead, under Johnson, Nixon, and beyond, the government has plunged in one direction and then another. Government programs have become party-centric, biased, and undependable. The evolution of a squabbling Democratic base fighting a deftly managed Republican base makes Johnson's mistakes all the more intractable.

Billionaire pundit Ray Dalio observed that media trust collapses when the media becomes a tool of the powerful, who use propaganda and distortion to "gain support and destroy the opposition." (Dalio, 2021) Dalio observes that media truth dies in "Stage 5" of his "Big Cycle" of empire rise and fall: empires (like the USA) progress from their (1) founding, to (2) building, to (3) peaceful prosperity, to (4) bubble-financed excesses, to (5) wealth and values gaps, bureaucratic paralysis, and financial, populist, class and extremist internal conflicts, and finally ending in (6) civil wars, revolutions and new orders. However, Dalio also observes that the timing of big cycle stages is uncertain. For example, the Roman Empire "fell" several times in the view of its population, but until 536 AD, it kept resurrecting itself; then its luck ran out and bad leadership destroyed the

Western Empire; even then, the Eastern Empire took over 900 more years to fully die. Johnson helped bring on Stage 5 for the USA. Kennedy was the kind of leader that could have inspired our culture to new heights and establish good feelings that could have long delayed Dalio's "Stage 5" societal collapse.

Oswald's ego-driven mistake is still hurting America in 2021, just as Walter Cronkite predicted. We are paralyzed by polarities.

# 17

# RECOVERING

Oswald shot at John Connally and accidentally killed President John F. Kennedy. Oswald's ego forced him to shoot at Connally even when it was clear that hitting a moving target would be very difficult and even when another man was getting in the way. Oswald's ego prevented him from backing out of a very stupid act.

The tragedy was we lost a great man. Or maybe more accurately:

*"[Kennedy] was a man who could have become great or could have failed, and now we'll never know. That's what's so awful." (Mailer, 1968)*

The idea that one man can change the course of history is sadly proven by Oswald.

Historians have argued that economic forces were the driving factors in history. Marx, and presumably his self-tutored "disciple" Oswald, believed that economic forces drive an evolution of class societies towards a classless, free, communist utopia.

Some modern historians have applied Marxian-like evolution to individual empires, but without any happy utopian endings: Ray Dalio's "Big Cycle" of empires makes a strong case for inevitable doom (and rebirth) based on his research of the life and death of every major "empire" for the last two millennia.

Marx was probably right when he ridiculed history taught as 'high-sounding dramas of princes and states.' It is likely that, in many cases, the visible kings had little to do with the history of their state. The proliferation of a tame herd of figurehead Hapsburgs and other European dynasties does suggest that the real workings of European states had much more to do with their secretive financial and corporate processes. But sometimes, a single person, a Napoleon, does break through the machinations of "smoke-filled back rooms."

Other historians treat financial structures as one of several forces in the evolution of society. They describe history as driven by "the masses" and the evolving conditions of those masses – a "history from below." Certainly, the major changes in the condition of the masses have been driven by the evolution of technology and the combination of engineering and financial support for applying new technology.

Some historians draw a parallel with science – where "great men" are more a product of timing and media hype than truth: science is a wavefront of knowledge that can be pushed along by anyone, anytime – a "discovery" by one person is never either made on its own nor will it not be soon discovered independently by someone else when the wavefront engulfs the idea. In contrast, the history of any individual is not a wavefront at all: each person, tribe and state gets only one chance to make each decision, and once made, that decision point is gone. While the great tide of history may eventually rebound towards a similar future, it will not be the same future. One need only consider Genghis Khan to understand the colossal impact of one individual on history.

·   ·   ·

**Johnson Was Not the Man We Needed**

At the end of 1963, most Americans knew little of Johnson - generally, he had done little in the Kennedy administration. He was described as a man who knew a very great deal about the congress and who pressured votes in the House and Senate. Some thought him kind, generous, compassionate, and a fighter for the underprivileged. But those who worked with him generally thought he was blindly ego-driven, needy, grandiose, vengeful, unprincipled, cruel, and always shifting blame to others.

As 1964 began, the US was at a turning point. LBJ made the wrong turns. America's path to polarization was set when LBJ fumbled key issues: civil rights, the fight against Communism, and the inspiration of individuals. Since 1963, American convictions of "ideology, race, and religion" have been weaponized to "render America's divisions unusually encompassing and profound." (Carothers, 2019) In a word, polarized.

Normally, divisive issues come and go. Ideological anti-communism has become a muddle: the fall of the USSR, the capitalist competitiveness of China, and the creeping socialism needed to support infirm Americans have weakened that once-pure "essence" into Progressive versus Conservative tribalism. Likewise, the pure religion fights of Catholics versus Protestants versus Jews versus Moslems versus the a-religious have reduced to making other people conform, for example, to ideas on abortion and birth control.

But one issue has never gone away. What remains at the embarrassing root from which American divisiveness endures and metastasizes: Racism. Racism is the embarrassing unspoken foundation of America's polarization.

**Polarized by Exploited Racism**

Racism is not an absolute of human nature. If it were, no JFK could help us. But it is not a fundamental trait. What is fundamental in humans is fear of the unknown. "Unfamiliar individuals are viewed with suspicion across the entire animal kingdom." Were we to acquaint ourselves and our children with fellow humans of all shapes and colors [and those humans behaved respectfully], we could eliminate knee-jerk racism (Bressan, 2023). Unfortunately, we do not live in utopias. Racist fears have been an easy tool for political polarization, locking in a motivated voting base.

Kennedy had reached the point when racial justice had become his "most important problem." The issues of integration were already thoroughly studied after decades of commissions and reports such as Moynihan's 1964 report (Moynihan, 1965). Kennedy understood that racist fears pervaded society and were usually ingrained by young adulthood. Further, dangerous behaviors are not evenly distributed among rich and poor, nor is reporting even-handed; perceived violent criminal behaviors can force stereotyping for protection. Reducing ingrained racism requires time, inter-racial exposure, mutual respect, and a great commitment to avoid crimes and exploitation. As Kennedy observed, we cannot end racism by legislation – we must end irrational fears in ourselves. Great and persistent leadership was needed. Kennedy had the knowledge, the unique capability, and the unique situation: he could have made real progress.

Kennedy's unique opportunity was built painstakingly by Black non-violent activists like MLK. By decades of turning their other cheek, they had created a reservoir of goodwill among most Americans. Unfortunately, that work was undermined when LBJ's overselling and under-supporting produced overwhelming frustrations, disrespect, and violence. JFK's unique chance was lost with Johnson's mistakes.

Race relations got worse and have never gotten much better. The speeches of the late 1960s can almost be repeated unchanged in 2021. For minorities, and particularly for Black people, the gaps in social equality, political equality, and legal equality have shifted somewhat but remain depressingly familiar.

The 1965 McCone Report, written to prevent another Watts-type riot, seems like good advice in 2021: "The consequences of inaction, indifference, and inadequacy would be far higher in the long run than the cost of correction." It recommended: (1) cooperative training and employment, (2) aggressive pre-school and remedial education in small classes and specialized treatments to at least make sure that fifth-graders can read, (3) improved police treatment of citizens and citizen complaints, especially avoiding police brutality, racism and abusive language, (4) empower a civilian police review board, (5) improve community relations to foster respect for law and police in citizens, however disadvantaged, and (6) enforce regulations to improve services such as food quality, healthcare and public transportation.

The 1968 Kerner Report researched the civil disorders of 1964 through 1967. It surveyed Black and white attitudes, detailed the problems and recommended solutions, echoing the McCone Report. It was widely read, with millions of copies made. It warned that violence would bring repression, not justice. One month after the Kerner report was released, rioting erupted in over 100 cities following the assassination of MLK. In 2021, the Kerner report could be reissued almost without change.

Distinguished Harlem psychologist and HARYOU founder Dr. Kenneth Clark observed that the 1968 Kerner Report was like reports composed after investigations of the 1919 Chicago riot, the 1935 Harlem riot, the 1943 Harlem riot, and the 1965 Watts riot. Said Dr. Clark, "I must in candor say to you members of this [Kerner] commission -- it is a kind of Alice in Wonderland -- with the same moving picture re-shown over and over again, the same analysis, the same recommendations, and the same inaction."

Since 1968, other reports have echoed the Kerner Report. From 1919 to 2022, over one hundred years have gone by with little progress on key integration issues. Nearly every approach has been suggested and tried, often multiple times, often without "critical mass." Model Cities came and went, as did the many projects started under the EOA. AmeriCorps (the 2020 parent of VISTA) and Senior Corps have "zombie" budgets and have been threatened with shutdowns. They certainly are not set up to take on a "required year of service" from all citizens, for example. Further, the divisive political environment has thus far prevented any aggressive approaches. Polarization has bred ever more polarization.

We had a great chance with the efforts of the peaceful protests in the ten years before JFK's death and a rare "Great Leader" in Kennedy. We cannot resurrect that chance. Instead, we must use reason to fashion a robust, gradual path to remedy Oswald's damage.

If we've tried everything and failed, what do we do now? We must assess the failures. Many good ideas failed with under-funding, but many more seem to have failed from exploitation or over-expectations. Practically speaking, our country needs some smaller successes before big projects can be identified, let alone funded. There have been some successes.

President Carter's "Habitat for Humanity" has been an impressive success. With more budget, more science and more training, it should be possible to help renovate some inner-city housing as a participatory effort. Teaching people to provide basic maintenance helps keep neighborhoods from deteriorating. All homeowners and conscientious renters should know how to rid living spaces of pests like ants, cockroaches, mice, and rats. Habitat for Humanity could expand to help free citizens from depending on landlords for fixes to their homes.

In 2008, the USA elected a Black President. Sadly, he was elected into a straightjacket of threatened world financial collapse and real-world recession. He had problems that, to his credit, he had to give higher priority. In two short years, control of the Senate went to the opposition party; thereafter, any remotely radical new programs became impossible except by executive order. Even when Obama had a party majority in the Senate, he would have to face opposition from conservative Democrats and from filibusters. Obama focused on healthcare as a root problem for all poor people - and a bankruptcy threat for all middle-class Americans. Eventually, Obama passed a compromise ACA that was acceptable to the AMA and health insurance industries but, by 2023, was helping half as many poor as expected, at three times the cost; to turn that around, it seems to mean that the medical and medical insurance industries were making three times the money for doing one half the ACA work.

President Obama accepted the sad proposition that an ongoing cause of the cycle of poverty was the single-parent family, as asserted earlier, even in JFK's time. Obama, both privately and by executive orders, was able to create his My Brother's Keeper Alliance (MBK) with the specific goal of breaking the poverty cycle among inner-city Black populations. MBK has been a minor success so far. Some criticize it as "putting the onus on Blacks to fix their own problems." MBK agrees that if single-parent families must persist, then they must be supported with role model mentors as well as material help. MBK's mentoring could provide good role models outside classrooms. VISTA volunteers could team with MBK for greater effect.

What is a "good role model?" Obama's MBK is working with the "5,000 Role Models of Excellence Project" for over 8000 Miami-Dade boys of color. Each is mentored for eight years in grades 3-12. They are prepared for the real world of work and responsibilities, breaking the "school-to-prison pipeline" with improved discipline, attitudes, and academics – by "instilling the values of mainstream America while respecting the existing values of the individual." Since 1993, they describe thousands of successes and are lauded by their wider Miami community. Some decry "mainstream values" as "white" – but those values are the result of evolution towards improved society of life, liberty, and the pursuit of happiness. If a different value system is desired, for example, a "ghetto-specific culture," then let it be detailed, debated, and evaluated as delivering value: Less racism? Better jobs? Better food? Better schools? Better service? Better housing? Better policing? Better safety? Sustainable asset accumulation? Better lives?

Obama is not the only Black leader calling for greater personal responsibility. Robert Woodson, in "Red, White and Black," observes that absolving anyone of personal responsibility is often fatal to their personal development. He focuses on "what Black Americans have the power to do for themselves, their neighbors, and their country." His "1776 Project" says, "The U.S. is a flawed but very good country, where it is simply not terribly hard to succeed, given hard work and personal responsibility" (Woodson, 2021). Woodson re-establishes respect for great leaders such as Jefferson and Lincoln, who, despite their surrounding culture, made important contributions to all Americans. His position and the 1776 Project are considered extreme by many, but his emphasis on self-determination as individuals is likely to provide a better foundation for long-term success for any American. Johnson destroyed JFK's intended directions towards individual duty and responsibility and substituted a welfare state approach, which is not working. LBJ's welfare mentality perpetuated or even increased systemic racism in America: "The aftermath of the Great Society is arguably the most salient threat facing Black America." (Woodson, 2021)

Woodson has oversimplified the problem: many poor Blacks have a tougher childhood environment long before they are old enough to make their own way in Woodson's individualism. That is where Americans must help. All of us should give Obama's MBK and its partners the clear-headed, unbiased, respectful attention they deserve. They provide a realistic way forward that can be funded and supported by moderates of all parties. It is not too late to reconsider a VISTA-like contribution: active people of any race could work with MBK as part of a revised VISTA. As Kennedy said, "ask what you can do…"

We need unbiased evaluation of programs that have already been tried: why did they succeed or fail? Even programs as "obviously successful" as Head Start need real evaluation and adjustment. Studies have reported that the test score successes generated by Head Start are erased by sixth grade. A new study revealed that many pre-K kids are not ready to focus on reading and math skills and that those skills are quickly acquired later; that new study suggests skills that should be taught to some in pre-K: attention, social development, working memory, and persistence in small group play (Hirsh-Pasek, 2022) But it could also be that kids are not ready because their single parent did not have time to teach them self-control, the alphabet, words, and numbers.

Poverty remains a fact of life for over 11% of Americans. Black people are more than twice as likely to suffer poverty. But poverty is not inevitable. VISTA could serve as a source of jobs and perhaps a basis for universal service. Perhaps universal service can create the inter-personal contacts that can replace fear with respect.

We should pay attention to what works for others. China was able to lift 800 million Chinese out of severe poverty by providing equal access to education, jobs, health care, and other services. Viet Nam has had similar success through improvements in employment, productivity, health care, education, and infrastructure. Austria is trying an experiment for universal jobs. Germany is raising the minimum wage and subsidizing necessities. Several countries have experimented with guaranteed incomes (although mostly well below a living wage). Several countries implement "workfare," requiring that able welfare recipients find paid or unpaid employment. The USA's workfare (TANF) has reduced welfare payments by 90% (inflation-adjusted); unfortunately, TANF also increases poverty rates and hurts poor children. We need "lifecycle" assessments of these and many other projects to see what works for whom and why.

We don't want to fail by "refighting the last war." For example, we should consider the effects of Artificial Intelligence on each of us. What skills will we absolutely need to excel in the coming "AI world?" Can AI help us better prepare ourselves? Can AI be an equalizer for the underprivileged?

.  .  .

All underprivileged Americans need help. History has shown that many Black people, in fighting through systemic racism, need special help. Is MBK the right helper? MBK restricted its members to Blacks, primarily because it is imperative that Black people be trained as leaders who can inspire "people who look like them." There are many advocates for Blacks - but few non-Black leaders who can get Black people themselves to be the best they can be despite a racially biased USA (Obama, 2015).

Black Lives Matter has gained the country's and the world's attention, driven by stories of apparent police brutality against Black people: their "BREATHE Act" lays out extensive changes in governments (The Breathe Act, 2020). Yet few ghetto parents appear to support less policing; police violence is far from the most dangerous killer of Blacks. More damaging threats to inner city lives are nutrition, obesity, health care failings, single-parent poverty, and gangs.

Nevertheless, JFK recognized that police violence was a major source of destructive unrest: he suggested expanding the role of the Federal Government in stopping state and local police tyranny. We should consider a Federal "Equal Justice Agency" at FBI level to provide professional review of the country's police forces as well as immediate arbitration assistance in times of unrest. We have the technology now, for example, to let an AI-based "instant replay" or "instant advice" technology provide real-time support to police through their body cams, car cams, and drones; police could opt to use that support in difficult interactions, both to eliminate mistakes and recriminations and to improve on life-threatening decisions. An AI could act as a social worker, psychiatrist and wingman coordinated with real-time data.

Reviews of past success show that real, lasting successes are often the product of Black leaders. The White Hats of Tampa and Atlanta controlled dangerous riots much more effectively than outside forces, for example. In Detroit, Black neighbor-hood groups were best at keeping their streets safe. We need to support Black leaders as core improvers for Black Americans, starting with mentorships and leader training in, for example, the MBK of Barack and Michelle Obama. Then, a broadened, multiracial involvement of VISTA/AmeriCorps can work under the local direction of Black leadership. When Black excellence is recognized, we can integrate on equal terms.

**Political Party Polarization**

Racism is not currently admitted to be the leading issue causing polarization. A recent Pew Research Center analysis indicates that "admitted" racial polarization has declined slightly since 1994, while the dominant divider is now "party affiliation."

## As partisan divides over political values widen, other gaps remain more modest

*Average gap in the share taking a conservative position across 10 political values, by key demographics*

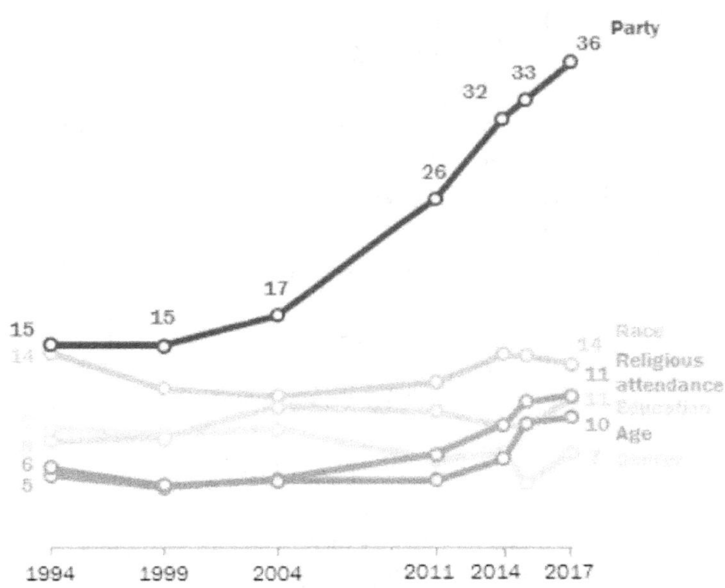


Notes: Indicates average gap between the share of two groups taking the conservative position across 10 values items. Party=difference between Rep/Lean Rep and Dem/Lean Dem. Race=white non-Hispanic/black non-Hispanic. Education=college grad/non-college grad. Age=18-49/50+. Religion=weekly+ religious service attenders/less often.
Source: Survey conducted June 8-18 and June 27-July 9, 2017

**PEW RESEARCH CENTER**

*(Pew Research Center, 2017)*

This sudden rise of "party affiliation" seems misleading. People do not join a party because of its "name." They join because they feel it represents their issues. In looking at real issues, the Pew Research Center found these issues most separated the voters of the two parties.

The notation used below: "(75%, 28% ⇒47)" means the

number of Republicans who agree (75% in this case), the number of Democrats who agree (28% in this case) and the division between Republican and Democratic agreement (47 in this case, = 75% - 28%):

1. (18%, 84% ⇒-66) Support Black Lives Matter ideas in general (Pew polling, 2023).
2. (19%, 80% ⇒-61) Others do not see racism where it exists (Pew polling, 2023).
3. (75%, 28% ⇒47) Poor Blacks are responsible for their own condition.
4. (65%, 18% ⇒47) The needy have it easy because of free government benefits.
5. (69%, 24% ⇒45) Government can't afford more help to the needy.
6. (57%, 14% ⇒43) Abortion should be illegal in most or all cases (Pew Fact Sheet, 2024).
7. (53%, 13% ⇒40) Military strength is the best path to peace.
8. (45%, 85% ⇒-40) Help "illegal" immigrants to stay (Pew polling, 2022).
9. (79%, 39% ⇒40) Increase deportations of "illegal" immigrants (Pew polling, 2022).
10. (58%, 20% ⇒38) Government environmental regulations are more bad than good.
11. (63%, 30% ⇒33) Government business regulations are more bad than good.
12. (44%, 12% ⇒32) "Illegal" immigrants hurt more than help.
13. (52%, 24% ⇒28) Most business profits are fair and reasonable.
14. (69%, 45% ⇒24) Government is almost always wasteful, inefficient.
15. (37%, 13% ⇒24) Government should discourage homosexuality.

(Pew Research Center, 2017) except where noted.

·  ·  ·

In the above, we see that the top five most polarizing persistent issues pertained to race or what, to many, is a euphemism for poor People of Color. There are many other issues that show polarization, for example:

- fear of fascism
- fear of a plutocracy or hidden elite
- fear of government indoctrination
- fear of science overreach in vaccines
- fear of guns
- fear of the FED
- fear of fake news, fake images, fake speaking, and soon fake movies
- fear of social media mind control and indoctrination
- fear of school and college indoctrination
- fear of unions or capitalism
- fear of the national debt and deficits
- fear of China, Russia, Iran, ...

Some of these issues seem to arise as an attempt to undermine whatever the other side is saying. Others seem to be generated almost equally for each party. Others are the subjects of long-running conspiracy investigations.

Transgender rights became, briefly, the most polarizing issue in the 2024 Presidential election.

(69%, 18% ⇒51) Disallow teaching gender identity in elementary schools.

(85%, 37% ⇒48) Allow play only for teams matching sex at birth.

(67%, 20% ⇒47) Allow use only of public restrooms matching sex at birth.

(72%, 26% ⇒46) Deny health care for transgender transitions to <18.

(59%, 17% ⇒42) Treat parents helping transgender transitions to <18 as child abuse.

(48%, 80% ⇒-32) Protect transgender rights for housing, jobs, and public spaces.

(48%, 80% ⇒-32) Provide medical insurance for transgenders.

While transgender rights became a leading "wedge issue" for 2024, it will likely be resolved by state laws. It does not seem likely to have the persistence of the other polarizing issues listed above.

Given the above, it is reasonable to conclude that the underlying basis of American Polarization is a residual race problem. There is no simple way out of that worsening polarization. The Federal Government has tried basically everything and mostly failed to repair the racism at the root. The solution may be to "think like JFK." Each of us has the individual power to end our racist actions, if not our racist thoughts. That goes for doing racist actions, but it also goes for using race as an excuse.

We will not achieve equality because we are simply not equal. We can't force equality because history shows that it will hurt us all. When we respect each other, we can reduce polarization. When we reduce polarization, we can expect our government to provide helping hands without death by filibuster. Oswald ruined our "easy way" forward of having a trusted government and feeble polarization, freeing the hands of a brilliant leader.

### A Fool with a Gun

Oswald would have been aghast at the disasters he triggered by his stupid arrogance. Oswald wanted to help Kennedy improve America with:

1. An end to racial discrimination: systemic racism remains entrenched.

2. An end to exploitation of the downtrodden: the rich/poor divide has deepened.
3. An end to ultra-factionalism: Americans are more polarized

His accident replaced a good leader with a self-aggrandizing egomaniac. It was an accident that Oswald had so much contact with the hidden world of intelligence. It was unfortunate that Oswald died before his trial. It was natural for everyone to hide their issues once Oswald was dead since no trial was possible. It was unfortunate that the new President undermined trust in government. It was natural for the financial and corporate powers to fill the void of mistrust by generating their own narratives to divide and conquer the voters. It was natural that once polarization began, the oligarchy of financial and corporate powers would expand and exploit that polarization.

Rebalancing the oligarchy and government must start by breaking down artificial divisions that polarize us. Now, in 2024, we are beset by alternative media narratives that generate mistrust of anything outside our own bubbles. Each believer thinks other facts are dangerously insane while ignoring the contradictions in their own "facts." We have let special interests use false narratives to divide us and conquer us. We can do nothing substantive as long as we remain polarized.

Our polarized bubble is reinforced by a steady stream of misinformation. Most of us do not have the time and background to see through the dividing disinformation. Regulation seems like the only way out of this media mire. It is time to re-institute a "Fairness Doctrine," the personal attack rule and the "political editorial" rule. It was the removal of these rules that precipitated wholesale lying in the media. There must be a way to make a cost for lying, but in an international internet world with AI-driven "bots," it will take a lot of care. The constitutional issues are complex (Ruane, 2011).

•  •  •

The oligarchy think tanks are trying to protect their advantage e.g., (Matzko, The Fairness Doctrine Was Terrible for Broadcasting and It Would Be Terrible for the Internet, 2019). They will push for laws to prevent any future controls on lies (Pence, 2011). But disinformation is killing our society. There has to be a way to aggregate, tag, and track claims so that their truth or falsehood can be developed over time.

We do not need a "1984" Department of Truth. We would be worse off if we created an agent of repression. But we do need a government we can trust. If we regulate lying outside the government, then we must also regulate lying by the government.

Once we shake off the fog of disinformation, Kennedy's challenge of June 11, 1963, remains before us:

*Difficulties over segregation and discrimination exist in every city, in every State of the Union, producing in many cities a rising tide of discontent that threatens the public safety. Nor is this a partisan issue. In a time of domestic crisis men of good will and generosity should be able to unite regardless of party or politics.*
*... We are confronted primarily with a moral issue.*
*...The heart of the question is whether all Americans are to be afforded equal rights and equal opportunities, whether we are going to treat our fellow Americans as we want to be treated.*
*... not every child has an equal talent or an equal ability or an equal motivation, but they should have an equal right to develop their talent and their ability and their motivation, to make something of themselves.*

## Let Us Begin

Rashly fired bullets from one "patriotic" egomaniac unleashed another egomaniac on the USA. Let us recognize that misfortune and misinformation have divided us. Lacking understanding, we make the divide greater each day.

·   ·   ·

Can we rebuild the Kennedy Spirit that was ripped from our hearts in 1963?

*Where there is no vision, the people perish.*
*Proverbs 29*

We can work together to sift out an agreed truth. We can accept personal responsibility for our fate and our collective fates. We can resolve to do our best. Then, let us move forward with mutual respect to help each other evolve a new "New Frontier."

*All this will not be finished in the first 100 days. Nor will it be finished in the first 1,000 days, nor even perhaps in our lifetimes on this planet. But let us begin.*

*President John Fitzgerald Kennedy, 1961*

Aguilar, D. G. (2014, September 27). *Medical Experts and the JFK assassination*. Retrieved from www.c-span.org: https://www.c-span.org/video/?321702-3/ discussion-medical-evidence-kennedy-assassination

Alvarez, L. W. (1976). A Physicist Examines the Kennedy Assassination Film. *American Journal of Physics Vol. 44, No. 9*, 813-827.

Anatomical Surrogates Technology. (2009, July 25). *JFK Assassination Magic Bullet Test (Part 2)*. Retrieved from https://educationforum.ipbhost.com: https://www.youtube.com/watch?v=PZRUNYZY7Ig

Assassination Records Review Board. (1998, September 30). *The Assassination Records Review Board Report*. Retrieved from National Archives www.archives.gov: https://www.archives.gov/research/jfk/review-board/ report

Associates, R. D. (Director). (1960, 1961, 1963). *The Kennedy Films* [Motion Picture].

Ayton, M. (2014). *Beyond Reasonable Doubt*. Rock Hill, SC: Strategic Media Books.

Belkin, M. (1979). Wound Ballistics. *Progress in Surgery*, pp. 16:7-24.

Buchanan, T. (1964). *Who killed Kennedy?* New York: G. P. Putnam's Sons.

Bugliosi, V. (2007). *Reclaiming History: The Assassination of President John F. Kennedy*. New York: W. W. Norton. Retrieved 5 23, 2021, from https://books. google.com/books?id=7jrKTKDhvfkC&pg=PA1533#v=onepage&q&f=false

Carothers, T. A. (2019, Sep 25). *How Americans Were Driven to Extremes*. Retrieved from Foreign Affairs: https://www.foreignaffairs.com/articles/ united-states/2019-09-25/how-americans-were-driven-extremes

CBS News Inquiry. (1967). *The Warren Report - part 4*. Retrieved from c-span.org: https://www.c-span.org/video/?454598-1/cbs-news-inquiry-warren-report-part-4

Church Committee Report, n. 9.-7. (1976). *The Select Committee to Study Governmental Operations with Respect to Intelligence Activities, Foreign and Military Intelligence*. Washington, D. C.: United States Congress.

Clarke, T. (2013). *JFK's Last Hundred Days*. NYC: Penguin Press.

Cohen, J. (1992, June). *Yes, Oswald Alone Killed Kennedy*. Retrieved from Fred Litwin - On the Trail of Delusion: https://www.onthetrailofdelusion.com/ post/yes-oswald-alone-killed-kennedy-by-jacob-cohen

Costella, J. (2021). *Which way does JFK's head move from Frame 312 to Frame 313 of the Zapruder Film?* Retrieved from johncostella: https://johncostella. com/jfk/headmove/

Costella, John, and James Fetzer, eds. (2013). *Assassination Research*. Retrieved from http://assassinationresearch.com

Dalio, R. (2021). *Principles for Dealing with the Changing World Order: Why Nations Succeed and Fail.* New York: Avid Readers Press/Simon & Schuster.

Daniel, J. (1963, Dec 14). *Unofficial Envoy: A Historic Report from Two Capitals.* Retrieved from jfklancer.maryferrell.org: https://jfklancer.maryferrell.org/cuba/links/JeanDaniel/jdan_complete.pdf

David S. Lifton. (1980). *Best Evidence: Disguise and Deception in the Assassination of John F. Kennedy.* New York: Carroll & Graf.

Dawson, J., & Sleek, S. (2018, Sept 28). *The Fluidity of Time: Scientists Uncover How Emotions Alter Time Perception.* Retrieved from www.psychologicalscience.org/: https://www.psychologicalscience.org/observer/the-fluidity-of-time

DeRonja and Holland. (2016, 5 9). *A Technical Investigation Pertaining to the First Shot Fired in the JFK Assassination.* Retrieved from https://www.acsr.org/: https://www.acsr.org/wp-content/uploads/2016/05/DeRonja-Holland-2.pdf

Discovery Channel (Director). (2008). *JFK: Inside the Target Car* [Motion Picture].

Dorman, E. (1963, November 22). *jfk assassination films-elsie dorman - Mike Prokes.* Retrieved from www.dailymotion.com: https://www.dailymotion.com/video/xeszrk

Eaton, R. (1984). *Neural Mechanisms of Startle Behavior.* New York: Plenum Press.

Fallstrom, B. (2013, Nov 25). *Embalmer also connects area to the assassination.* Retrieved from herald-review.com: https://herald-review.com/special-section/jfk/embalmer-also-connects-area-to-the-assassination/article_b4c2715c-55c6-11e3-a056-0019bb2963f4.html

Farid, H. (2011). *A 3-D Lighting and Shadow Analysis of the JFK Zapruder Film (Frame 317).* Retrieved from https://farid.berkeley.edu/: https://farid.berkeley.edu/downloads/publications/tr10a.pdf

FBI Questions Rachley. (1963, 11 23). *https://mcadams.posc.mu.edu.* Retrieved from FEDERAL BUREAU OF INVESTIGATION interview of VIRGIE RACHLEY: https://mcadams.posc.mu.edu/russ/testimony/rachley.htm

Ferguson, N. (2008). *Virtual History: Alternatives And Counterfactuals.* NYC: Basic Books.

Fetzer, J. (2007, The International Journal of the Humanities: Annual Review). *Reasoning about Assassinations: Critical Thinking in Political Contexts.* Retrieved from https://www.academia.edu/: https://www.academia.edu/93272641/Reasoning_about_Assassinations_Critical_Thinking_in_Political_Contexts?email_work_card=view-paper

Fiester, S. (2013). *Enemy of the Truth: Myth, Forensics, and the Kennedy Assassination.* Southlake, TX: JFK Lancer Productions and Publications, Inc.

Friedman, M. P., & Ferreira, R. G. (2022, Winter). Making Peaceful Revolution Impossible: Kennedy, Arévalo, the 1963 Coup in Guatemala, and the Alliance against Progress in Latin America's Cold War. *Journal of Cold War Studies*, pp. 155-187.

Gallup Polls - Swift, A. (2013). *Majority in U.S. Still Believe JFK Killed in a*

*Conspiracy.*        https://news.gallup.com/poll/165893/majority-believe-jfk-killed-conspiracy.aspx.

Gillon, S. (2009). *The Kennedy Assassination: 24 Hours After.* New York: Basic Books.

Haag, L. A. (2013). *Cold Case JFK.* Retrieved from Nova: Cold Case JFK on pbs.org:   https://aguilarforensics.weebly.com/firearms--tool-marks/nova-jfk-cold-case-full-video

Haag, L. a. (2013, November 13). *The Shot That Missed.* Retrieved from https://www.youtube.com Posted by NOVA l PBS: https://www.youtube.com/watch?v=iiUv2WQKBjo

Harrison Livingston. (2004). *The Radical Right and the Murder of John F. Kennedy.* Victoria, BC: Trafford Publishing.

Hartmann, W. (1978, Sep 11). *HSCA Volume II: Testimony of William Hartmann.* Retrieved from www.aarclibrary.org: https://www.aarclibrary.org/publib/jfk/hsca/reportvols/vol2/pdf/HSCA_Vol2_0911_2_Hartmann.pdf

Henry R. Luce. (1963, November 29). President John F. Kennedy. *Life Magazine.*

Hill, C. (2013). *Five Days in November.* NY: Simon & Schuster Inc.

Hirsh-Pasek, K. e. (2022, Feb 28). *Making pre-K work: Lessons from the Tennessee study.* Retrieved from https://www.brookings.edu/: https://www.brookings.edu/blog/education-plus-development/2022/02/28/making-pre-k-work-lessons-from-the-tennessee-study/

Holland, M. (2015, 12 3). *The Zapruder Film Reconsidered.* Retrieved from Roosevelt House Public Policy Institute at Hunter College: https://www.youtube.com/watch?v=t8Hp9ZqVxGA

Hosty, J. (1996). *Assignment: Oswald.* NYC: Arcade Publishing.

House Select Committee on Assassinations. (1979). *Findings and Recommendations.* Washington: U. S. Government Printing Office; https://www.archives.gov/research/jfk/select-committee-report/title-page.html.

iHeartPodcasts, w. R. (2023, October 23). *Who Killed JFK?* Retrieved from iHeartPodcasts: My Book

Itek. (1967). *Nix Film Analysis.* Lexington, Massachusetts: Itek Corporation.

Itek Corporation. (1967, November 20). *LIFE-ITEK Kennedy Assassination Film Analysis.* Retrieved from http://jfk.hood.edu: http://jfk.hood.edu/Collection/Weisberg%20Subject%20Index%20Files/I%20Disk/Itek%20Corporation/Item%2022.pdf

James Bookhout, FBI. (1963, November 23-5). *Commission Exhibit No. 1988.* Retrieved from www.history-matters.com: https://www.history-matters.com/archive/jfk/wc/wcvols/wh24/html/WH_Vol24_0018b.htm

James Reston Jr. (1989). *The Lone Star: The Life of John Connally.* New York: Harper & Row.

James Reston Jr. (2013). *The Accidental Victim: JFK, Lee Harvey Oswald, and the Real Target in Dallas.* New York: Zola Books.

Jefferson Morley. (2016). *CIA & JFK: The Secret Assassination Files.* Kindle - The Future of Freedom Foundation.

John Latimer, e. a. (1996). *Differences in the Wounding Behavior of the Two Bullets That Struck President Kennedy; An Experimental Study.* Retrieved from https://mcadams.posc.mu.edu/:        https://mcadams.posc.mu.edu/pdf/lattimer.pdf

John Lattimer M. D., E. S. (1977). *President Kennedy's Spine Hit by First Bullet. Bulletin of the New York Academy of Medicine*, 280-291.

L. Koene, R. H. (2013). *Projectile Ricochet from Wooden Targets*. FREIBURG, GERMANY: 27TH INTERNATIONAL SYMPOSIUM ON BALLISTICS.

Landis, C. a. (1939). *The Startle Pattern*. New York: Farrar and Rinehart.

Lemmino. (2023, July 24). *The Kennedy Assassination: Inside the Book Depository*. Retrieved from https://www.lemmi.no/: https://www.lemmi.no/p/the-kennedy-assassination-inside-the-book-depository

Litwin, F. (2023). *Oliver Stone's Flim-Flam: The Demagogue of Dealey Plaza*. NothernBlues Books.

Macintyre, B. (2018). *The Spy and the Traitor: The Greatest Espionage Story of the Cold War*. NYC: Crown.

Mailer, N. (1968). *The Idol and the Octopus*. New York: Dell.

Manchester, W. (1962). *Portrait of a President*. Philadelphia: Curtis Publishing Company.

Mark Lane. (1963, December 19). Oswald Innocent?—A Lawyer's Brief. *National Guardian*, pp. 5-..

Mark Lane. (1966). *Rush to Judgment*. London: The Bodley Head.

Martin, J. T. (1963, 11 22). *John T. Martin film*. Retrieved from https://emuseum.jfk.org: https://emuseum.jfk.org/objects/36908/john-t-martin-film

Matzko, P. (2019, 6 12). *The Fairness Doctrine Was Terrible for Broadcasting and It Would Be Terrible for the Internet*. Retrieved from CATO Institute: https://www.cato.org/blog/internet-regulation-fairness

Matzko, P. (2020, March). *How JFK Censored Right-Wing Radio*. Retrieved from www.cato.org: https://www.cato.org/policy-report/march/april-2020/how-jfk-censored-right-wing-radio

McAdams, J. (2011). *JFK Assassination Logic: How to Think about Claims of Conspiracy*. Washington, D. C.: Potomac Books.

McFadden, D. (2021, Nov 16). *Why Did the Earwitnesses to the John F. Kennedy Assassination Not Agree About the Location of the Gunman?* Retrieved from www.frontiersin.org: https://www.frontiersin.org/articles/10.3389/fpsyg.2021.763432/full

McHugh, W. (1967, Oct 17). *George G. Burkley, Oral History Interview*. Retrieved from https://www.jfklibrary.org/sites/default/files/archives/JFKOH/Burkley%2C%20George%20G/JFKOH-GGB-01/JFKOH-GGB-01-TR.pdf

Meagher, S. (1966). *Subject Index to the Warren Report and Hearings & Exhibits*. New York: Scarecrow Press.

Meagher, S. (2013). *Accessories After the Fact: The Warren Commission, the Authorities & the Report on the JFK Assassination*. Skyhorse.

Mellen, J. (2016). *Faustian Bargains: Lyndon Johnson and Mac Wallace in the Robber Baron Culture of Texas*. New York: Bloomsbury USA.

Minutaglio, B. &. (2013). *Dallas 1963*. New York: Hachette Book Group.

Mohrenschildt, G. d. (1977). *HSCA Volume XII: George de Mohrenschildt*.

Retrieved from www.aarclibrary.org: http://www.aarclibrary.org/publib/jfk/hsca/reportvols/vol12/pdf/HSCA_Vol12_deMohren.pdf

Mohrenschildt, G. d. (2014). *Lee Harvey Oswald as I Knew Him.* Lawrence: University Press of Kansas.

Moore, J. (1991). *Conspiracy of One: The Definitive Book on the Kennedy Assassination.* Fort Worth, Texas: The Summit Group.

Moynihan, D. P. (1965). *The Negro Family: The Case For National Action (aka The Moynihan Report).* Washington, DC: Office of Policy Planning and Research, US Department of Labor.

Myers, D. (2007, June 1). *Epipolar Geometric Analysis of Amateur Films Related to the John F. Kennedy Assassination.* Retrieved from www.jfkfiles.com: http://www.jfkfiles.com/jfk/html/report_download.html

Nalli, N. R. (2018, April). *Gunshot-wound dynamics model for John F. Kennedy assassination.* Retrieved from https://www.ncbi.nlm.nih.gov/: https://www.ncbi.nlm.nih.gov/pmc/articles/PMC5934694/#br0120

Nellis, D., & Taylor, C. (2013). *JFK: A President Betrayed.* Retrieved from JFK A President Betrayed off_air recording: youtube.com/watch?v=WoQntFvH_cw

Nijhuis and Janssen, e. a. (2007, 10 1). *Choice reaction times for human head rotations are shortened by startling acoustic stimuli, irrespective of stimulus direction.* Retrieved from The Journal of Physiology 2007 Oct 1: https://www.ncbi.nlm.nih.gov/pmc/articles/PMC2277050/

Norman Mailer. (1996). *Oswald's Tail: An American Mystery.* New York: Ballantine Books.

Obama, B. (2015). *My Brother's Keeper Alliance.* Retrieved from MBK Alliance: https://www.obama.org/mbka/

Olivier and Dziemian. (1965, March). *Wound Ballistics of 6.5 mm Mannlicher-Carcano Ammunition.* Retrieved from https://www.maryferrell.org/: https://www.maryferrell.org/showDoc.html?docId=62296

Olson, D. A. (1971, Sep 23). Photographic Evidence and the Assassination of President John F. Kennedy. *Proceedings of 23rd Annual Meeting of the American Academy of Forensic Sciences, Vol 16, No. 4,* pp. 399-410.

P Brown, B. L. (1991). The effect of posture on the normal and pathological auditory startle reflex. *Journal of Neurology, Neurosurgery and Psychiatry,* 892–897.

Paul Hoch. (1975, March 24). *CIA Activities and the Warren Commission Investigation.* Retrieved from archives.gov: https://www.archives.gov/files/research/jfk/releases/2018/104-10196-10027000l.pdf

Pence, M. (2011). *H.R.642 - Broadcaster Freedom Act of 2011.* Retrieved from Congress.gov: https://www.congress.gov/bill/112th-congress/house-bill/642?s=1&r=7

Perry, D. (2021). *Tales of Deception and Imagination.* Grapevine, TX: self.

Pew Research Center. (2017, Oct 5). *Partisan divides over political values widen.* Retrieved from https://www.pewresearch.org/: https://www.pewresearch.org/politics/2017/10/05/1-partisan-divides-over-political-values-widen/

Pew Research Center, Washington, D.C. (2021, May 17). *Public Trust in Govern-*

*ment: 1958-2021.* Retrieved from https://www.pewresearch.org/: https://www.people-press.org/2019/04/11/public-trust-in-government-1958-2019/

Pierre Sundborg. (2016). *Tragic Truth: Oswald Shot Kennedy by Accident.* CreateSpace Independent Publishing Platform.

Posner, G. (1993). *Case Closed.* Warner Books. Retrieved 5 23, 2021

Priscilla J. McMillan. (2013). *Marina and Lee.* Hanover, NH: Steerforth Press.

Prouty, L. F. (1992). *JFK: The CIA, Vietnam, and the Plot to Assassinate John F. Kennedy.* New York: Carol Publishing Group.

Rahn, K. a. (2004, October 25). *Neutron Activation Analyses Proves Oswald Acted Alone In JFK Assassination.* Retrieved from www.sciencedaily.com: https://www.sciencedaily.com/releases/2004/10/041025131255.htm

Randich, E. a. (2006, Sep 6). *Proper Assessment of the JFK Assassination Bullet Lead Evidence from Metallurgical and Statistical Perspectives.* Retrieved from www.osti.gov: https://www.osti.gov/servlets/purl/900118

Reiman, R. (2019). *Six 'Shots' in Dallas: 'Framing' the Perpetrator of the Kennedy Assassination through the Zapruder Film, 1963-2013.* Retrieved from www.academia.edu: https://www.academia.edu/107580900/Six_Shots_in_Dallas_Framing_the_Perpetrator_of_the_Kennedy_Assassination_through_the_Zapruder_Film_1963_2013

Roberts, C. (1967). *The Truth About the Assassination: The Answer to the Warren Report Critics.* New York: Grosset and Dunlap.

Ruane, K. (2011, 7 13). *Fairness Doctrine: History and Constitutional Issues.* Retrieved from Congressional Research Service: https://fas.org/sgp/crs/misc/R40009.pdf

Russell, B. (1964, September). *16 Questions On Kennedy Assassination.* Retrieved from https://www.colombotelegraph.com: https://www.colombotelegraph.com/index.php/16-questions-on-kennedy-assassination/

Sabato, L. J. (2013). *The Kennedy Half Century: The Presidency, Assassination, and Lasting Legacy of John F. Kennedy.* New York: Bloomsbury.

Salinger and Vanocur, e. (1964). *A Tribute to John F. Kennedy.* New York: Dell.

Sauvage, L. (1965). *The Oswald Affair.* Paris: Les Editions de Minuit.

Schlesinger, A. M. (2007). *Journals: 1952-2000.* London: Penguin Books.

Select Committee on Assassinations, 9. C. (1979). *Report of the Select Committee on Assassinations.* Washington: U.S. GOVERNMENT PRINTING OFFICE.

Shaw, D. J. (2016). *The Memory Illusion: Remembering, Forgetting, and the Science of False Memory.* Cornerstone Digital.

Storing, T. L. (2019). *In Search of Veritas: Kennedy Assassination Conspiracy Theories and the Emergence of An American Culture of Suspicion, 1963-1993.* Retrieved from https://orc.library.atu.edu/: https://orc.library.atu.edu/cgi/viewcontent.cgi?article=1024&context=etds_2019

Sturdivan, L. (2005). *The JFK Myths: A Scientific Investigation of the Kennedy Assassination.* St. Paul: Paragon House.

Susan Cheever. (2013). *Drinking in America: Our Secret History.* Kindle - Twelve.

*The Breathe Act.* (2020). Retrieved from breatheact.org: https://breatheact.org/

Then, C., Nelson, K., Vogl, T. J., & Roth, K. E. (2022, May 2022). *Computational ballistic analysis of the cranial shot to John F. Kennedy.* Retrieved from https://

www.sciencedirect.com/: https://www.sciencedirect.com/science/article/pii/S0379073822000949

Thompson, J. (1967). *Six Seconds in Dallas*. Retrieved 6 4, 2021

Thompson, J. (2021). *Last Second in Dallas*. Lawrence: University Press of Kansas.

Thompson, J. (Accessed on 2/26/2022). *Bedrock Evidence in the Kennedy Assassination*. Retrieved from https://www.maryferrell.org/: https://www.maryferrell.org/pages/Essay_-_Bedrock_Evidence_in_the_Kennedy_Assassination.html

Time Magazine. (1963, October 4). *Nation: BOX SCORE FOR '64*. Retrieved from https://content.time.com: https://content.time.com/time/subscriber/article/0,33009,875229,00.html

Time Magazine. (2011). *Top 10 Historically Misleading Films*. Internet: https://entertainment.time.com/2011/01/26/top-10-historically-misleading-films/slide/all/.

Titovets, E. (2020). *Oswald: Russian Episode*. Independently Published.

Usdin, S. T. (2018). *Bureau of Spies: The Secret Connections between Espionage and Journalism in Washington*. Buffalo: Prometheus.

Vaughn and Myers. (2016, 11 22). *http://jfkfiles.blogspot.com*. Retrieved from Holland's Magic Bullet: A forensic ballistician examines a dubious theory: http://jfkfiles.blogspot.com/2016/11/hollands-magic-bullet.html

Verhoeven, B. (2015, July). *The Rearguard of Freedom: The John Birch Society and the Development of Modern Conservatism in the United States,1958-1968*. Retrieved from University of Nottingham Ph. D. Theses: https://eprints.nottingham.ac.uk/28893/1/VerhoevenThesisNottinghamFinalVersion.pdf

Warren Commission. (1964). *Warren Commission Hearings and Exhibits*. United States Government Printing Office. Retrieved 5 24, 2021, from http://www.maryferrell.org/mffweb/archive/docset/getList.do?docSetId=1006

Weisberg, H. (1965). *Whitewash: The Report on the Warren Report*. Skyhorse Press; originally self-published. Retrieved 5 23, 2021

Weisberg, H. (1994). *Case Open: The Omissions, Distortions and Falsifications of Case Closed*. New York: Carroll & Graf.

William D. Rubinstein. (2014). *Shadow Pasts: 'Amateur Historians' and History's Mysteries*. Milton Park, UK: Routledge.

William Manchester. (1967). *The Death of a President*. New York: Harper & Row.

Wilson, A. J. (1992). The injuries to JFK. *JAMA, 268*(13), 1681-1681. Retrieved 5 24, 2021, from https://jamanetwork.com/journals/jama/fullarticle/400233

Woodson, R. (2021). *Red, White, and Black: Rescuing American History from Revisionists and Race Hustlers*. Amazon Kindle: Emancipation Books.

World Heritage Encyclopedia. (1998). *John F. Kennedy Autopsy*. http://self.gutenberg.org/articles/John_F._Kennedy_autopsy.

Zapruder, A. (1963, November 22). *Online Collection: Abraham Zapruder film*. Retrieved 5 24, 2021, from The Sixth Floor Museum at Dealey Plaza: http://emuseum.jfk.org/view/objects/asitem/classification@Films/1/title-asc?t:state:flow=3d5a735c-1f99-41ca-b653-8333b79f424b

Zapruder, A. (2016). *Twenty-Six Seconds: A Personal History of the Zapruder Film*.

New York: Grand Central Publishing.